Sabbatian Heresy

THE TAUBER INSTITUTE SERIES FOR
THE STUDY OF EUROPEAN JEWRY
Jehuda Reinharz, General Editor
Sylvia Fuks Fried, Associate Editor
Eugene R. Sheppard, Associate Editor

THE BRANDEIS LIBRARY OF MODERN JEWISH THOUGHT
Eugene R. Sheppard and Samuel Moyn, Editors

This library aims to redefine the canon of modern Jewish thought by publishing
primary source readings from individual Jewish thinkers or groups of thinkers in reliable
English translations. Designed for courses in modern Jewish philosophy, thought, and
intellectual history, each volume features a general introduction and annotations to each
source with the instructor and student in mind.

Sabbatian Heresy: Writings on Mysticism, Messianism, and the Origins of Jewish Modernity
Paweł Maciejko, editor
Modern Middle Eastern Jewish Thought: Writings on Identity, Politics, and Culture, 1893–1958
Moshe Behar and Zvi Ben-Dor Benite, editors
Jews and Diaspora Nationalism: Writings on Jewish Peoplehood in Europe and the United States
Simon Rabinovitch, editor
Moses Mendelssohn: Writings on Judaism, Christianity, and the Bible
Michah Gottlieb, editor
Jews and Race: Writings on Identity and Difference, 1880–1940
Mitchell B. Hart, editor

FOR THE COMPLETE LIST OF BOOKS THAT ARE FORTHCOMING IN
THE SERIES, PLEASE SEE HTTP://WWW.BRANDEIS.EDU/TAUBER

Sabbatian Heresy

Edited by
Paweł Maciejko

WRITINGS ON
MYSTICISM, MESSIANISM,
AND THE ORIGINS OF
JEWISH MODERNITY

Brandeis University Press

Waltham, Massachusetts

BRANDEIS UNIVERSITY PRESS
An imprint of University Press of New England
www.upne.com
© 2017 Brandeis University
All rights reserved
Manufactured in the United States of America
Designed by Eric M. Brooks
Typeset in Albertina and Verlag by Passumpsic Publishing

For permission to reproduce any of the material in this book,
contact Permissions, University Press of New England, One Court
Street, Suite 250, Lebanon NH 03766; or visit www.upne.com

The research leading to these results has received funding from
the European Research Council under the European Union's Seventh
Framework Programme (FP/2007–2013) / ERC Grant Agreement
no. 263689—"TCCECJ."

Library of Congress Cataloging-in-Publication Data
NAMES: Maciejko, Paweł, 1971– editor.
TITLE: Sabbatian heresy: writings on mysticism, messianism, and the
    origins of Jewish modernity / edited by Paweł Maciejko.
DESCRIPTION: Waltham, Massachusetts : Brandeis University Press, [2017] |
    Series: The Tauber Institute series for the study of European Jewry |
    Series: The Brandeis library of modern Jewish thought |
    Includes bibliographical references and index.
IDENTIFIERS: LCCN 2016049423 (print) | LCCN 2016050001 (ebook) |
    ISBN 9781611687279 (cloth: alk. paper) | ISBN 9781512600520 (pbk.: alk.
    paper) | ISBN 9781512600537 (epub, mobi & pdf)
SUBJECTS: LCSH: Sabbathaians—History. | Jewish messianic
    movements—History.
CLASSIFICATION: LCC BM199.S3 S25 2017 (print) | LCC BM199.S3 (ebook) |
    DDC 296.8/2—dc23
LC record available at https://lccn.loc.gov/2016049423

For Adam, *the first*

Contents

Foreword

It is with great enthusiasm that we greet the publication of this volume on Sabbatianism and its significance in modern Jewish thought. Everything about Sabbatai Tsevi's life (1626–1672) and thought was shot through with world-changing theological convulsion. The dates of his birth (9th of Av) and death (the Day of Atonement) point to the symbolic significance of the movements and traditions he initiated and inspired, either directly or indirectly, up through the nineteenth century. Catastrophe, exile, and divine abandonment became the necessary conditions out of which the urgent promise of personal and collective redemption could be anticipated. And in these radical orientations, the reestablishment of connections with the divine required a breaking and reordering of normative structures. The spiritual and intellectual impact and legacy of Sabbatian thought courses between apocalyptic, messianic, and redemptive signification. The entire Jewish world changed after the 1660s with the appearance of a Jewish messiah, who then converted to Islam while on his way to assume his kingship over a third Jewish commonwealth in the Land of Israel. This volume addresses the global reverberations of Sabbatai's announced messianic arrival, his apostasy, and the reconfigurations of interreligious practice and belief that came in their wake. Gathered here are central texts that offer a glimpse into the notoriously secret and stigmatized world of Sabbatianism, and present the reader with texts from Sabbatai Tsevi, his contemporary disciples, subsequent prophets, Sabbatian controversies that emerged in Europe and in the Ottoman Empire, as well as later iterations of Sabbatian ideas and literary representations. The editor, Paweł Maciejko, has challenged us to assess the reception of Sabbatian mystical thought as something that went well beyond its more common portrayal as a misadventure in messianic manipulation and salacious rituals of transgression and to consider Sabbatianism as a substantive tradition marking the origins of modern Jewish thought.

Eugene R. Sheppard and Samuel Moyn, Editors
The Brandeis Library of Modern Jewish Thought

Introduction

Jesus of Nazareth and Sabbatai Tsevi were the two most important Jewish messiahs in history. The former became the founder of the world's largest religion, whose theological traditions and liturgical practices have been flourishing for the past two thousand years. The truth of his messianic mission has been the central article of faith for millions of believers. His teachings, as recorded in the Gospels, have served as inspiration for countless works of genius and take their place in the treasury of humanity's moral and religious heritage. The latter, for his part, never became a household name: to the extent that he is known outside the narrow circle of scholars specializing in early modern Judaism, he is generally considered a colossal failure of messianic hopes and aspirations. The spiritual awakening initiated by Sabbatai Tsevi (arguably also a new religion in the making) spectacularly collapsed less than a year after its inception. The creed of his faith, largely forgotten, seems too bizarre to merit a serious discussion. Any lingering traces of belief in his messianic mandate have long since disappeared from living memory. For most of those who do remember him, Sabbatai Tsevi and his messianism constituted a burst of short-lived religious enthusiasm fueled by naïveté and credulity. An inexplicable oddity. A bubble on the current of history. An intriguing anecdote—at best. Yet behind these simplistic images, a more complex reality lurks. Sabbatai's messianic allure, transitory though it was, calls for serious reflection: aside from Jesus, Tsevi was the only Jewish messiah whose gospel gained sufficient momentum to break through the confines of a particular social group or a specific geographical milieu. The countless would-be saviors of the Jews (or redeemers of the world) who appeared between antiquity and the modern period might have been important in their local settings, but remained practically unknown outside their own communities. Breaking this mold, Sabbatianism, as the movement founded by Tsevi came to be called, for a brief period captured the entire Jewish world and all strata of Jewish society— Jews of the Orient and Occident, rich and poor, learned and illiterate, men and women. Further, Christianity excepted, Sabbatianism was the single messianic upheaval among the Jews that exerted a significant impact on the surrounding societies. The eruption of religious fervor around Sabbatai Tsevi in the 1660s was probably the highest-profile event involving Jewish communities prior to the twentieth century. It echoed in innumerable contemporary letters, memoirs, travelogues, and newspaper reports. Rulers of empires as well as high-ranking Muslim and Christian clergymen were actively involved in shaping the course of events affecting Sabbatai and his followers, and devised strategies of response to the spreading of messianism among the masses. Some—albeit very few—non-Jews became ardent believers in Tsevi. Leading intellectuals of the age creatively engaged with Sabbatianism and wrote passionate rejoinders to its momentous emergence and stunning downfall.

The importance of Sabbatai Tsevi transcends his immediate period. If we consider as Sabbatianism not only the outburst of public messianic ardor that briefly surrounded Tsevi, but also the entire debate triggered by his advent, then the movement was less short lived than often assumed: most of the controversies that took place in the Jewish world between the mid-seventeenth and the mid-nineteenth century were associated in one way or another with Sabbatianism. Sabbatai's followers developed a set of theological doctrines in which Jewish tradition was reinterpreted in novel and highly unorthodox ways and was merged with Muslim and later Christian elements. These doctrines, as well as the (allegedly or actually) licentious and transgressive behavior of many Sabbatians, provoked intense opposition (and therefore significant polemical literature) from rabbinic authorities. The patterns of polemics that emerged on the occasion of Sabbatianism formed the basis for other disputes. Quarrels between Sabbatians and their detractors had a profound impact on the contours of central controversies of later Judaism, such as debates surrounding the emergence of Hasidism, the Haskalah, and the Reform movement. In the twentieth century, numerous works of art and literature attest to the deep fascination with the figure of Sabbatai Tsevi. For some major Jewish thinkers, his rise and fall constitutes the key to the most crucial phenomena of modern Jewish history: Zionism and the establishment of Jewish political sovereignty and the secularization of traditional Jewish society. In short, any real discussion of the early modern and modern Jewish experience must take into account Sabbatianism. In such reflection, both the internal diversity of Jewish society and a cross-sectional view of Jewish, Christian, and Muslim relations during the past three hundred years can be considered.

An outline of the messiah's biography is in place. Sabbatai Tsevi was born on the 9th of Av, August 1, 1626, in Smyrna (Izmir), on the Aegean coast of Anatolia. He received the preliminaries of traditional Jewish education from the leading scholars of his natal city, Rabbis Isaac de Alba and Joseph Escapa. At the age of fifteen, Tsevi abandoned the yeshivah and embarked on a path of solitary study and meditation, dabbling in Kabbalah and esoteric lore. He also began to experience states of profound depression interspersed with moments of ecstatic euphoria. During the latter, Tsevi performed strange acts and invented bizarre rituals, some of which involved blatant violations of Jewish law. In 1648, in a moment of ecstasy, he pronounced aloud the Ineffable Name of God and proclaimed himself the messiah. Nobody took this claim seriously; most of those who knew him considered him mentally ill. However, the messianic pronouncements and outlandish actions continued, and the Smyrna rabbis eventually expelled Sabbatai from the city. Throughout the 1650s, Tsevi wandered through Greece, Thrace, Turkey, and Egypt, to settle, in 1662, in Jerusalem. Doubting himself and overcome with an intense sense of guilt, he tried to suppress both his messianic visions and his abnormal behavior. Sabbatai became a normative (if possibly slightly strange) member of the Jerusalem Jewish community, on whose behalf he undertook a journey to Cairo. On his way back in April 1665, he met in Gaza the Kabbalistic prodigy Nathan Benjamin Ashkenazi. Several months prior to this meeting, Nathan had experienced a revelation, the centerpiece of which was the image of the messiah Sabbatai Tsevi engraved upon the Throne of Glory. The encounter was a turning point in both their lives; Nathan managed to convince Sabbatai to accept the truth of his messianic destiny, and provided him with conceptual tools allowing for an explanation of his nonnormative conduct. Idiosyncratic acts and rituals (termed by Nathan *ma'asim zarim*, strange deeds) were signs of Tsevi's elevated messianic rank and the basis for future rites of his faithful. The cycles of depression and euphoria were external expressions of the messiah's internal struggle against the powers of darkness. In May 1665, in Gaza, Sabbatai Tsevi again publicly proclaimed himself the messiah. This time, the entire community was swept up with him. Nathan had several other prophetic visions, and he composed theological pronouncements elaborating on them. These were copied and sent to distant Jewish communities as circular epistles, which triggered the spread of the messianic enthusiasm first in Palestine and Egypt and subsequently also in other parts of the Ottoman Empire and most of Christian Europe. By October 1665, Jewish communities from Persia to Morocco and from Yemen to Poland were engulfed in religious frenzy. Ecstatic trances, prophecies, apparitions, and other supernatural phenomena multiplied. Poems and songs in honor of the messiah were composed, enthusiastic sermons were preached, and celebrations of the imminent redemption were held; in most Jewish communities skeptics and opponents of Tsevi were a tiny—and at times persecuted—minority. Diaspora Jews began selling their properties and clos-ing businesses in expectation of the approaching move to the Land of Israel, where the final stage of redemption was to take place. At this point, Sabbatai Tsevi's predilection for transgressive actions reached its peak: he ate prohibited foods, abolished fasts and established new festivals, instituted new blessings and prayers, called upon women to read the Law, dismissed rabbis and communal leaders, and appointed "kings," among whom he divided the world. He also de-clared that before long he would seize the crown of the Ottoman sultan.

In December 1665, Tsevi sailed to Constantinople. Worried about the spread of religious fervor, the Turkish authorities intercepted his boat on the open sea. Sabbatai was brought in chains to the fortress of Gallipoli, where he remained until the summer of the following year. To the great surprise of his detractors, the Turks treated the prisoner with honor, allowing him to hold court and to send and receive envoys, among them rabbinic and Kabbalistic luminaries. Muslim respect coupled with the continuing spread of the prophetic propa-ganda among the Jews brought the messianic hopes to an apotheosis: during his imprisonment, Sabbatai issued several pronouncements signed "I am the Lord your God Sabbatai Tsevi," and among some of his believers he came to be con-sidered a divine figure. The anticlimax came in September 1666: on the fifteenth of that month Sabbatai was brought before Sultan Mehmed IV in Adrianople. Accounts of this meeting are riddled with contradiction, but one thing is certain: from the meeting with the ruler of the Ottoman Empire, Sabbatai Tsevi emerged a Muslim.

Following his conversion, Sabbatai Tsevi received instruction in the tenets of Islam, studied the Qur'an, began praying in a mosque, and developed contacts with Muslim mystics, including members of Dervish orders. He also continued to study the Zohar and other Kabbalistic writings, prayed at home in Hebrew, and observed, apparently with the silent consent of the authorities, most ritual commandments of Judaism. During his recurrent states of illumination, he maintained his earlier erratic pattern of behavior, repeatedly proclaiming the continuance of his messianic mission despite his conversion, inventing yet more festivals and rites, and allegedly engaging in numerous immoral practices. It seems that the Turks turned a blind eye to Sabbatai's enduring adherence to Jew-ish customs and his excesses because they planned to deploy him as a mission-ary among the Jews. Indeed, at moments of euphoria, Tsevi made several calls on his followers to embrace Islam, causing a conversion of some two hundred Jewish families. Yet if the Ottoman authorities hoped for a large Jewish apostasy and quick integration of the converts into the dominant society, they miscalculated. Acting on the explicit instruction of the messiah, the converts avoided mingling with born Muslims and preserved close ties with those followers of Sabbatai who remained within the framework of official Judaism. Thus, a tightly knit sectarian group that consisted of nominal Muslims and nominal Jews and whose primary religious identity was neither Jewish nor Muslim but Sabbatian was formed.

In August 1672, Sabbatai was denounced to the authorities for his duplicitous and licentious behavior. In January of the following year he was exiled to Ulcinj (Dulcigno) in Albania. He continued writing letters and dispatching emissaries, and some of his believers, including Nathan of Gaza, managed to visit him there. He died on the Day of Atonement, September 17, 1676.

For a mass messianic movement, Sabbatianism produced scarcely any theology. Precious few Sabbatian texts were composed during its heyday, before Sabbatai's conversion to Islam. After the conversion, Tsevi came to epitomize for most Jews as well as for many Christians and Muslims the notion of a "false messiah." He was subsumed under the familiar categories of religious impostor, charlatan, and sect leader. These labels were taken up—rather uncritically—by early historians of Sabbatianism. Yet they are highly problematic. First and foremost, as a term of scholarly analysis, "false messiah" is a poorly constructed concept. It is an obvious oxymoron: a messiah who is false is simply not a messiah; a messiah who is a messiah cannot, by definition, be false. Further, benchmarks of falsity invoked (or implicitly presumed) by those who use the term "false messiah" are in themselves problematic. Even if we argue (and this is a risky proposal) that in the course of the historical development of the Jewish religion, all Jews have accepted some universal standards of messiahship (such as Maimonides's Laws Pertaining to the Messiah), such standards are not operative categories of scholarship but rather its subjects. Claims that a particular messianic pretender was false according to set criteria should be *studied* by scholars; they should not be *made* by them. Finally, the term "false messiah" implies a value judgment. Scholars of early Christianity are not in the habit of offering disclaimers concerning the fact that Jesus of Nazareth was and indeed is considered a false messiah by some, nor are they accustomed to making declarations concerning their belief or disbelief in the matter. Scholars of Sabbatai Tsevi should, perhaps, exhibit the same restraint.

Even prior to Sabbatai Tsevi's conversion it was obvious to all that he did not fit any of the existing conceptions of the messiah. He and his followers knew it perfectly well; they never pretended he did. Some of the Sabbatians rejected the very possibility of formulating criteria of messiahship akin to the ones formulated by Maimonides; others proposed their own messianic parameters; yet others turned the argument on its head and contended that the very lack of fulfillment of traditional criteria by Sabbatai signaled the truth of his mission. The significance of Sabbatianism for Jewish messianic speculation is not merely that it was the largest movement of its kind or that it had a profound impact on other religious and political phenomena; most critical is that it was the most important attempt in the history of post–Second Temple Judaism to define (or to redefine) the very category of messianism. Sabbatianism's singularity was that an act which should have marked the utter failure of the purported redeemer, his conversion, did not put an absolute end to the belief in his messianic vocation. For the vast majority of Sabbatai's followers, pious Jews that they were, the apostasy did disqualify his claims to a messianic mandate. Their adventure with messianism ended the minute the object of their hopes became a Muslim. For a few, however, the conversion was merely a stage for the unfolding redemption drama. In fact, Sabbatianism as a highly original form of thought began precisely where Sabbatianism as a mass messianic movement ended. Sabbatian thought took off as an attempt to explain the inexplicable: to imbue Tsevi's apostasy with religious meaning. The conversion of the messiah was a necessary step in his salvific mission.

The notion of the necessary apostasy of the messiah constituted the inner kernel of Sabbatianism. The social profile and theological tenets of the Sabbatian religion were determined not so much by Tsevi's claims to be the messiah, but by his conversion to Islam and the novel way the conversion was conceptualized in the writings of his prophets and disciples. The foundations of this conceptualization have been reconstructed in the seminal works of Gershom Scholem. While Scholem was by no means the first scholar to tackle Sabbatianism (important contributions to the reconstruction of the history of the movement had been made by David Kahana, Majer Bałaban, Heinrich Graetz, and Simon Dubnow, among others), he was the first historian to move beyond the false messiah paradigm. Rather than a priori dismissing Tsevi as an impostor or madman and his followers as delusional fanatics, Scholem sought to unearth the social and intellectual substructure of the movement. Undeterred by the ostensible absurdity of the doctrines of the messiah's "strange actions" and his necessary apostasy, he took the ideas of the Sabbatians with utmost seriousness and proposed to understand them on their own terms. His was the first

—and in many ways unsurpassed—attempt to tease out the inner workings of Sabbatianism.

According to Scholem, Sabbatian theology "in all its infinite varieties" had its common root in efforts to resolve the "contradiction" between "the inner and the outer reality of redemption."[1] For the believers, redemption became an "unmediated reality," an "overwhelming experience,"[2] whose inner certainty had to be reconciled with the empirical reality of historical events. Since the majority of the Jews accepted—if only for a brief period of time—Sabbatai as the true messiah, "the sheer quantitative magnitude of the revival had become a qualitative factor."[3] Faced with Sabbatai's apostasy, a number of his adherents "refused to submit to the sentence of history,"[4] and continued to follow him despite the fact that he had become a Muslim. Accordingly, they sought in classical Jewish texts allusions to the notion that the messiah would *perforce* apostatize.[5] This search promptly yielded fruit, and a number of theological "ideologizations"[6] of this deed were developed. First, the conversion was interpreted as a descent of the powers of righteousness embodied in the messiah into the world of evil and impurity (*kelippot*, husks, in the terminology of Kabbalah). The purpose of this descent was further expounded as an endeavor to bring about the total destruction of the *kelippot* or, conversely, as an attempt to save the sparks of holiness trapped among them. While all those who continued to adhere to Sabbatai Tsevi after the apostasy accepted one of the variants of this basic theological paradigm, Scholem distinguished at this point two major wings within the movement: "moderate" Sabbatians held that the messiah's conversion was a sui generis act, one that was not intended to serve as an example for others, whereas "radical" Sabbatians maintained that he should be followed all the way into apostasy.[7] The most important representatives of the latter wing were, according to Scholem, the Dönmeh of Salonika, who converted to Islam in 1683, and the 1759 Frankist converts to Catholicism in Poland. These radicals among radicals drew ultimate conclusions from Sabbatai's "constitutive act"; they turned conversion into a positive commandment and argued that the "true faith cannot be a faith which men publicly profess."[8] Thus, in its most extreme expressions Sabbatianism led to a fundamental impasse: the impossibility of reconciling one's true religious identity with one's social role.[9] In the final analysis, Sabbatianism was for Scholem "religious nihilism," wherein values and spiritual tenets of normative Judaism were shattered beyond repair, while seemingly orthodox practices of moderate Sabbatians—and even more so, new religions adopted by their radical brethren—were mere disguises lacking any deeper meaning or significance.

The notion of religious nihilism did not imply simply a rejection of values or mores associated with normative religion. Rather, as Scholem put it: "By this concept I do not mean nihilism with regard to religion but rather a nihilism that appears in the name of religious assertions and follows from religious tenets. It adopts religious discourse but it completely denies the authority, which this discourse claims to possess. It does not attempt to replace the old structures with new ones, but tries only to destroy them."[10] Sabbatian conversionary theology was nihilistic, for it simultaneously repudiated "vulgar" or "unenlightened" religious experience, and recommended the conscious and systematic desecration of the values of traditional religion as the way of the elect to true redemption. Although Scholem qualified his analyses by saying that many Sabbatians combined their belief in the messiah with perfectly orthodox Jewish observance, he also affirmed clearly that the antinomianism that stemmed from Tsevi's "strange deeds" was not found on the accidental fringe of the Sabbatian movement, but rather constituted its very core. *All* Sabbatianism, from its very foundations, was nihilistic: antinomian practices logically followed from the Sabbatian worldview, regardless of whether or not a particular believer actualized them in practice. Scholem's most famous statement on the subject (perhaps his most famous publication of all) is titled *Mitsvah ha-Ba'ah be-Avera* (literally: a commandment that is fulfilled by the breaking of another commandment). The phrase, especially after its mistranslation into English as *Redemption through Sin*, came to be regarded as the catchword of Sabbatianism.

In calling Sabbatianism religious nihilism, the author of *Redemption through Sin* by no means meant to condemn the movement. The description, instead, was intended to frame it as a necessary stage in the all-encompassing "dialectic of Jewish history." The function of Sabbatianism in this dialectic was that of an "antithesis": the most radical excesses of Tsevi's believers were to annihilate the petrified forms of religion, while at the same time sowing seeds for future developments. Scholem relentlessly advanced the view that despite its antinomianism and frontal attacks on normative religious authorities, even despite the apostasies it inspired, from its very beginning till its last vestiges Sabbatianism was "distinctly Jewish in character": it was a "grandiose though abortive attempt to revolutionize Judaism from within."[11] Hence, Scholem argued, "Sabbatianism must be regarded [. . .] as a single continuous development which retained its identity in the eyes of its adherents regardless of whether they themselves remained Jews or not, but also, paradoxical though it may seem, as a specifically Jewish phenomenon to the end."[12]

Gershom Scholem's theorization of Sabbatianism (whose spirit and characteristic idiom I tried to preserve in the preceding paragraphs) is nothing short of a grand narrative. Pre-Scholem Jewish historiography outlined fairly well the history of Sabbatai Tsevi and his following, yet it failed to propose an interpretative paradigm for an understanding of its sources and importance. Sabbatianism was treated as an artificial implantation on the healthy body of the Jewish people. Its sudden appearance and staggering success among both the rabbinic elite and the Jewish masses had no internal logic and could be explained only by reference to foreign pressures and stimuli. Scholem's insistence on the Jewishness of Sabbatianism allowed him to paint a more coherent and inclusive picture of Sabbatai Tsevi's messianism; it also permitted him to present it as a legitimate element within the wider framework of the history of Judaism and of the Jewish people. Sabbatianism came to be presented as a distinctive "movement," stemming from the same impulses, responding to the same needs, and expressing itself in different variants of the same theology. Varied and disparate phenomena spanning a period of more than one hundred and fifty years were subsumed under the same rubric. Different theological positions as well as different—and at times antagonistic—splinter groups associated with Sabbatianism were points on the same spectrum, whose poles were marked by a distinction between "moderate" and "radical" Sabbatians. While initially intended as a distinction between those followers of Sabbatai Tsevi who remained formally Jewish and those who followed him into apostasy, Scholem later extended this dichotomy into other aspects of Sabbatian theology and praxis, such as the antinomian excesses of the radicals versus traditional observances of the moderates or the acceptance of the divinity of the messiah by the former versus the belief in his purely human nature by the latter. In Scholem's view, Sabbatian concepts were valid (if at times highly idiosyncratic) reinterpretations of canonical Jewish sources. The ideas put forward by Sabbatian prophets and Kabbalists were taken up and further creatively transformed by normative Jewish thinkers and thus reintegrated into mainstream Jewish culture. The movement had a spiritual and intellectual genealogy (in Lurianic Kabbalah) and progeny (in Hasidism,[13] Haskalah,[14] and ultimately Zionism).[15]

Scholem's commitment to the homogeneity, unity, and especially the "specifically Jewish" nature of Sabbatianism had two important corollaries. The first was an emphatic denial of any substantial external influence on the movement (the author of *Redemption through Sin* performed intellectual somersaults to demonstrate that the outbreak of Sabbatianism "owed absolutely nothing" to contemporary non-Jewish millenarianism and messianism). Scholem did not deny the influences on the later Sabbatian theology, but he claimed that "the crisis in Judaism came from within and it would hardly have taken any other course had there been no Christian influence."[16] The second corollary was his equally emphatic stance that alien religious creeds adopted by some Sabbatians were "merely external façade[s],"[17] "which they regarded of course as purely extrinsic"[18] (expressions such as "of course" and "obviously" are sprinkled liberally throughout the different formulations of this point in all of Scholem's essays on Sabbatianism). Sabbatian converts were "voluntary Marranos,"[19] who superficially adopted other religions, while secretly preserving Judaism as they understood it. They became Muslim or Christian, but in the words of Scholem, "remained Jewish in their hearts."[20]

Gershom Scholem's imposing hermeneutical edifice defined the parameters of the subsequent scholarly debate. Not only did his interpretation permit the integration of Sabbatianism in a larger historical scheme, but most crucially, it amounted to a rewriting of Jewish history in light of Sabbatianism. For Scholem, messianism was certainly a chapter in the history of the Jewish people and one of many factors in the development of Jewish religion. But it was much, much more than that. The entirety of Jewish history was, on a deeper level, the history of messianism; messianic "energies" were hidden engines behind the development of virtually all major religious and political phenomena that shaped Jewish life through the ages.

The immensely persuasive power of Scholem's writings on Sabbatianism stem from their scope and boldness, as well as from their pure literary beauty. His studies are worth reading independent of any discussion on the validity of his interpretation: they are masterpieces. This said, for many readers his interpretation of Sabbatianism became not one of its many possible interpretations; it became Sabbatianism per se. While numerous scholars have added important —and some truly excellent—contributions that challenged particular points raised by Scholem, corrected some of his factual inaccuracies, or discussed texts or individuals associated with Tsevi's sect that were never the object of his attention, scholarship has largely upheld his conceptual apparatus and even his characteristic phraseology. Few serious attempts to challenge Scholem's broader perspective or propose a truly different view on Sabbatianism have been made. No scholar after Scholem has shared his ambition of rewriting the history of the Jewish people as the history of messianism, exploring Sabbatianism's genealogy in the Middle Ages, or tracing its impact on modern and contemporary religious and political phenomena. No one has written a monograph of the movement in its entirety or even a single phase of its unfolding. Instead, we have brief essays, each engaging with a particular Sabbatian personality or suggesting a close reading of a specific Sabbatian text.

I wish to draw attention to two approaches to Sabbatianism that reach beyond Scholem and his explanatory paradigm as it has been taken up and extended by other scholars. In so doing, I do not mean to imply the lack of validity on the part of Scholem's reading (and as noted, his reading hardly lacks elegance). It seems to me, however, that all that can be seen from Scholem's particular perspective has already been seen. Repeating his interpretative moves in light of yet another Sabbatian text or yet another event from the movement's history would simply belabor the point.

The first avenue of reflection touches on the syncretic or, better, transreligious facet of Sabbatianism. Sabbatai Tsevi must have solved the thorny issue as to which Islamic practices to adopt and, conversely, which Jewish observances to carry over to his life as a Muslim (till the end of his life, Sabbatai's religious praxis consisted of a curious admixture of Jewish and Muslim rituals). All subsequent Sabbatian converts had to negotiate a dual religious identity. Yet even for the Sabbatians who did not convert, the question of selective reception and rejection of alien notions and practices became a primary preoccupation. In Nathan of Gaza's theology, as reconstructed by Scholem, Sabbatai Tsevi converted to Islam in order to fight satanic forces on their own territory: conversion had the twin purpose of eradicating evil from within and saving the sparks of sanctity that had been ensnared by the demonic. For the messiah's followers, this idea had far-reaching implications: the world into which Sabbatai Tsevi (and those of his faithful who joined him in apostasy) entered could no longer be considered an undifferentiated dominion of darkness. It demanded careful study, both for the purpose of "learning your enemy" and in order to trace and rescue the elements of holiness that might have gone astray therein. Thus, from the very outset, Sabbatian thought displayed a keen interest in other peoples and other religions: from the moment the messiah entered the foreign realm of the nations of the world, questions concerning foreign traditions became key points of Sabbatian theology. The aspect of this problem that has received the most scholarly attention is the syncretic character of some Sabbatian rites and tenets of belief.

The question of the syncretic motif of Sabbatianism was first raised by Scholem himself, if only in a single paper that stands in opposition to the main line of his inquiry. In his masterful essay on Berukhiah, the leader of the Koniosos, a Muslim Sabbatian subsect in Salonika, the Israeli scholar expounded the doctrines of programmatic syncretists, who understood their conversion to Islam as a step in the redemptive process of fusing different religions. For the radical group of Koniosos, Islam was not only a mask for heterodox Judaism. They believed in the unity of all faiths and consciously included in their creed alien and diverse tenets.[21] Scholem went to great pains to emphasize that this particular aspect of Berukhiah's teachings was highly unusual even against the backdrop of other Sabbatian doctrines, including those of other Sabbatian subgroups of Salonika. In his view, the syncretistic tendency and positive attitude toward non-Jewish religions was not an organic development of Sabbatianism, but derived from the encounter with Muslim sectarian groups of the Ottoman Empire such as the Bektashi dervishes, whose rituals and teachings likewise included a strong syncretistic component involving elements of Christianity, Gnosticism, Shia Islam, as well as various pagan and animistic beliefs. The Koniosos did not belong to what he termed "classical Sabbatianism." Accordingly, among Scholem's studies on Sabbatianism, the Berukhiah essay remains a one-off oddity: his other works (including his other articles on the believers of Salonika) rehearsed the rhetoric of non-Jewish religions understood as "merely exterior façades" and "voluntary Marranism."

Scholem's presentation of Berukhiah's syncretism as exceptional and of all Sabbatians as "true Jews at heart" regardless of their "external" roles and religious affiliations might suit some strands of Sabbatianism (and might attest as well to his extraordinary ability to read the human heart). However, it does not account for the ubiquity among many Sabbatians of elements of rites and beliefs that could not be derived, except by the most strained arguments, from Jewish tradition. It also does not engage the wider—and more important—issue of Sabbatians' conscious attitude to such elements. The key question is not *if* Sabbatianism incorporated elements of other religions; the key question is *why* it did so. Scholem's notion that Sabbatianism contained a syncretic element, yet this element appeared only on the fringes of the movement, has been challenged by Yehudah Liebes. According to Liebes, a transconfessional feature was present in the main line of development of Sabbatian theology from the very beginning and can be discerned not only in the Tsevi's attitude to Islam, but also in Nathan's announcement that the true messiah would redeem even Jesus. The "dialectics" (Liebes approves of and appropriates Scholem's use of the concept) expressed itself here in attempts to mediate between the nihilistic position expressing itself in disdain or enmity for non-Jewish religions seen as the realm of *kelippot*, and the syncretic thrust that sought in all of them positive sides.[22] Seeking positivity in other religions might have led to conversion, but did not necessarily do so. Indeed, according to Liebes, in its most developed expressions Sabbatian syncretism amounted to a "religious renewal" of Judaism by other faiths.[23] Liebes mostly engaged eighteenth-century Sabbatianism in Christian Europe; in his view, during this period the syncretic aspect of Sabbatian thought became so pronounced that Sabbatianism could have been understood by Christian missionaries (including converted Jews familiar with intra-Jewish debates) as a kind of "crypto-Christianity."[24]

I fully concur with Liebes's view that it was precisely the mainstream, and not the fringe, of Sabbatianism that absorbed non-Jewish concepts and practices. I also believe that research on Christian and Christianizing undercurrents of Sabbatian thought is particularly auguring. Oddly for a group whose leader converted to the Muslim religion, Sabbatians, including those in the Ottoman Empire, seemed to be much more preoccupied with Christianity than with Islam. Nathan of Gaza's messianic pursuits included a visit to Rome, and his texts invoke Jesus but not Mohammad. His treatises contain Hebrew calques of Latin technical expressions of religious discourse.[25] No systematic research has been carried out on this issue, but it seems that he had at least some familiarity with Christian theological texts. Avraham Miguel Cardozo, Sabbatianism's principal converso theologian, received a thorough Christian education before leaving the Iberian Peninsula and returning to Judaism in Venice. Although Cardozo consistently downplayed his Christian past (and ferociously fought accusations of carrying vestiges of Christianity into his Judaism), there is no doubt that he retained a deep interest in theological questions that had occupied him in his Christian youth. Cardozo served as a main channel for the transmission of Christian ideas into Sabbatianism; his works contain numerous quotations and paraphrases of the texts of the Church Fathers and medieval theologians. These citations are hardly ever referenced, and they were likely not recognized as Christian in origin by most of his Jewish readers. Still, through Cardozo this thought entered the universe of Sabbatian discourse and became further elaborated in encounter with canonical Jewish texts. Cardozo's main disciple, Nehemiah Hayon, is a case in point. Hayon developed a Sabbatian doctrine of a Triune God. Like his teacher, he emphatically denied any Christian sympathies or influences and argued that the Christian concept of the Trinity is merely a distortion and vulgarization of its proper, that it to say Jewish, version. It is an open question whether Hayon took his own denials seriously. What is crystal clear, however, is that he could not avoid questions about the relationship of his teachings to those of the Christians. For Sabbatianism, Christianity became an unavoidable point of reference.

Scholem's and Liebes's analyses of Sabbatian syncretism opened up a full gamut of fascinating possibilities of inquiry. Yet the way in which these scholars formulated their main hypotheses and lines of argument seem to me overly narrow. Even sidestepping the methodological debate about the usefulness (or adequacy) of the notion of syncretism in the general study of religions, the key concept strikes me as ill fitted with regard to the specific case of Sabbatianism. Syncretism is far from peculiar to Sabbatianism (every religion, including normative Judaism, is syncretic to some degree). Sabbatianism's singularity was that in it fusing interreligious elements became a positive, and possibly even a supreme, value. It is not merely that different religions "exerted influence" on Sabbatian groups or that some of their tenets were "absorbed" by the Sabbatians; it is that combining elements of different religions became a nexus of a religious program in itself. It is for this reason that Liebes's notion that a syncretic trend in Sabbatianism amounted to enriching Judaism by tenets and rites of other religions may be misleading. The movement's transreligious push did not entail supplementing one religion with elements of others. Rather, it involved a conscious blending of all of them. Judaism was in no way privileged in this process of religious amalgamation. Indeed, in the writings of Cardozo, Jacob Frank, and arguably also Eibeschütz, it was considered in some respects inferior to other faiths.

Syncretism in fact may not be a wholly helpful frame for analysis of the interreligious trait of Sabbatianism. But it certainly does touch a nerve: preoccupation with the non-Jewish world and worldview is one of the most striking features of Sabbatianism. While Sabbatians did not always display a positive or even tolerant attitude toward non-Jews, they never ignored other religions and traditions. They studied them with an intensity that sometimes bordered on obsession (according to contemporary testimony, Rabbi Jonathan Eibeschütz developed an "uncontrolled urge to read books of the priests"[26]).

The importance of the study of Sabbatian syncretism goes beyond the immediate subject of research on the movement initiated by Sabbatai Tsevi. Jewish historiography generally has it that the Jews' prevailing attitude toward non-Jews during the premodern period was guided by solely practical considerations of, on the one hand, defense against political or ecclesiastical encroachments on the Jewish way of life and, on the other, establishing the boundaries of halakhically permissible contact between Jews and Gentiles. References to non-Jewish notions, in this view, were dictated by the demands of polemics, necessitated by the need to find legal frames for everyday interactions, or mere incidental curiosa. Alien faiths and cultures of other peoples might have constituted mortal dangers, but were neither real temptations nor serious challenges forcing a true redefinition of Jewish concepts. Jews were not, so to speak, genuinely interested in the outside world.[27] Sabbatianism, however, gives the lie to this classic claim. The profound fascination of many Sabbatians—including many of those belonging to "classical Sabbatianism"—with the non-Jewish world requires explanation. The Sabbatians were certainly the most ecumenical of early modern Jews. While mainstream Jewish discourse habitually bundled all "nations of the world" and their faiths together, Sabbatianism carefully distinguished between different creeds and denominations, often drawing lines not only between large religious formations such as Islam and Christianity, but also between different sects and subgroups, such as different Protestant churches or different Sufi orders. As noted before, the engagement of Sabbatianism with Christianity seems deeper than its engagement with Islam. Some Sabbatians were most knowledgeable about the particulars of Christian theology. For them, the encounter with Christian theological literature was akin to that experienced by Christian Hebraists, who "discovered" in Jewish texts what they knew from their own tradition. They presumed estrangement and found familiarity. In fact, if Christian Hebraism is understood as a Christian interest in Judaism that transcends the immediate needs of contemporaneous religious polemics, it might be argued that some strands of Sabbatianism amounted to a "Jewish Christianism" among the Jews.

The second avenue of inquiry that I wish to propose has to do with the personality of Sabbatai Tsevi and the ideas introduced by the messiah himself, rather than by his followers and interpreters. For Scholem, Sabbatai Tsevi was but a plaything of wider historical processes. The messiah, a yeshivah dropout, lacked not only basic knowledge of Judaism, but the elementary capacity for self-reflection. Indeed, he needed his prophet to explain him to himself. In the reading put forward by the author of *Redemption through Sin*, all early Sabbatian ideas stemmed from Nathan of Gaza's extraordinarily creative interpretations of Sabbatai's incongruous actions.[28] Nathan's speculations, in turn, were "dialectical elaborations" and "sublimations" of deeper and unconscious spiritual energies or conceptual superstructures built upon clashes of social and religious forces that had nothing to do with Sabbatianism as such and existed, in latent form, long before its inception. These forces had been "denied the political and historical outlets [they] had originally anticipated."[29] Sabbatianism was their historical moment coming to the fore.

In his early writings on Sabbatianism, Scholem claimed that Sabbatai Tsevi "left no writings and, what is more important, he is not credited with a single unforgettable word, epigram, or speech. As a Kabbalist and a scholar he does not appear to have raised himself above mediocrity."[30] Yet as more and more of Sabbatai's letters were unearthed by scholars, Scholem could no longer assert that Sabbatai wrote nothing. Still, he continued to speak of the figure of the messiah with undisguised derision, and continued to maintain that Tsevi's thought was wholly unoriginal and uninspiring. Scholem was so convinced by this stance that when Sabbatai's letter expounding his own understanding of apostasy to Islam was discovered, he incorporated fragments of it into the revised version of his monograph, carefully omitting all passages that might have undermined the interpretation he had been advancing. Published in full by Abraham Amarillo, the letter was given a fascinating reading by Yehudah Liebes. First, it turned out that from the outset Tsevi had had his own vision of messiahship, a vision that differed from and to a large extent contradicted that of his prophet Nathan. The messiah placed radical emphasis on a strictly personal relationship with God (in that letter and his other writings Sabbatai repeatedly referred to God as "my God," "the God of my faith," "the True Living God," or "the God of Sabbatai Tsevi"). He contrasted this personal rapport with God with rabbinic, and importantly, Kabbalistic abstract speculations about the Absolute. Moreover, Tsevi did not consider Islam, his adopted faith, a demonic realm; his attitude toward the Muslim religion was much more complex, inclusive, and affirmative. Sabbatai, unlike for some of his followers including Nathan and Cardozo, did not portray his own conversion as an effect of external pressure, but an existential choice, consciously and freely made. This choice was not driven by Kabbalistic teachings about the liberation of the sparks of the holy from the impure, but a leap of faith, a response to the unfathomable command of the living God, whom "he alone knew." Further, and similarly, Sabbatai's "antinomian" actions were not, in his own view, antinomian at all. Like the conversion to Islam, they emerged seamlessly from the messiah's existential proximity to the Creator, who was inaccessible and inconceivable to anyone but Sabbatai himself. The wisdom of the Living God was stupidity in the eyes of the world: the notorious pronunciation aloud of his Ineffable Name was not an intentionally blasphemous act of rebellion against the sacred norms of Judaism, but "Sabbatai Tsevi's calling his close personal friend, God of Israel, by His private name."[31]

Liebes's argument is far-reaching in consequence. Sabbatai Tsevi is here appreciated as a persona of his own merit and author of original writings, with Liebes demonstrating that Sabbatianism indeed originated in its messiah, not only in his commentators. As against Scholem, Sabbatai was not a blind tool of wider historical forces but a free agent acting on the basis of his own religious insights. Yet these insights carried destructive potential that needed to be defused. According to Liebes, Jewish messianic belief has had a long history of struggling with the "dialectical tension" (here too, Liebes embraces Scholem's notion of dialectics) between "functional" messianism propounding political visions of national restitution and "mythological" messianism focused on the persona of the messiah.[32] Sabbatai Tsevi disturbed this delicate balance. The world of his personal mythology consisted of only him and his God, leaving no room for visions of communal redemption or, for that matter, for any interest in a wider collective.[33] Nathan of Gaza's theological tour de force was directed at restoring the lost dialectical moment and thereby saving Sabbatian mythology for Judaism as the religion of the Jewish people. Nathan—who "understood Sabbatai Tsevi better than Sabbatai understood himself" (which is to say, understood both the power of Sabbatai's myth and its destructive potential)—succeeded: he managed to translate the messiah's persona into terms that had transpersonal and national value and therefore could "revive and fertilize Judaism."[34]

The personalistic or existential theology of Sabbatianism constitutes a highly fruitful avenue of future study. As yet, no scholar has considered the wider ramifications of Tsevi's ideas and their possible impact on later Sabbatian thought. Liebes, who initiated this line of research, considered it a dead end: Sabbatai's notions had already been reinterpreted by Nathan of Gaza in a way that removed their sting. Fascinating in themselves, the messiah's views were not known among later Sabbatians and had no impact on subsequent developments (none of Liebes's work on syncretistic eighteenth-century Sabbatianism draws upon his essay on Sabbatai's personal God). I take exception to this final-curtain characterization. To begin with, there *does* seem to be further transmission of these ideas in their original form, with all their destructive potential. Avraham Miguel Cardozo and Jonathan Eibeschütz appear to have been familiar with and further developed Sabbatai's views, and Jacob Frank directly quoted Tsevi's letter, a document that he clearly knew very well. Yet even more important than establishing the chain of transmission is another topos. Sabbatian theology is deeply personal (in the sense in which all good theology is deeply personal). The juxtaposition of the existential concept of God directly experienced by an individual and the abstract deity of reified traditions blindly enforced by the religious establishment appears in the writings of all important personalities of what we today consider the Sabbatian movement, whether or not they were familiar with Tsevi's own writings. The dualism that permeates all Sabbatian teachings from Sabbatai Tsevi's "God of my Faith" and "God of the rabbis," through Avraham Miguel Cardozo's differentiation between the Prime Cause and the God of Israel, until Jonathan Eibeschütz's explorations of the dangerous liaisons between *Atika Kadisha* and *Malka Kadisha*, is, in my opinion, not so much a Gnostic dualism of the good alien God and the evil demiurge, as a Pascalian dichotomy of the living God of Abraham, Isaac, and Yaakov and the lifeless Absolute of soulless religious functionaries.

While strict logic did not link the Sabbatian interreligious outlook and its personalistic theology, I would argue that the latter, in its disregard for external boundaries as well as its rejection of inherited or unreflexively accepted norms and principles, made the former not only possible but highly likely. Sabbatai Tsevi's God could not be bound to any religion, including Judaism, the religion in which He first revealed Himself. Hence, He could be sought in all religions. No higher authority could guide this quest for the True God or predict its results. No exclusive claims to clues and regarding His will or nature could be made about any single sacred textual canon. (Nehemiah Hayon proposed to treat *all* books as Kabbalistic books and argued for unbound freedom of their interpretation.) Considering Sabbatianism through the prisms of transreligious approach and theological personalism yields two additional points of inquiry.

First, such a discussion disenchants Sabbatian antinomianism: Sabbatai's "strange deeds" were not absurd acts of a madman explained away by his followers, but strenuous efforts to follow the unfathomable wishes of his personal deity. To the extent that his adherents indeed tried to imitate their messiah, they attempted to emulate not his odd behavior as such but his quest for the understanding and fulfillment of the true God's will. They were prepared to fulfill this will even if it led them to violations of Mosaic Law or to the abandonment of official Judaism, but they never claimed that such violations had inherent value in themselves. Sabbatian patterns of behavior might have been "antinomian" or "blasphemous" in the eyes of contemporary observers, but Sabbatianism never produced a systematic ideology of antinomianism—such an ideology is an artifact of academic research. More important, even these contemporary observers were significantly less impressed by Sabbatian violations of Mosaic Law than modern scholars. While the principal enemies of the Sabbatians (e.g.,

Jacob Sasportas, Moses Hagiz, Jacob Emden) did fulminate against the Sabba-tians' "licentiousness," they were much more concerned about their flirting (and sometimes open romance) with "the other" than with any libertine excesses. Mixing religious identities and values, not antinomianism, was the prime target of polemics.

"Redemption through sin" (*Mitsvah ha-Ba'ah be-Averah*) is a catchy phrase and a wonderful title for a scholarly essay. Yet to the best of my knowledge, the no-tion does not appear in any Sabbatian text: the concept itself is rabbinic (it is first used in the Babylonian Talmud)[35] and the only Sabbatianism-related source that invokes it is a confession of a repentant Sabbatian, in which, using rabbinic terminology, he denounces his former fellow believers.[36]

Second, the Sabbatian noninsularity and its provision of a God of living expe-rience give the best inkling into the mystery of Sabbatianism's appeal and long duration. What Sabbatai Tsevi's religion offered to its believers was an acces-sible world and an accessible God. In Sabbatianism, Judaism ceased to be self-referential: Sabbatian thought developed in conscious dialogue with other faiths. The world's religious and cultural diversity was explored and explained. This satisfied the curiosity of believers, but it also infused with new meaning the con-stitutive Jewish experience, the experience of exile. Sabbatianism is usually con-ceptualized as a form of messianism. This conceptualization certainly accords with the heroic phase of the movement, from its eruption till, roughly, the death of Sabbatai Tsevi. Although later Sabbatian thought does contain some specula-tions concerning Sabbatai's "second coming," messianism as a privileged theme of reflection disappeared from the believers' discourse by the late seventeenth century. Scholem noticed this disappearance and understood the difficulty it presents for scholars trying to define the scope of their inquiry and answer the knotty question of whether or not a particular individual or text was Sabbatian. For Scholem, it is not the common subject matter that links different texts clas-sified by him as "Sabbatian," but common terminology.[37] Countering Scholem here, I submit that a topical thread does indeed run through Sabbatian texts. This common concern is a sustained reflection on the meaning of exile, both in the sense of political exile of the Jews among the nations and the metaphysical exile of the Shekhinah among the *kelippot*. Tsevi's belonging-not-belonging to both Judaism and Islam was a profound expression of the messiah's elemental homelessness. Sabbatian converts were thrown into alien worlds and remained stretched between attraction and repulsion; the Sabbatian preoccupation with non-Jewish creeds and practices can be read as an attempt to make sense of the drama of redemption both for the peoples of the world and for the Jews, who were scattered among them. Sabbatian thought was thus a dialogue with the world into which the Jews are exiled—neither able to fully join it nor to escape it.

As Sabbatianism dialogued with the world, it also dialogued with its God. The Sabbatian God was a God who could be reasoned with, even argued with; one who intervenes in temporal affairs; one who sometimes answers pleas and is sometimes painfully silent. For Sabbatai Tsevi, this God was first and foremost the God of direct personal encounter. Sabbatai's moments of ecstasy brought him into intimate proximity with *his* God. He "knew," with absolute certainty, that this God existed, acted in this world, and that he, Sabbatai Tsevi, was loved by Him and fulfilled His will. Yet this celebration of the existential immediacy of God had a darker side: Sabbatai's moments of intimate closeness to the "God of his Faith" could not be freely produced by an act of will. The intimacy was interlaced with periods of God's "silence," in which Sabbatai experienced an excruciating sense of abandonment and utter uncertainty regarding the right course of action. In Sabbatai's letters, the tension between God's proximity and distance was an existential howl (the best minds of his generation were destroyed by prophecies); in the writings of later Sabbatians, it was elaborated with infinite subtlety. Sabbatianism put forward a concept of a God who is simultaneously cherishing and untrustworthy. The Sabbatian God entered into personal rapport with his messiah and then inexplicably abandoned him. He is the God of Israel, who gave commandments to Moses and demanded that Moses's descendants break them. He made a covenant with his people and reneged on his part of the bargain. During the periods of his silence, the faithful lack any clue as to the course of redemption or even everyday behavior: traditional religious norms do not provide a basis for action—after all, God Himself has shown that they might be abolished—and the existential experience of God's guidance is impermanent and unsummonable.

It was precisely this concept of God that contained the seeds of Sabbatianism's own destruction. Sabbatianism after the death of Sabbatai Tsevi was conspicuously bivalent—the call to base religious life on personal religious experience clashed head-on with its inability to craft this experience into a coherent set of religious norms and practices. Perhaps the best contemporary analogy for Sabbatianism is offered not by millenarian or messianic movements in Christianity and Islam, but by the early modern nonconfessional Christianity ("Christians without a church") discussed in the classic study of Leszek Kołakowski.[38] Sabbatianism was a religion characterized by an irremovable antagonism between its own most fundamental values and any translation of these values into institutions, structures, social hierarchies, standardized practices and rituals, or fixed tenets of belief. It attacked the existing religious structures, but was intrinsically unable to transform itself into such a structure. It was a religion of permanent rebellion, of unending motion. Like Kołakowski's nonconfessional Christians, the Sabbatians' heretical character was not accidental but essential: it was not a function of its condemnation by a *particular* religious authority, but rather emerged from its organic inability to establish—and to reconcile itself with— *any* religious authority.

In its most consistent—and therefore most radical—expressions, Sabbatian thought was perfectly aware of the ultimate consequences of its own position. Neither the tension between the God who is intimately close and the God who is frightfully distant nor the tension between faith and functionalism were ever resolved on some higher dialectical plane. If Nathan of Gaza indeed tried to soothe the sting of Sabbatai Tsevi's ideas by counterbalancing them with dialectical oppositions, he failed miserably. Early Sabbatianism gloried in the existential proximity of God and celebrated the discovery of spiritual freedom of approaching redemption. Later Sabbatianism expressed itself in sophisticated theological constructions, which engendered radical reinterpretations of the early optimistic Sabbatian soteriology. The religious sentiments of mid-eighteenth-century Sabbatai believers were epitomized not by the dialectical writings of Nathan of Gaza, but by a remark of an anonymous Sabbatian, who attributed to his messiah the following truly Faustian statement: "Sabbatai Tsevi declared: Since the God of Israel did not choose to fulfil my messianic destiny I will punish Him by causing thousands to abandon his faith."[39] Eighteenth-century Sabbatianism was a much darker creature than its seventeenth-century counterpart. The rebellion against the petrified structures of normative religion conducted by the "spiritualists" fighting the rabbis in the name of a new "utopian Judaism" (Scholem) or attempts to "revive and fertilize the Jewish religion" (Liebes) was to a large extent replaced by a rebellion against Sabbatai Tsevi, and in some cases a rebellion against the God of Israel Himself.

Notes

1. Gershom Scholem, "Zum Verständnis des Sabbatianismus: zugleich ein Beitrag zur Geschichte der 'Aufklärung,'" *Almanach des Schocken Verlags auf das Jahr 5697* (1936–37): 36; Scholem, "Redemption through Sin," in *The Messianic Idea in Judaism and Other Essays on Jewish Spirituality*, trans. Hillel Halkin (New York: Schocken Books, 1971), 88, 92.

2. Scholem, "Zum Verständnis des Sabbtianismus," 35.

3. Gershom Scholem, *Sabbatai Sevi: The Mystical Messiah 1626–1676*, trans. R. J. Zwi Werblowski (London: Routledge, 1973), 688.

4. Scholem, "Redemption through Sin," 88; Gershom Scholem, *Major Trends in Jewish Mysticism* (New York: Schocken Books, 1954), 306.

5. Scholem, *Sabbatai Sevi*, 720.

6. Halkin renders this as "rationalizations"; see Scholem, "Redemption through Sin," 88. Compare, however, the Hebrew original of Scholem's essay, "Mitsvah ha-Ba'ah be-Averah," in *Mehkarim u-mekorot le-toledot ha-Shabbeta'ut ve-gilgulehah* (Jerusalem: Byalik, 1974), 18.

7. Scholem, "Redemption through Sin," 101–9; Scholem, *Major Trends*, 314.

8. Scholem, "Redemption through Sin," 109.

9. Scholem, "Zum Verständnis des Sabbtianismus," 37.

10. Scholem, "Der Nihilismus als Religiöses Phänomen," in *Judaica* 4 (Frankfurt: Suhrkamp Verlag, 1984), 134.

11. Scholem, *Major Trends*, 288.

12. Scholem, "Redemption through Sin," 84.

13. Scholem, *Major Trends*, 327.

14. Scholem, "Redemption through Sin," 140–41; Scholem, "Ursprünge, Widersprüche und Auswirkungen des Sabbatianismus," in *Judaica* 5 (Frankfurt: Suhrkamp Verlag, 1992), 130.

15. Gershom Scholem, "Die Theologie des Sabbatianismus im Lichte Abraham Cardozos," in *Judaica* 1 (Frankfurt: Suhrkamp Verlag, 1977), 146; compare Jacob Katz, "Relationship between Sabbatianism, Haskalah, and Reform," in Katz, *Divine Law in Human Hands: Case Studies in Halahkic Flexibility* (Jerusalem: Magnes Press, 1988), 23.

16. Scholem, *Major Trends*, 307; compare Scholem, *Sabbatai Sevi*, 211–17, 283.

17. Scholem, "The Crypto-Jewish Sect of the Dönmeh (Sabbatians) in Turkey," in Scholem, *The Messianic Idea*, 146, 160.

18. Scholem, *Major Trends*, 304.

19. Ibid., 315; Scholem, "Redemption through Sin," 98, 110, 147.

20. Scholem, "The Crypto-Jewish Sect," 142; see also Gershom Scholem, "Die Metamorphose des häretischen Messianismus der Sabbatianer in religiösen Nihilismus im 18. Jahrhundert," in *Judaica* 3 (Frankfurt: Suhrkamp Verlag, 1978), 214.

21. Scholem, "Berukhiah—Rosh ha-Shabbeat'im be-Saloniki," in Gershom Scholem, *Mehkarei Shabbeta'ut* (Jerusalem: Am Oved, 1991), 352–53.

22. Yehudah Liebes, "Ha-Meshihi'ut ha-Shabbeta'it," in Liebes, *Sod ha-Emunah ha-Shabbeta'it* (Jerusalem: Byalik, 1995), 19.

23. Ibid.

24. Liebes, "Al Kat Sodit Yehudit-Notsrit she Mekorah be-Shabbeta'ut," in Liebes, *Sod ha-Emunah*, 221.

25. Chaim Wirszubski, "Ha-Ideologia ha-Shabbeta'it shel Hamarat ha-Mashiah," in Wirszubski, *Bein ha-shittin* (Jerusalem: Magnes, 1990), 225.

26. Jacob Emden, *Bet Yehonatan ha-Sofer* (Altona, 1762), 16v.

27. For the most synthetic account of this historiographic position, see Jacob Katz, *Ex-*

clusiveness and Tolerance: Studies in Jewish-Gentile Relations in Medieval and Modern Times (London: Oxford University Press, 1961).

28. See, for instance, Scholem, *Major Trends*, 296.

29. Scholem, "Redemption through Sin," 109; Scholem, *Sabbatai Sevi*, 69.

30. Scholem, *Major Trends*, 293.

31. Liebes, "Yahaso shel Shabbetai Tsevi le-Hamarat Dato," in Liebes, *Sod ha-Emunah*, 25.

32. Liebes, "Ha-Shabbeta'ut ve-Gevulot ha-Dat," in Rachel Elior, ed., *Ha-halom ve-shivro. Ha-tenu'ah ha-Shabbta'it u-sheluhoteha: Meshihiyut, Shabbeta'ut u-Frankizm* (Jerusalem: Magnes, 2000), 7.

33. Ibid., 14.

34. Ibid., 21.

35. See BT Berakhot 47b.

36. Jacob Emden, *Sefer Shimush* (Altona, 1762), 20v.

37. See Scholem, *Major Trends*, 302–3.

38. Leszek Kołakowski, *Świadomość religijna i więź kościelna. Studia nad chrześcijaństwem bezwyznaniowym siedemnastego wieku* (Warsaw: PWN, 1965).

39. Joseph Prager, "Gahalei esh," Bodleian Library, Oxford, Ms. Mich. 106–8 (Neubauer no. 2189), vol. 1, 32r.

1 | Sabbatian Movement prior to Sabbatai Tsevi's Conversion to Islam

The spread of messianic enthusiasm in the summer and autumn of 1665 generated much interest among the Jews of the Ottoman Empire and Christian Europe. During this period, Sabbatai Tsevi's prophet, Nathan of Gaza, composed a series of epistles describing the advent of the messiah and foretelling the impending momentous events. While addressed to particular people, these letters were intended for wide circulation and were copied and passed from community to community. The most important of Nathan's epistles was a missive to Sabbatai Tsevi's main supporter in Egypt, one of the leaders of the Cairo Jewish community, Çelebi Raphael Joseph. The letter was a manifesto of the rapidly expanding messianic movement; it was read in Smyrna, Constantinople, Rome, Venice, Hamburg, and Amsterdam, among other places. In addition to conveying the turbulent atmosphere of the times and providing a glimpse into the mindset of Sabbatai's prophet, it offers a first outline of the tenets of Sabbatian theology that will be fully elaborated in the writings composed after the messiah's conversion. Nathan's notion of the messiah recalls few traditional Jewish ideas of this figure. He is not a political liberator triumphing over Israel's enemies, gathering the exiles in the Holy Land, and reinstating the sacrificial service in the Jerusalem Temple. Rather, first and foremost, the messiah is a suffering servant atoning for the sins of his people. His afflictions have a salvific value of themselves: the great, "inconceivable and limitless" suffering that Sabbatai Tsevi undergoes on behalf of the Jewish people earns him a special place in the economy of salvation. This elevated position affords him special prerogatives: by a pure act of grace, he may absolve sins and save even the worst wrongdoer ("including even Jesus of Nazareth"). Indeed, Nathan goes further. Approaching the Calvinist conception of "double predestination," the prophet argues that Sabbatai Tsevi may not only remit the transgressions of sinners; he may also condemn the righteous irrespective of their good deeds. The fate of an individual (or at least of an individual Jew) does not depend on his or her actions. Rather, it hinges on the sovereign act of will of the redeemer who, as he pleases, grants salvation or decrees damnation. Moreover, this redeemer requires not the observance of the commandments, but "pure faith" in him, unsupported by signs or marvels. The Jews are to accept Sabbatai Tsevi as their savior despite the fact that he does not fulfill any criteria of messiahship, does not prove the truth of his mission by any miracle, and despite all appearances to the contrary. From its very outset, Sabbatianism breaks the link between human deeds and divine salvation: redemption is an act of grace wholly unconnected to the fulfillment of the commandments. Finally, no bloody apocalyptic conflict and Jewish revenge on Gentile haters of Israel is found here as a trope: Tsevi triumphs "without any warfare" "through the hymns and praises." (Indeed, Sabbatai was exceptionally musical, and singing and dancing constituted an important part of Sabbatian rites.) Sabbatianism is a religion of faith rather than deeds.

Thomas Coenen's *Ydele verwachtinge der Joden getoont in den Persoon van Sabethai Zevi* (*Vain Hopes of the Jews as Revealed in the Person of Sabbatai Tsevi*) belongs to the genre of Christian anti-Jewish polemic emphasizing the "blindness" of the Jews that causes them to reject the only true redeemer, Jesus Christ, and leads them to the continuing reckless acceptance of false saviors. The "blind obstinacy" of the Jews is simultaneously their crime and their punishment. In other words, the Jews' inability to see reality constitutes both the reason for disregarding the "obvious" truth of Christianity and the retribution for the rejection of this very truth. Coenen was a Calvinist minister serving the community of Dutch merchants in Smyrna between 1662 and 1671. Despite its clear bias, his book, printed in 1669, is invaluable as the fullest account of Tsevi's biography written by a contemporary and the only account of the messiah's early days in Smyrna written by a direct observer. Coenen was an eyewitness to the Sabbatian fever in Anatolia, and he met personalities central to the drama, including Nathan of Gaza and Sabbatai's brothers, Joseph and Elijah. The Dutch clergyman may be seen as the first historian of Sabbatianism: in addition to recording his direct experience, he attempted to gather additional evidence juxtaposing conflicting testimonies, and he even published several Sabbatian texts in Dutch translation. In the eighteenth century, sections of *The Vain Hopes* were translated into Hebrew and formed the basis of the Jewish anti-Sabbatian writings of Leyb ben Ozer and Rabbi Jacob Emden.

Jacob Sasportas (1610–1698) was born in North Africa and served as rabbi in a number of Sephardic communities in Western Europe. During the Sabbatian frenzy, he was living as a private individual in Hamburg. Sasportas became the main strategist and principal ideologue of anti-Sabbatianism before the conversion of the messiah. In December 1665, he composed two letters to the rabbis of Amsterdam, the center of Sabbatianism in Europe. Therein, the rabbi expressed doubts about messianic rumors and attacked the conceptions expounded by Nathan in his letter to Raphael Joseph. The responses he received from Aaron Sarfatti and Isaac Nahar show the depth of the Sabbatian convictions of many rabbinic leaders of the time. These letters, together with Sasportas's rejoinders and many other documents, were compiled by Sasportas into a book titled *Tsistat Novel Tsevi* (*The Fading Flower of Tsevi*; a pun on Is 28:4).

Sasportas's open opposition to Tsevi at the height of the movement earned him little sympathy and reportedly even endangered his life. After the conversion, the erstwhile Sabbatians were eager to efface the memory of their families' involvement in the Sabbatian fever. *Tsitsat Novel Tsevi*, prepared for publication, was suppressed by community leaders. The work was published in its entirety only by the twentieth-century scholar Isaiah Tishby.

1 | Nathan of Gaza, A Letter to Raphael Joseph

Source: Jacob Sasportas, *Tsitsat Novel Tsevi*, ed. Isaiah Tishby
(Jerusalem: Mosad Byalik, 1954), 7–12.

To our fruit of holiness enwrapped in praise, our man of deeds rich in accomplishment, the exalted prince and honored rabbi. May your light shine like the rising sun, blossom like the flowers! May an abundance of life and peace rest upon your head, never (please God) to depart!

I write to acknowledge receipt of your letter, and to convey my delight that, Lord be praised, you are a believer in this faith, which is clear as the sunlight and admits no dispute or any doubt whatever. This is the faith though which the Jewish people shall achieve their "inheritance" from the Lord, meaning the Jubilee that is to be revealed at this time, and come into their "rest," meaning the self-revelation of the Holy Ancient One within the Irascible One that is to occur in the year 5430 [1669–70].[1] [. . .]

Nowadays we again face opposing forces. They are wholly ineffective, however, and injure no one but themselves. For the final End is now upon us.

This being so, you must not wonder by what special merit our generation has come to deserve it. In addition, there are the dreadful agonies, inconceivable and limitless, that Rabbi Sabbatai Tsevi has suffered on behalf of the Jewish nation. Consequently, he has full power to do with this nation whatever he pleases, to justify or (God forbid) condemn them. He may justify the most depraved sinner in existence—even someone like Jesus—or condemn anyone who doubts him, even if he be the most pious man alive, to unspeakable torments.

You must treat the following principle as absolutely certain: *The Jewish people cannot attain to life other than by believing these things without any sign or miracle.* All

---

1. [The language of "rest" and "inheritance" is taken from the Bible, e.g., Dt 12:9. In Lv 25, the "Jubilee" is the fiftieth year, in which slaves are set free and all the children of Israel reclaim their ancestral holdings. In Kabbalah, it is a representation of the maternal *sefirah* (divine aspect) named *Binah*, called Jubilee. The "Irascible One" (*Ze'ir Anpin*; literally, "small of face") is the central male divinity in the Kabbalistic system, roughly equivalent to the biblical God, frequently manifesting Himself in judgment, while the "Holy Ancient One" (*Attika Kaddisha*, sometimes called "Ancient of Days") is the loftier, more esoteric divine manifestation, who consists of pure Grace.]

this is God's purpose, enacted in this generation worthy to see the beginnings of Redemption. You must have no concern whatever for those who do not believe, even if they happen to be your personal friends.

Now I will tell you how events are to unfold:

A year and some months from now, [Sabbatai Tsevi] will take dominion from the Turkish sultan without any warfare. Through the hymns and praises he will utter, all the nations will be brought into submission. Wherever he turns to conquer, he will take with him the Turkish sultan alone. All the kings will become his tributaries; the Turkish sultan alone will be his personal slave. There will be no bloodshed among the Christians, other than in the Germanic lands. The ingathering of the Diaspora will not take place at that time; rather, the Jews will enjoy high status in their present localities. Nor will our splendid Temple be then rebuilt. But the rabbi [Sabbatai] will reveal the place of the altar and offer sacrifices, and [reveal] the ashes of the Red Heifer.[2]

This will go on for four or five years. The rabbi will then travel to the river Sambatyon,[3] appointing the Turkish sultan as his deputy for the interim and instructing him how to treat the Jews. After three months, however, the [sultan's] advisers will entice him to rebel. Many woes will then befall, and the prophecy be fulfilled, *I will test them as one tests gold, and smelt them as one smelts silver* [Zec 13:9].[4] No one will be spared these woes apart from those living here [in Gaza], for here will be the center of dominion.

[...]

The eschatological signs prophesied in the Zohar will take place at the end of this period, which will extend until the coming Sabbatical year.[5] This will be the "seventh year" in which "the son of David will come," and in that seventh year we shall have our Sabbath [cf. Lv 25:4], King Sabbatai.[6]

That is when the rabbi will return from the river Sambatyon with his consort, the daughter of Moses our Master. It will then become known that Moses has

2. [Which according to the ritual prescribed in Nm 19, long fallen into disuse, were to cleanse individuals of their corpse impurities and allow them to visit the site of the Temple.]

3. [The legendary river that separates the Lost Ten Tribes of Israel from the rest of the world.]

4. [Nathan reverses the biblical order of the phrases.]

5. [The year 5432 (1671–72).]

6. [Whose name is from the Hebrew word for "Sabbath." The quotation is from BT Sanhedrin 97a.]

been alive for the past fifteen years, and that [Sabbatai's] blessed bride, Rebecca by name, is now thirteen years old.[7] The rabbi's current wife will become a slave girl, his new wife the Lady. While he is outside Jerusalem, the slave girl will be the Lady. Know, however, that a private conversation will be required for you to understand this.

In that year he will come from the river Sambatyon mounted on the lion of Bei Ila'ei,[8] a seven-headed snake for its bridle, fire blazing from his mouth [2 Sm 22:9]. When they see this, all the nations and rulers will certainly throw themselves to the ground before him. On that same day the Diaspora will be ingathered and the Temple manifest itself, fully built, from on high. There will be seven thousand living in the Land of Israel at that time, and on that same day the Land will witness the resurrection of those who died there and will expel those who do not deserve to remain. The resurrection outside the Land will take place forty years afterward.

From this you may gather some slight notion of his greatness [Jb 26:14]. You must take these things on absolute faith and through this faith merit to experience them. Out of my affection for you, in recognition of your pious devotion [Gn 22:12], I have revealed to you everything.

Thus shall prosperity and contentment flourish and never wane, for you and all who hold to the faith and also for

Your humble well-wisher,
Abraham Nathan

Translated by David Halperin

7. [Moses has presumably been living with the Lost Tribes of Israel on the other side of the Sambatyon, where he has sired the messiah's destined bride.]

8. [A mythical beast described in the Talmud, Hullin 59b. "Bei Ila'ei" can be understood as "the exalted places," and perhaps Nathan so intends. In his letters, Sabbatai speaks of himself as the "lion of Bei Ila'ei" and the "gazelle of Bei Ila'ei" (also from Hullin 59b, a huge animal equated with the unicorn).]

2

Thomas Coenen, Vain Hopes of the Jews

Source: Thomas Coenen, *Ydele verwachtinge der Joden Getoont in den Persoon van Sabethai Zevi* (Amsterdam: Joannes van den Bergh, 1669).

The messiah walked in front, carrying a silver-plated fan in his hand. When he passed houses of Jews, they reverently spread tapestries on the ground. Once it happened that they encountered the city guards who, seeing them as a properly behaved company, against their custom just let them pass. Greatly astounded by the politeness of the Turkish guards, the Jews interpreted it, in the absence of miracles that should confirm the mandate of the true messiah, as a miracle in itself: as if the fan in his hand was like Aaron's staff with which he wrought miracles.

While there were still a considerable number of Jews who wouldn't accept such vanities right away, their number lessened by the day. The partisan divide between them and the supporters of Sabbatai Tsevi had grown so much that nothing less than a schism was to be expected. It was feared that the bitterness would wax until they would murder one another like cats and dogs. For it had come so far that words of abuse came to deeds. The wrathful mob was mobilized. They set off to the house of one of Sabbatai's opponents, a rich and respectable Jewish citizen of this city, and showered its door and windows with stones. There was no lack of people who, armed like well-equipped soldiers, went to kill this Jew named Kahin Pegna [Hayyim Peña], or at least to beat him up and loot his house. But fortunately it did not come that far. As it was Friday around the hour that Sabbath would commence, they contented themselves for the time being with throwing stones.

Although things already had gone so far, this was not the end. Sabbatai Tsevi heard that Pegna had neither been stoned to death nor physically abused, but instead was still alive and unrepentant in his opinions. Sabbatai was very dissatisfied with this and thought it necessary to do something extraordinary to frighten his other [opponents]. He assembled his followers, consisting in part of fishermen and salesmen of poultry and eggs, and in part craftsmen or laborers, some servants, and the sort of nobles of whom the richest have nothing to lose. He then decided to send an order on the Sabbath to the superintendents of the Portuguese synagogue to throw [Peña], whom Sabbatai Tsevi had banned as a heretic because he had refused to believe in him, out of the synagogue. The superintendents and other Jews could not understand why, according to this strange innovation, [they] should expel a well-respected man solely on the basis of his word and without any legal reason.

Then Sabbatai Tsevi himself approached, followed by around five hundred of the scum, paying no attention whatsoever to the Sabbath and the devotions of the Jews who gathered there. Having arrived, he took an ax (even though, according to their superstitious belief, Jews on that day are not allowed to touch a tool or instrument). To doubly profane the Sabbath, he shattered the door of the synagogue. Pegna had slipped away in order to escape the fury of the raving and desperate mob, and fled through a trapdoor or the roof. When the agitated mob entered and searched the entire synagogue, and did not find the person they were looking for, Sabbatai ordered the prayers to be read and had them commence where it pleased him. He climbed on a chair and committed several excesses as great as a Jew can commit. The first one should have been called wisdom had it come from the heart and had [it] not been accompanied by frivolities. He clutched his fist as if he were blowing a trumpet to the four parts of the earth, lifted his eyes toward heaven, and began speaking to the Jews: "What did Jesus the Nazarene do that you abused him so? I will yet place him among the prophets." The color [of his face] changed, and he displayed great anger toward four or five *kachams* [rabbis] of Smyrna, threatening them, throwing them out of the synagogue, and banning them.

Each of them he addressed personally. One he named a camel, another a hare, the third one a pig, the fourth one he called a rabbit—all names of animals that according to the ceremonial law are impure. To this he added that he would give each of them only that specific meat to eat. Afterward he went to the arc in which the Holy Bible is locked. Carrying it, he sang a Spanish song that, if I succeed in explaining it well, means: "Ascending a mountain, and descending into a valley, I met Melisselde the emperor's daughter, who came out of the bathhouse to wash her hair. Her face was shining like a rapier, her eyelids like a steel bow, her lips as corals, her flesh as milk, etc." He expounded several Psalms and passages from the Song of Songs, and also explained their hidden sense, but everything in a very condensed manner. Finally, he declared himself the messiah. Kacham Ben Veniste [Hakham Hayyim Benveniste, the chief rabbi of Smyrna], who also was in this synagogue, asked him: "What kind of sign will you show us that you are the messiah?" Sabbatai placed him under the ban and ejected [him] from the synagogue. He also demanded that he beg for forgiveness and threatened that he

[Sabbatai] would make him eat camel meat. Afterward he made several people pronounce aloud the name of God that is expressed in four letters; they were all very excited.

Even the Jews who before had not believed in him began to accept him for the true messiah, even though they should not have done so seeing all his absurdities. For it is incredible how many whims he served them and yet what great honor they bestowed on him. He knew how to give apparent explanations of all his actions, and in particular to expound the word "camel," which he reduced to its Hebrew root, which does not refer to the name of an animal, but denotes "the one who pays, or remunerates, good." This is what he said when he was asked [why] he had given the aforementioned kacham such an abusive name. [. . .]

The escalating situation inspired me to conduct my own research in order to find the roots of this folly. Since for a long time I haven't been to enjoy the company of a Jewish physician whose services Christians often use and who reportedly had been appointed king of Portugal [by Sabbatai Tsevi], I instead sought an occasion to speak with the first princes of blood, the great monarch's brothers, who are the agents of a Dutch house. I found only the older one, who [had] just returned from the Dardanelles filled with vain hope. But the younger, who had been appointed king of Judea and who the day after receiving this office had appointed a viceroy and confirmed this in an official writ confirmed by a notary and witnesses (in October of last year this person sold his patent of viceroy with all its entitlements for a lion dollar), held his brother company over there. [. . .]

I therefore changed the subject to that of his brother, the alleged messiah, wanting to know on what basis he supported his folly. To this he did nothing other than praise the holiness of his brother, claiming that from his childhood on [his brother] had occupied himself with nothing other than reading and researching the law of the fathers, and that God had revealed to him that he would be the messiah. To which I responded that this could not be taken as a good ground because so many pious people read and that reading was also my own daily exercise. Arguing in a friendly manner, I also quoted to him several scriptural passages that spoke of the coming of the messiah, such as the well-known passage in Gn 49.10 which states that the messiah should come from Judah when the scepter of the tribe has not yet been taken away entirely; that he should be born while the Second Temple was still standing (according to Hg 2:7–10); that he was to be born in Bethlehem in Judah (Mi 5:1); and other biblical verses. None of these could apply to his brother, since their [Judah's] power and rule did not exist anymore, the Second Temple had been destroyed, the genealogies were confused, and his brother was born in Smyrna. The only answer I received was that God, when He would declare his brother the messiah, would make that all known to me. In the absence of a better and deeper answer, I had to content myself with this one. He only asked me if it wasn't miraculous that, after having been so many months in the hands of the Great Turk, his brother was still alive and was even fed on account of that Lord, and was also treated politely by the Turks themselves? That divine protection increased his hope and promised him a good outcome. I let him know that I had wondered about that myself as well because sinners in this empire are sometimes punished all too hastily, especially when someone would dare to have royal aspirations, but that this is not reason on which to base one's hope. But I noticed that I was dealing with a person who presently was not open to healthy scriptural arguments because he was so excited and complacently blinded by those elevated thoughts about his brother's case. Hence I did not succeed in receiving any interesting matters concerning these new events, and I concluded my conversation with him.

Translated by Alexander Van der Haven

3

A Letter of Rabbi Aaron Sarfatti of Amsterdam to Rabbi Jacob Sasportas of Hamburg

Source: Jacob Sasportas, *Tsitsat Novel Tsevi*, ed. Isaiah Tishby (Jerusalem: Mosad Byalik, 1954), 26–29.

To the man who is our splendid crown, our Torah's glorious ornament—ever present before our eyes, amply learned, deeply wise; wings outstretched, he gains the skies—massively erudite, incisive in argument, he sits ensconced on wisdom's judgment seat—the honorable Rabbi Jacob Sasportas!

Praise the Lord, who has appointed the prophet Nathan as a true and just prophet for His people Israel, and His splendid Beauty[1] as our righteous messiah! O our joy! Our great good fortune! Our delightful lot! That we are permitted to experience in our time that which was denied to Rabbi Shimon ben Yohai and his band of saints,[2] and all the generations from then to the present. How could we possibly have merited seeing God's goodness in this earthly life, were it not for the sheer abundance of His grace and mercy that has preserved us to see this day? For in what way can we have deserved to see his goodness while we are yet on earth? Let us therefore call upon the Lord our God to grant power to His king and grace to His messiah, "the messiah of the God of Jacob" [2 Sm 23:1].

My dear brother! Whom I love like my very soul! I must tell you how deeply you troubled us with those letters of yours that I saw with my own eyes, and pained our ears to hear them. Not only did you show yourself a doubter and a waverer, you went so far as to launch your quibbles (which surely you have not forgotten) against the Most High. One by one, "Jacob, I will marshal them" [Mi 2:12].

First you led off with this: how ludicrous you find it that our king should be mounted on an exalted lion and not "a donkey foaled by a she-ass" [Zec 9:9].[3] How can it have escaped you that he was to fulfill both prophecies? He did indeed ride a horse or an ass, just as the prophet said. A full seven days, according to report, he rode circling Jerusalem amid a people whose brutish cruelty you

---

1. [*Tsevi*, a play on Sabbatai's name.]
2. [The traditional authors of the Zohar.]
3. [So Nathan had predicted in his letter to Raphael Joseph.]

and your ancestors have well known. None dared whisper a protest. Was it not obvious to them all that God's power was at work? When he returns from the river Sambatyon, however, the exalted "lion of Bei Ila'ei" is to be his mount, as we learn from a writing of our prophet which I have sent to my dear son that he might place it before your learned gaze—"so fond am I of Jacob" [Mal 1:2].

You went on to speak of the "twisting serpent," which detail you professed to find astonishing . . . Would it not have been more appropriate for a thinker of your stature to have searched out the inner meaning of the prophecy, "Awake, awake, clothe yourself with splendor . . . it was you that hacked Rahab in pieces, that pierced the Dragon" [Is 51:9]? Did you find nothing strange in what our ancient rabbis said of Nebuchadnezzar (on the basis of the verse "I have even given the wild beasts to him" [Jer 28:14]) that he used to ride on a lion, carry a snake in lieu of a staff?[4] How much more properly may this be asserted of the one who is called "loftier than Abraham, uplifted higher than Moses, more exalted than the angels"[5]—and who is surely destined to be mightier and more splendid than any Eastern potentate . . . !

How you struggle to shake the faith of those who believe! How might it be possible, you say, for the Turkish king to "take off his turban, remove his crown and set it on the messiah's head in so paltry a space of time as a single year"? This [Is 21:16] "inspires in me the most sorrowful considerations" regarding him, "inducing me to suspect that some commandment of the Torah may have been breached."[6]

Well, for heaven's sake! The reverse is the truth. I put no stock in the earlier letters for just this reason, that their tidings spoke of something happening gradually, whereas our God works His salvation in the blink of an eye. "[He] shall come to His Temple suddenly," says the prophet [Mal 3:1]; while the Rabbi[7] says that "a divinely ordained constitution arises of a sudden, by His willing it to exist, like the creation of the world." The entirety of my sermon last Sabbath, in fact, was devoted to demonstrating to all that the Lord's salvation comes in the blink of an eye.

4. [According to the Talmud, Shabbat 150a, Nebuchadnezzar "rode upon a male lion to whose head he had tied a snake" to serve as reins.]

5. [Tanh. Buber *Toledot* no. 20 (p. 70a), expounding Is 52:13 to refer to the messiah.]

6. [Presumably, the biblical command to test the legitimacy of anyone claiming prophecy; Dt 18:15–22.]

7. [The spokesman for Judaism in the dialogue *Kuzari* (I, 81) by the twelfth-century Iberian philosopher Judah Halevi.]

I quoted the verse, "Even if it tarries, wait for it still; for it will surely come, without delay" [Hb 2:3]—which seems to contradict itself. Ah, but the meaning of "if it tarries, wait for it" is that the messiah's arrival has been predicted for many occasions, but when he is ready to reveal himself, *it will surely come* of a sudden, *without delay*. Thus did I expound, "I the Lord will speed it in due time" [Is 60:22]: when the *due time* for the end is here, then *I will speed it* without any delay. And what will you say if you hear in another three or four weeks that not one of the prophetic words has failed, that the Turkish king has set the royal crown on [Sabbatai's] head and given over to him all the land of Judah and Jerusalem? "Won't Jacob then be ashamed of himself?" [Is 29:22] . . .

I have no more appetite for engaging with your verbiage, which unlike my time is endless. It is now midnight, and I must be up before dawn to pour out prayer and supplication to our God. Our whole community is sanctified to a degree beyond words' power to express. You yourself, if you could only see it, would admit it is the Lord's doing. The synagogue is thronged all day and all night, as on Yom Kippur; Sabbath donations have amounted to ten thousand guilders; benches have been added to our study house as on one glorious day of the past. You would see a world topsy-turvy: all the dicing houses and lotteries forsaken through the initiative of the people themselves, without any prodding from their leaders. Instead they immerse themselves in God's Torah all day and all night, performing the perfect penance [of self-flagellation] demonstrated by Rav Judah,[8] all their conversation of our holy Torah, "the word sent by the Lord to Jacob" [Is 9:7].

I beg you therefore, dear brother Jacob: take my advice and save yourself. Politely request that the honorable Rabbi Isaac Aboab[9] send your letter back to you. Then burn it in the ash pit, along with this letter, like leaven on Passover eve. Let no trace of it remain as evidence against you, to haunt you and become your downfall. You must thereafter, with sincerest regret, banish all such thoughts from your mind. [. . .] What a pity it would be if you were to share the fate of Rabbi Jacob Hagiz, still under censure for his unbelief! A pity indeed, if you were to become "in treachery and deceit, a brother to that Jacob"! [Jer 9:3, Mal 1:2].[10]
[. . .]

8. [BT Yoma 15a, 54b, Zevahim 38a.]

9. [Sephardic chief rabbi of Amsterdam.]

10. [Jer 9:3: "every brother takes advantage"; Mal 1:2: "Esau is Jacob's brother." Sarfatti weaves together the two verses, hinting at Sasportas's equivalence with the biblical villain Esau.]

Once again, therefore, I must implore you to do as I advise, so that "Jacob's wrongdoing may be thoroughly covered over" [Is 27:9].

I need say no more, but only pray that the Most High soon brings us to a life renewed, when we shall be found worthy to witness Zion's consolation and to behold God's delights and the countenance of our glorious messiah, when we shall climb the Lord's mountain "to the House of the God of Jacob" [Is 2:3]. [. . .] O God, "show Jacob the truth!" [Mi 7:20].

Your brother, who loves you truly,
Aaron Sarfatti

Translated by David Halperin

4

Exchange of Letters between Isaac Nahar of Amsterdam and Jacob Sasportas of Hamburg

Source: Jacob Sasportas, *Tsitsat Novel Tsevi*, ed. Isaiah Tishby
(Jerusalem: Mosad Byalik, 1954), 49–57.

I. NAHAR TO SASPORTAS (9 FEBRUARY 1666):

To my teacher and friend of time past, the illustrious Rabbi Jasper[1]—Friday, a day of marvelous news!

For want of time I have not written to you. I am aware, moreover, that your student Rabbi Maimon Hiyya has already written you the splendid news from Izmir: absolute, formal, juridical verification of the fact that Nathan is a prophet of the Lord and Sabbatai Tsevi our lord, our king, God's messiah. The great rabbis of Izmir, who educated him and now stand at his side, have on his authority abolished the fast of the Tenth of Tevet and declared it a day of feasting and celebration.[2]

It is peculiarly auspicious that this news arrived just as we were completing our Tuesday fast—a token, let us hope and pray, that the Lord has accepted our penitence.

Now that the truth has been so clearly attested [2 Chr 32:1], it is no longer possible for any intelligent person to harbor doubts. Those self-appointed experts, so sure of the power of their eloquence, so ready to make the righteous the butt of their arrogant mockery and to treat this whole subject as a joke—all of them must now humbly eat their words. And in view of the disturbing reports current among the people (whose voice must be considered equivalent to that of God Himself), I cannot refrain from speaking my mind.

"Rabbi Jasper," they write us from [Hamburg], "makes no secret of his private opinion that he has never given credence to any of this. On the contrary, he has

1. [Sasportas regularly signed his letters with the nickname *yashpeh*, "jasper," an acronym for **Ya'akov Sasportas ha-katan**, "humble Jacob Sasportas."]

2. [A legal act of great moment, fulfilling the prophecy of Zechariah 8:19: "The fast of the fourth month, the fast of the fifth month, the fast of the seventh month, and the fast of the tenth month shall become occasions of joy and gladness, happy festivals for the House of Judah."]

sent a letter to Livorno, intending it to reach the prophet in Gaza, in which he brazenly proclaims that no attention is to be paid to anything one may have heard about him, according to his arguments." I have heard many people criticizing you for this! "Is this how a rabbi behaves?" they say. "One day he delivers a sermon in praise of the messiah and the prophet; he writes that he has absolute faith in them. Then he turns around and says it is all nonsense. What an inconstant person he must be! Or else, perhaps, he has been bribed to trick people with smooth-talking duplicity" [Ps 12:3].

Some demand to know how you can have been so cocksure as to send your letter announcing your objections and disagreements to the prophet himself. How can you have been unafraid to provoke the fiery rage of this man, whose words are like glowing coals, whose honor is championed by God? Current report has it that "Jacob (God forgive him!) has abandoned his piety." All the learned and devout, all those active in communal affairs, are astonished at your outpourings, wondering why you have not followed Jeremiah's maxim that "the best course is to wait in silence for the Lord's salvation [Lam 3:26]."

If only you knew, sir, how I have struggled to defend you! To find some justification for the things you have said! "No, no," I told them, "he has always thought of this as a reasonable possibility. He only wants to reserve judgment until the facts become clear." But everyone then retorts, "No, on the contrary, he arrogantly presumes to dictate his opinion to all and sundry," and with that my arguments are silenced; I have no way to answer.

If what they are saying about you is true, you really have no choice but to recant your essential stance and to let that recantation be a starting point for your repentance. Our friendship demands that I speak to you candidly out of my deep concern for your sacred honor, which the ignorant will surely find opportunity to besmirch. I beg you therefore to tell me the truth. You will emerge justified, and I will be able to silence your critics and put an end to the gossip.

God grant that we merit the sight of our messiah and king, and that he lead us marching proudly to our land!

Tuesday, week of the Torah portion: "This is what you must do [Ex 29:38]," year of "I will *rescue* My people [Zec 8:7]."[3]

Your humble correspondent,
Isaac Nahar

3. [*Rescue* has the numerical value 426, representing the year 5426. The date indicated is Tuesday, 4 Adar I 5426 = 9 February 1666.]

II. SASPORTAS TO NAHAR (16 FEBRUARY 1666):[4]

To the man who is called "Damascus" and "Hadrach" [Zec 9:1]—*Damascus*, in that he draws water from the Rivers of his wisdom and allows us to drink from it, and *Hadrach*, in that he is proclaimed our tender father[5]—the honorable Rabbi Isaac Nahar, upon whom I would pour out as a River my wishes for peace.

I have given my closest attention to your letter, written in your own hand, in which I am exhorted to "recant" and "repent" of my evil ways as though I were some godless scoundrel. There is not a single rabbi in any region who has the right to speak to me that way even if I had committed some acknowledged misdeed, far less to turn my virtues into faults.

Truth to tell, you have been so ready to believe slanders, your transports of joy have so addled your good sense, that you are prepared to treat virtue as though it were a felony. You consequently tell me to my face that I "have no choice but to let my recantation be a starting point for my repentance"—language I have never heard in my life, even from my illustrious teacher. What has become of your good manners and your upbringing? What has moved you to misuse your tongue and pen as weapons, as whips to inflict agonizing wounds, as arrows in the bow of a greedy, unscrupulous hunter, as hooks with which to drag off my good reputation, using for that purpose lines far removed from the nobly established line of the truth? [. . .]

But what can I do? I have already granted you my approval [cf. Eccl 9:7]; I have made no secret of my pride in you. "This is precisely the sort of man," I have said, "whom you ought to appoint as rabbi." I have conferred on you the authority of the twin flames of Written and Oral Torah, before the entire educated public. Before all the learned, I have extravagantly praised you; if anyone tried to besmirch you, I gave him a lesson he did not soon forget. "Let him give rulings," I

---

4. [The letter exists in two versions: the original text Sasportas entered into his notebook, and an edited version he later prepared for public consumption once Sabbatai and his followers had been safely discredited. The "edited" version represents Sasportas as speaking out far more boldly against Sabbatai and Nathan than he would have dared in February 1666, when the messianic excitement was at its height and those who doubted were wise to keep their mouths shut. The original text has been translated here.]

5. [Sasportas fancifully expounds the biblical place names in accordance with *Midrash Genesis Rabbah* 90:3 and its parallels, and twice puns on the name "Nahar," Hebrew for "river."]

would reply to anyone who inquired of me, "let him make judgments."[6] I have established your good repute the world over; how can I now ruin it? How can I go back on my solemn word? No! I must overlook the injury and naked insult [cf. Prv 27:5–6] that seem to be the rewards of this friendship. I must judge you as charitably as I can.

Had it been anyone else, however, who trampled on my dignity—who presumed to admonish me, instruct me, and illuminate for me the ways [Jb 38:19] of the Jewish faith as though I were some unfledged convert—I do not care if he is the greatest authority of our time, his court a veritable Sanhedrin, I would unleash against him a rage so bitter and scorching he would think death to be preferable. [. . .]

For I declare myself to be innocent, sinless before God. I have said nothing I must be ashamed of; I have not corrupted the faith and the tradition that I received from my holy ancestors and teachers, whose wisdom nourishes me to this day. On the contrary, I claim it as my virtue that I stand firm in the truth, refusing to discard the smallest detail of the doctrine of our ancient rabbis or to blemish the principles of the Oral Torah. Who, after all, is to guard these teachings, if not I and my fellow scholars? It is by this achievement that I measure myself and am measured by others, greater than I, who modestly defer to me. [. . .]

I initially judged [the claim that the messiah had appeared] to be a remote possibility. I never denied it might be true. [. . .] I had no right to label it a certainty; in the absence of a court certification, no scholar would have had that right. [. . .] The situation changed only with the arrival of the news that the court had upheld the ruling that the fast of the tenth month be abolished and turned into a day of feasting and celebration [cf. Zec 8:19].

This decision, I reasoned, must have been made by the rabbis' consensus after being shown some evidentiary miracle. There exists no court superior to theirs, nor could any report be so firmly established. To seek the opinion of any other court would be needless; it is with regard to cases like this that the Talmud says, "There is no need to provide against an erring court" [Bava Batra 138b].

To be sure, one would not want to take any action on the basis of a document like this one, an expression of individual opinion without the proper legal formulations. It is nevertheless clear evidence, of a kind hitherto unseen, concerning a matter whose truth is sure to be revealed. Until now we had only

6. [The language of rabbinic authorization, taken from the Talmud, Sanhedrin 5a.]

a generic sort of attestation, founded on hearsay, lacking any manner of court certification, as close analysis of the details will prove to any critical inquirer. But now we have eyewitnesses; we have the specifics of the guarantors; we have a legal act of no small consequence [. . .].

This and more:[7] The rabbi of Altona has received a letter, the authenticity to which he can attest, from a relative in Jerusalem itself. This letter provides general confirmation of the truth of [Nathan's] prophecy, and bears the great good news that our salvation is at hand.

> From this day forward I abandon all doubt, as did the rabbis of Izmir and others deemed "sage" by God and their fellows. Never would I impugn their sanctity or their faith on account of their initial skepticism and denial of the evidence. I take it as a given that these men, their wisdom and piety guided by Written and Oral Torah, could not justifiably have embraced this faith without proper attestation. It would have been perfect idiocy for them to do otherwise. [. . .]

As for what these untimely birthed souls have written to you from here [Hamburg]—warped, insolent beings, fit only to be swept away by a boiling River[8]—I account it the sheerest baby talk, the jabber of those aborted unripe, pretending to an expertise they do not have and never will. Hardly astonishing, of course. We live in messianic times, when "insolence will increase, the young shall bully the old, youths will put old men to shame, and the wisdom of the learned will degenerate."[9] [. . .]

I cannot convey the pleasure I feel as I watch these adolescents, these worthless brats, installed in civic office and credited with wisdom and piety superior to my own. This may be Ahijah's curse;[10] it is my consolation. Who knows? It may indeed have been out of stupidity or innate viciousness that I rejected this faith

7. [This and the next paragraph are entirely suppressed from the "public" version of Sasportas's letter.]

8. [Sasportas's unnamed critics, whom Nahar had quoted in his letter. Sasportas draws on the exegesis of Job 22:16 in the Talmud, Hagigah 13b–14a (with a pun on the name Nahar, "river") to characterize them.]

9. [Combining Talmud, Sotah 49b, with Is 3:5.]

10. [Talmud, Sanhedrin 105b–106a describes the curse of the prophet Ahijah (on the basis of 1 Kgs 14:15), but as Tishby remarks, it seems to have no relevance to Sasportas's point. Tishby is surely right to suppose that Isaiah's curse (Talmud, Hagigah 14a, following Is 3:1–5) is intended.]

of yours. And they may indeed become the messiah's ministers and his deputies, while I am set to cleaning the manure out of his stables.

With this I will conclude. I dislike making lengthy excuses for myself where no excuse is necessary. Those who caused offence against me and God, if they did not act out of some flighty credulity, may be able to plead piety as their excuse. I know that God will champion my honor, if not for my sake then for that of His Torah, which is the Torah of my fathers and teachers. [...]

Tuesday, week of the Torah portion "My angel shall go before you" [Ex 32:34] and "he who has sinned against me, him only will I erase from My record" [Ex 32:33], year of "a people *delivered* [Dt 33:29]";[11] here at Hamburg.

Jasper

III. NAHAR TO SASPORTAS (21–27 FEBRUARY 1666):

Year 1 of our king, our messiah, and our prophet

To our shining lamp [BT Sanhedrin 14a], on whom I pray the light to shine —my teacher and friend of time past, the flawless rabbi, the most learned and noble Rabbi Jasper, upon whom I would pour out as a River my wishes for peace [cf. Is 66:12].

I have received your letter. I shall make no rejoinder. I trust I am to be numbered among God's true friends, who hear indeed but do not answer back.

I write to let you know that I shall set forth this coming month (which we hope to be auspicious) for our beloved Land of Israel, in the company of my revered mother, my wife, my son, and the gentleman Abraham Pereira. We have not yet decided whether to go via France or Germany. I pray God grant us a smooth journey for His name's sake, bring us safely to the place where we long to be, and deem us all worthy to witness the consolation of Zion.

I devoutly hope, too, that I may see you either en route or in Livorno, so that we can enjoy the pleasures of our friendship [Prv 7:18] as we did in the old times. I shall ever be, as I have always and everywhere been, your faithful friend. My affection for you is permanent and immoveable; it does not depend on any external honor, popularity, or acclaim, since (thank God) I have no need for any such things. I do not pursue honor, but only the disinterested love for the Good.

My brother, the honorable Rabbi Moses Nahar, sends you his best regards.

11. [*Delivered* has the numerical value 426, representing the year 5426. The date indicated is Tuesday, 11 Adar I 5426 = 16 February 1666].

It is my fervent prayer [Ps 69:14] that God lead us marching proudly to our land [cf. Lv 26:13] and deem us worthy of the sight of our messiah.

Amsterdam; week of the Torah portion "See, the Lord has singled [him] out by name" [Ex 35:30], year of I will *rescue* [Zec 8:7],[12] which is Year 1 of the reign of our messiah.

Translated by David Halperin

12. [*Rescue* has the numerical value 426, representing the year 5426. The week indicated is 16–22 Adar I 5426 = 21–27 February 1666].

11 | Sabbatai Tsevi's Conversion and Its Interpretation

Reports of the conversion of Sabbatai Tsevi sent shock waves among his followers and his detractors alike. At first, the most ardent believers flatly denied the truth of these tales. Others developed a position akin to the Docetistic doctrines found in early Christianity: it was claimed that the "real" Sabbatai Tsevi never met the sultan and remained faithful to Jews and Judaism; the one who converted was a mere phantom or simulacrum of the messiah. Very few who had dared to publicly attack Tsevi before he became a Muslim adopted a triumphant attitude (Rabbi Joseph Halevi of Livorno is a notable exception). Several erstwhile followers rewrote their biographies and portrayed themselves as skeptics or even early opponents of the messiah. Sabbatian prophecies were ridiculed. Rabbinic courts collected evidence about the earlier transgressions of the messiah and his followers. Hostile accounts were gathered and widely publicized. Fact and fiction mixed in these accounts, yet a conviction of the deep and long-standing corruption of Sabbatai and his circle became the order of the day.

The particulars of the meeting between Tsevi and the sultan are lost to history. The leading narrative had it that the messiah was forced to apostatize. It was rumored that the sultan offered him the choice of Islam or death preceded by terrible torture. This story was also told with a twist: the alternative to conversion was said to be violent reprisals against Jews throughout the Ottoman Empire. Thus, in this account, Tsevi converted in an effort to save his fellow Jews. Alternatively, his adoption of Islam was a ruse, used by a spy entering enemy territory. Moreover, the guise was a temporary one, a "descent for the purpose of ascent." Having conquered the forces of darkness in their own realm, Sabbatai Tsevi would return to Judaism and the People of Israel.

At some point during this tempestuous time, Tsevi penned his own version of the conversion scene. In this letter, the messiah's adoption of Islam was the conscious act of a lucid person. Fully volitional, it was a response to the call of the "True God." Sabbatai embraced Islam "with all his heart." Neither was the conversion temporary: Tsevi accepted Islam "until the time of the End." Moreover, he called on Jews whose "souls agreed with his" to follow him into apostasy. Sabbatai's account foregrounds his relationship with God, whom "he alone knew" and whose will was his ardent desire. Yet a further (and remarkably audacious) point was most pivotal for the development of later Sabbatian thought: a vision of a God who altered or annulled altogether the rules of the covenant he had established with his people. For Sabbatai, the True God had left Judaism, and: "without the True God, the Torah of Moses is no [longer] Torah." Islam was not for Tsevi intrinsically better than Judaism. Yet it *became* better once it became the abode of the True God. And Judaism, once the locus of the true revelation, became an empty shell. Sabbatai's God literally switched religions. In an arresting image, Tsevi did not merely follow the *will* of his God ordering him to apostatize; he followed God Himself: the messiah converted to Islam because the True God had "converted" before him.

Sabbatai's letter is undated, but it was certainly written shortly after the conversion. Toward the end of 1673, Tsevi produced a second extraordinary document. The epistle, addressed to his believers, asked that they cease calling him "messiah" or "king"; instead, they were to simply address him by his private name or as "friend." Specifically, Sabbatian festivals (such as the feast of the Ninth of Av) were to be cancelled and traditional Jewish observances were to be reinstated. Their belief in his messiahship should be kept quiet. Those who had separated from their communities should return home and reintegrate. All markers distinguishing the Sabbatians as a separate group should disappear. The "branches" of the Sabbatian faith should be "chopped down," with only the "root" remaining, "buried in the believers' hearts."

On the face of it, this last theological statement of Tsevi is a sign of capitulation. The "True God," whose unfathomable voice Sabbatai heard during his conversion, is conspicuously absent in this letter. Lacking divine guidance, Tsevi is forced to abandon his mission. However, the letter can be read differently. Sabbatai's call to "bury faith in the heart" may not be a call to discard it; rather, it may be a call to hide it from the world. The true test of Sabbatian faith is the public denial of this very faith. Ultimate messianism is the rejection of any messianic hopes. Sabbatianism, in the last articulation of its messiah, was to be a faith of pure inwardness, utterly incommunicable.

Nathan of Gaza's "Letter on Conversion," composed in 1674 or 1675, is the most comprehensive elaboration of mainstream Sabbatian theology attempting to explain the apostasy of the messiah. A Jewish prodigy, Nathan drew upon a wealth of rabbinic and Kabbalistic sources to demonstrate that the major canonical Jewish texts allude to a conversion of the true messiah. The thrust of his argument is that the apostasy—shocking as it may seem at first sight—is in fundamental agreement with the messiah's earlier pattern of behavior, Nathan's own prophecies, and most important, normative Jewish doctrines. The apostasy was not an abrogation of the Torah but its fulfillment, not a repudiation of Judaism but its affirmation. The rabbinic concept of "temporary injunction" is highly salient here: the commandments of the Mosaic Law were not abolished, but their validity was momentarily suspended. This suspension was limited to the messiah (in Nathan's view, Sabbatai's followers should under no circumstances follow him into apostasy) and had a strictly provisional character: before his death the apostate messiah would return to the Jewish fold. For now, the world was in a weird, indeterminate state, and Sabbatians were to observe most Jewish rites and commandments with the exception of the fast of the Ninth of Av within their own Sabbatian communities.

Nathan's letter attests to the tremendous intellectual and spiritual effort made to keep Sabbatianism within the framework of mainstream Judaism. Against his messiah's old and new detractors, Nathan contended that even the apostasy of the redeemer could be explained in traditional Jewish categories. This letter, however, had a deeper layer. I propose to read Nathan's epistle as a response to the two letters of Sabbatai Tsevi. Sabbatai presented his apostasy as voluntary; Nathan argued it was forced. Sabbatai emphasized he did not convert in a state of illumination; Nathan argued precisely that. Sabbatai stated that he adopted Islam "till the time of the End"; according to Nathan, the messiah's dwelling in the Muslim religion was not to last long. For Sabbatai, Islam became the true religion; for Nathan, it was a reservoir of demonic forces to be conquered. Sabbatai claimed that the Torah was abolished; Nathan affirmed the sacredness of the canon of Judaism and the underlying validity of its commandments. Against the messiah himself, his prophet argued that not even the founder of a religion has the right to undermine the fundaments of the religion he is founding: not even the messiah has the right to deny his messiahship. The natural-born church builder, Nathan knew perfectly well that, without clear markers of Sabbatian identity and a canonical interpretation of sacred texts, the Sabbatian "church" would not survive. He rejected both the messiah's call for all the Jews to convert from his first letter and his injunction to return the traditional fast on the Ninth of Av from the second (for many Sabbatians feasting on that date was the most important marker of difference between them and other Jews). In Nathan of Gaza's view, the Sabbatians were to be different from both Muslims and other Jews, remaining in suspension till the messiah's triumphant return to the faith and people of Israel. If this demanded the rejection of Sabbatai's most important theological pronouncements, that was a risk the prophet was prepared to take.

5

A Letter of Rabbi Joseph Halevi of Livorno to Rabbi Hosea Nantawa of Alexandria[1]

Source: Jacob Sasportas, *Tsitsat Novel Tsevi*, ed. Isaiah Tishby
(Jerusalem: Mosad Byalik, 1954), 187–91.

Tell me, dunce: are you quite certain you will have a blessed afterlife for believing, without any sign or miracle, in a man insane? Who perpetrated, moreover, one lawless act after another? In Izmir, for example, he spoke the sacred Name of God in the city streets; he taught the rabble and the children to do the same; he smashed his way into a synagogue on the Sabbath day to kill the rabbis who did not believe in him. [...] He closeted himself with a wife he had divorced, after she had been remarried; she pulled off his shoe and he did the same to her.[2] He offered Passover sacrifice outside the Temple, ate its forbidden fat, and made his companions eat as well. He made "Great Sabbath" out of a Monday, the twenty-second of Tammuz,[3] not to mention the Sabbaths and holy days he invented out of whole cloth. He cavorted with attractive married women. He slandered rabbis to the judge, claiming they had cursed the [Turkish] king.

Innumerable acts of this kind, lawless and improper, did he perform. How could you possibly have written that this "faith" is comparable to the Torah of Moses? ... How will you people live down your humiliation, now that your messiah has turned apostate and you have exposed yourselves as without any faith in God's unity or His Torah?

Even if he were the messiah, how could you have equated the servant's dignity with his Creator's? "To whom, then, can you liken God?" [Is 40:18]. From the very start of their exile, it was a new king whom the Jewish people expected and awaited, not some new god! We have one God and no more. You gave proof of your bad faith when you chose new gods, when you called [Sabbatai Tsevi] "the

1. [The letter was composed in November 1666, after the news of Sabbatai Tsevi's conversion reached Italy.]

2. [That is, he performed with her the ritual of *halizah*, prescribed in Deuteronomy 25:7–10 for a widow and her deceased husband's brother—only, with his penchant for ritual and liturgical innovation, he made the act reciprocal. Deuteronomy 24:1–4 forbids intimacy with an ex-wife who has remarried and again become single.]

3. [Actually the twenty-third.]

Almighty" after his Master's name, or—as the scoundrel Samuel Primo did in a letter he sent us—"the Lord our righteousness, King of kings of kings," and suchlike.

Was it the lying visionaries who led you astray, whose craftiness proved too much for you? The ones who recounted the past lives of everyone's soul, so that those with no spirit but an animal's became distributors of souls to the people? Tell me, clod: where do we find in Scripture anything of this sort? Where in the words of our Sages? [. . .] Your prophet, after all, had said that whoever does not believe in [Sabbatai] without any sign or miracle, even if he has Torah and good deeds to his credit, has no share in the blessed afterlife.[4] Well, tell me, numbskull: is it not true that the Israelites who left Egypt continued to doubt and question God until He showed Himself to them face to face at Mount Sinai, in spite of their having seen His mighty workings in Egypt and by the Red Sea? . . . Were they damned on that account? . . . Or consider Gideon, who doubted his own prophecy. Once he realized it to be genuine, he feared he might be punished for his disbelief and was told, "All is well [. . .] you shall not die" [Jgs 6:23]. For the Lord prefers the doubter who disbelieves out of faith over anyone who believes out of stupidity; and the Bible says, "A simple person believes anything" [Prv 14:15]. [. . .]

Tell me, simpleton: if your messiah really could do the awe-producing wonders you claim, how is it that when he stood before the king of the Turks—who condemned him to death, and everyone who was there told him, "If you have power to do anything at all, do it and save yourself from death"—how is it that his reply was that "I have no power to work any sign whatever," and that he had no choice but to choose the king's religion and become an apostate, publicly profaning God's name? Were those the "hymns and praises" that your prophet in Gaza promised him, that when uttered before the king would bring him at once to his knees, setting the royal crown on his head? [. . .] What became of all your throng of prophets and prophetesses who prophesied about him—no fewer than five hundred, you wrote us—Nathan of Gaza first and foremost among them?

Tell me, birdbrain: how could this [prophesying] have taken place outside the Holy Land? [. . .] And in Gaza! In Philistine Gaza the great prophecy manifested itself, while in Jerusalem—nothing whatever! [. . .] And there is more. Your prophet had the impudence to declare that the whole world would undergo suf-

---

4. [A paraphrase of Nathan's epistle to Raphael Joseph (see chap. I, this volume).]

fering, Jerusalem included—but not Gaza. His purpose, it would appear, was to degrade the Holy City and empower the Side of Impurity; he thereby betrays himself to have sprouted from the seed and root of Nimrod, who along with all his generation had that selfsame objective. [...]

Or was his intent rather to entrap the house of Israel with his words, so that the wealthy and powerful of the land would come settle in Gaza under his rulership, enriching him with their money? It is common knowledge, after all, that these scoundrels plotted to appoint for themselves a prophet, anoint a king, and establish an academy in Gaza. Thus they would wallow in the bribes sent from distant lands to supplicate the prophet, charge fees for all those coming to do him obeisance and seek mending for their souls, [and] drain off for themselves all the money raised by philanthropic folk for [the support of] God's house in Jerusalem. [...]

Tell me, blockhead: how did it happen that so many women received the gift of prophecy, so few men? From the day of Creation down to the time when prophecy ceased, there appeared a grand total of seven prophetic women, over against male prophets double the number of the Israelites who left Egypt, as we read in the first chapter of tractate *Megillah*.[5] How was it, then, that [in our time] the divine spirit rested on women menstruating, fresh from birthing, afflicted with fluxes—while the multitudes of learned scholars, veteran masters of religious law, were not granted so much as a prophetic dream?

Tell me, ninny: how did you presume to say that anyone disbelieving in your messiah might as well have denied the Torah of Moses and the resurrection of the dead? Those who disbelieved in him, after all, trusted the teachings of our ancient rabbis and found in [Sabbatai] nothing they had been led to expect. Where was Elijah, who was supposed first to come before the Great Court...? Where was the multicolored rainbow that was supposed to appear in the [messiah's] days, as the Zohar says in its commentary on the Torah portion *Noah*? Where were the miraculous signs enumerated in the last chapter of tractate *Sanhedrin*? [...]

How could any king be crowned while Jerusalem is in a state of ruin?... the earthly Jerusalem is exactly as she always was: every leper and every dripping gonorrheic entering at will into her most sacred precincts. [...]

Tell me, halfwit: [...] Was it really of [Sabbatai] that Habakuk [2:4] proph-

5. [BT, Megillah 14a, which lists the seven prophetesses as Sarah, Miriam, Deborah, Hannah, Abigail, Huldah, and Esther.]

esied, "The righteous shall live by his faith?"[6] Then kindly ask your prophet to tell you: in which "faith" shall he "live"? His original one? Or the new faith he has now entered into?

And I do humbly beg of you: ask that old man Mordecai, who you say saw on your messiah's head a crown of fire stretching up to the heights of heaven —what color was that crown? Was it perchance *silver*, the color of the money he collected from those who came from distant parts to pay him homage, whom he skinned alive to enrich himself and his gang of lying, thieving toadies? Or was it *white*, the color of the turban he now wears?

Translated by David Halperin

6. [*Tsaddik be-emunato yihyeh*, the initials of which spell the name "Tsevi." New JPS: "The righteous man is rewarded with life for his fidelity."]

6

**Moses Ben Habib, A Testimony Given
before the Rabbinic Court in Jerusalem[1]**

Source: Jacob Emden, *Zot Torat ha-Kena'ot* (Lvov: Michael Wolff, 1870), 53–54.

We were in a panel of three [judges] as one, and the chief rabbi, our teacher
and master, Rabbi Moses [ben] Habib, a Spaniard, came before us, and he testified in the language of the exiles from Spain [Ladino], and these are his words
translated into the Holy Tongue: I testify that it is well-known among the sages
of Jerusalem and Hebron that Sabbatai Tsevi, may his breath be extinguished,
before he became an apostate, fed ten Jews the fat of the kidneys, and also that he
commanded them to give the Passover offering outside of the Land of Israel and
fed them in the manner of the Passover sacrifice, and also composed a blessing
over the consumption of the animal fat, and this was its formulation: "Blessed
are you, Lord, who permits the forbidden."[2] I also heard this from another man,
who was a great scholar, who also did this thing, and then repented. I also heard
that in the year 5545 [1665] Sabbatai Tsevi revealed about himself that he was
the messiah of the House of David, and he gathered a large crowd from among
the people of Jerusalem, may it be rebuilt speedily in our days, to go to the grave
of the prophet Samuel and to prostrate themselves on his grave and pray there,
and among them was a villain who was also an informer and was suspected of
having forbidden sexual relations, and his name was Samuel Lazbani, and they
went there among the Muslims, and the beadles of the community decorated
the cave of Samuel the Prophet with some hundreds of candles and torches and
oil lamps, and all of the crowd went down to pray, and he, Sabbatai Tsevi, may
his name and his memory be blotted out, and ten people who were with him
did not want to pray, and they went up to one tower, a place of prayer for the
Ishmaelites, and were eating and drinking and carousing all night long, and did

---

1. [A testimony attributed to the chief rabbi of Jerusalem given around 1700. According
to Meir Benayahu, the author is not the Jerusalem rabbi but a Salonican scholar of the
same name (see E. E. Urbach, R. J. Zwi Werblowski, and Ch. Wirszubski, eds., *Studies in
Mysticism and Religion Presented to Gershom G. Scholem on His Seventieth Birthday by Pupils, Colleagues and Friends* (Jerusalem: Magnes Press, 1967), 35–40).]

2. [A pun on Psalm 146:7: "the Lord looseth the prisoners," reading *issurim* (prohibitions) for *asurim* [prisoners].]

not say the evening prayer, and the crowd waited for him to come and pray and he didn't want to, and because of this they were delayed until close to the crack of dawn, and close to the crack of dawn, after they had implored him, he went down and took a stick in his hand and struck the grave of Samuel the Prophet and spoke thus: 'Samuel, Samuel, I remove you from the status of prophet and I place under you this Samuel Lazabani,' and then he took the stick and broke all of the lamps and blew out all of the candles. And when the crowd saw this confusion, they each said the evening prayer on their own.

I heard further from the great sage, Rabbi Abraham Yitzchaki, the head of the court and the head of the Spanish Academy in the Holy City Jerusalem, may it be rebuilt speedily in our days, that he heard from his teacher, the great sage, our teacher and master Moses Galante, who said: "At the beginning I didn't scorn Sabbatai Tsevi, may his name and memory be blotted out, even though I didn't believe in him, only after I saw a letter of Sabbatai Tsevi, may his name and memory be blotted out, that he wrote to one of his believers here, and he signed it 'I am the Lord your God, Sabbatai Tsevi,' that is, he wrote the Holy Name as it is written, after this I condemn him every single day."

[. . .] And the famous doctor from Izmir, who is called Doctor Carun [?], told me how he and his son once went to Sabbatai Tsevi's home, and his son was a nice-looking youth, and Sabbatai Tsevi told him, go to that room and "whatever Sarah tells you, do as she says" [Gn 21:12], and Sarah was Sabbatai Tsevi's wife, and the young man went and she told him, "Close the door," and he did, and then she told him, "Take off my slippers," and he did, and then she told him to untie her trousers, and he yelled loudly, and his father heard and broke the door and asked him "What is this?" He told him the whole story, and the father began to curse and swear at Sabbatai Tsevi and his wife, and Sabbatai Tsevi said, "What is this that he did? If he had done her will, he would have made a great *tikkun* [in the world]."

I also heard from a sage, Samuel Zadok, that in the year 5545 [1665] Sabbatai Tsevi and Nathan [of Gaza] came to Salonika and did a few crazy things, and the sages drove him out; and he went to the nearby village, called Diran, and stayed in the home of one man, and this man had a single son, and the son became ill and died, and [Sabbatai Tsevi] said that he would bring him back to life, and he took the dead boy and took him to the synagogue, and he dug a hole and filled it with water, and he threw the dead body in it and closed the synagogue; and he was there with the dead body for eight days, and the smell of the dead body was so strong that dogs surrounded the synagogue and the neighbors could not sleep at night on account of the dogs, and the townsmen went and broke down the door, and they took the body and the meat was falling off of it in bits, and Sabbatai Tsevi said, "What have you done? If he had been but one more moment in there he would have come back to life."

I also heard from one of those men who apostatized as a result of Sabbatai Tsevi's incitement, [. . .] and he told how he himself saw that Sabbatai Tsevi, may his name and his memory be blotted out, put his phylacteries on his head and sodomized a young man and said it was a great *tikkun*; and I also testify that through this belief in Sabbatai Tsevi, a great stumbling block came out in Salonika, when Sabbatai Tsevi's wife came after his death, and said that Sabbatai Tsevi had come to her in a dream and told her that the soul of the righteous Joseph was conceived in her . . . , and after six months she took her brother, who was fifteen years old, and she closed herself up in a special room with him for three days and three nights, and when [s]he came out she said that the young man had died and nothing remained of him, not even a bone the size of a bead of barley, and that Sabbatai Tsevi had then come to her and had intercourse with her, and that she gave birth to the boy and suckled him, and he became as big as he was before, and that therefore he was the messiah of the house of Joseph, that is, that his father came from the line of David, and he is Sabbatai Tsevi, may his name and his memory be blotted out, and his mother from the line of Joseph, in fulfillment of the verse "Then Ephraim's [. . .] and Judah's harassment shall end" [Is 11:13].

[. . .] And the sage immediately commented that he had heard from a student of Sabbatai Tsevi, may his name and memory be blotted out, that it is well known that Sabbatai Tsevi said of himself that he was God, that the Holy One, Blessed be He, arose to His world and left the running of the worlds in his hand, and he interpreted this in a homiletic manner to refer to a passage in the New Zohar, Parashat Bereshit, to the verse "She then bore his brother Abel" [Gn 4:2], and he interpreted it regarding himself, that he was Cain, and regarding the Holy One, Blessed be He, etc., and more than this should not be put upon paper.[3]

Translated by Sara Tova Brody

3. [I.e., that Sabbatai Tsevi was Cain and the God of Israel, Abel.]

Source: Abraham Amarillo, "Te'udot Shabbetaiyyot," *Sefunot* 5 (1961): 266.

My brothers, my children, and my friends know this: I understood with great clarity that the True One, whom I alone have known for many generations and for whom I have strived so much, wants me to enter the religion of the Ishmaelites, the Law of Islam with all my heart. To permit what it permits and to forbid what it forbids and to abolish the Torah of Moses till the time of the End.[1] For the honor of His divinity and His revelation demand that I bring therein all whose souls agree with mine; after [the conversion] I will reveal to them the [mystery of] His divinity. This can be demonstrated with full necessity, strong as a molten mirror [Jb 37:18]: the supreme rank of His truth and the wondrous glory of the Cause of all Causes[2] and the Reason of all Reasons.[3] This is what is written: "It is time for you, Lord, to act; they have made void your Torah [Ps 119:126],"[4] as the Ishmaelites say; "The Torah of Moses is made void." This is also implied in [what God said to Moses]: "All strength to thee that thou breakest the Tablets of the Covenant" [after BT Shabbat 87a].

For the Torah of Moses without the True One is utterly worthless, as it is written: "For many [days] Israel has been without the True God and without Torah" [2 Chr 15:3]. As they [Israel] do not have the True God, his [Moses's] Torah is no Torah. Yet the Law of Islam is Law. The Holy One Blessed be He said: "I have laid down a statute; I have issued a decree! You cannot transgress My decree" [*Midrash Numbers Rabbah* 19:1]. This is what is written: "They have moved me to jealousy with that which is not God . . . and I will move them to jealousy with those who are not a people [Dt 32:21]," but the people of Ishmael. I will take [the Torah] to these people [the Muslims] and will make a new marriage contract with them.

And when Maimonides of blessed memory stated, "God will never amend or

1. [Cf. Dn 11:13.]
2. [Zohar I, 22b.]
3. [Zohar III, 128b.]
4. [BT Berakhot 54a already interprets this verse as allowance to suspend the Divine Law in special situations.]

change His religion,"[5] he was completely wrong, for he did not know the God of Truth, who is the God of Sabbatai Tsevi. As [the prophet] Jeremiah said: "The seed of Israel will cease from being a nation before me for all days [Jer 31:36]." "For all days" will not cease; "for some days" will cease. And the statements of the sages are not true till the faithful servant of the True God confirms them, and there is a time to every purpose [Eccl 3:1]. Enough said. [. . .]

And you must not think, my brothers, that I did this [converted to Islam] on account of an illumination [I was given]. Do not be afraid and say: "Today or tomorrow the illumination will depart from him, and he will regret what he said and will be anguished." This is not so; I did it myself, thanks to the great power and strength of Truth and Faith. No [adverse] winds, no sages, and no prophets of the world can move my resolution. Week of the Torah portion: "He was zealous for my sake among them . . . Therefore say, Behold, I give to him my covenant of peace [Nm 25, 11–12]."[6] Thus speaks the Lord of Truth and Faith, the Turco, and the Mesurman.[7]

Translated by Paweł Maciejko

5. [Sabbatai does not quote the original formulation of Maimonides, but rather the formulation of the Yigdal poem that is recited during the daily prayer services. He reads the phrase *ha-el* [*ve-*]*lo yamir dato* (God will not alter His Law) hyperliterally as "God will not convert [to another religion]."]

6. [Parashat Pinhas, second half of the month of Tammuz.]

7. [Scil. Muselman; Ladino: Muslim with r:l alteration.]

8

Sabbatai Tsevi, Bury My Faith![1]

Source: Avraham Elqayam, "Kivru Emunati," *Pe'amim* 55 (1993): 4–37.

My brothers, friends and teachers, believers wherever you may be! I throw myself in the dust at your feet, begging you most importunately to fulfill the request I am about to make of you, namely, that you chop down each and every one of the branches of this Faith, leaving only the root buried in your heart. So my soul has unequivocally desired, in clear awareness that this hope of mine has no prospect of speedy fulfillment unless this be done.

You must entirely cease the messianic celebration of the "Festival of the Ninth of Av"[2] and resume the full observance of the Ninth of Av itself according to your ancestral practice; your guilt do I take upon myself. Fully observe the rest of the fasts as well, according to your ancestral practice.

Nowhere shall you bless me as king, nor shall you speak of me as "our messiah" or "our King" or "our Lord," neither orally nor in writing. Call me just "Rabbi Sabbatai Tsevi, may his Rock preserve him"—that and no more—or else "the friend." If you write to me, address me as "My brother, my friend Rabbi Sabbatai Tsevi," or just plain ["Sabbatai Tsevi"]. Let no one speak of kissing my feet or my hands or anything like that; let no one send me any gift, even food or drink. Let no one fight or quarrel with anyone else on behalf of this Faith, in any manner whatsoever. All those wandering and exiled from their homes on account of this Faith—let them try as hard as they can to return peacefully homeward.[3]

1. [The translator, David Halperin, considers this letter a forgery written to reintegrate Sabbatai's followers into the Jewish community. Other scholars, including Avraham Elqayam, the scholar who first published the letter, as well as Paweł Maciejko, the editor of this volume, disagree.]

2. [Sabbatai's birthday, transformed (in accordance with the prophecy of Zechariah 8:19), from a fast day mourning the Temple's destruction into a celebratory festival.]

3. [The language is drawn from 1 Kings 22:17, "I saw all Israel scattered over the hills like sheep without a shepherd; and the Lord said, 'These have no master; let everyone return to his home in safety'" (*yashuvu ish le-veto be-shalom*). Sabbatai was rumored to have enigmatically echoed this biblical verse a few days before his death. "Each of you go back home [*shuvu ish el beto*]. How long will you adhere to me? Until you see beneath that rock that is on the seashore, perhaps?"]

You must wholly discard anything similar to these that may be considered a root of this Faith. In short, bury this Faith of mine deep underground.

I beg you, friends and companions, to show your great favor to me and my wishes by fulfilling this wish of mine, desired by my soul in a manner wholly unequivocal. Thus may our blessed God show you mercy, soon displaying to you that sight for which you have so longed, stinting nothing of His great goodness, provided only that you do as I ask. For if, as now appears (God forbid), there is no particle of truth in my claims—woe is me for the many evils this would entail!—then you will be relieved of this leprosy[4] (given that it is all a lie) as were the rest of our brothers who believed—God forbid! God forbid!—while I also will find relief in the concealment of my sickness and shame. But if they turn out to be justified and you do see them fulfilled, then your reward from me will be all the greater, corresponding to the greater magnitude of your faith, inasmuch as you took pity on my bitter, tortured soul and gave it satisfaction by granting its most impassioned wish.

If, however, you do not fulfill this request of mine, made of you with such pleading and supplication, this will show your faith to be severely wanting. For you would not grant satisfaction in this matter to the man in whom you have placed your faith, leaving him awash in bitterness on its account.

You must not think this a difficult thing that I ask of you. Your faith requires you to accept that [God's] supreme wisdom has thus decreed (as Scripture says plainly, "You have breached all his defenses [Ps 89:41]");[5] while if your concern is with your opponents, you have a perfect argument to offer them: "The man in whom we placed our faith urgently wished us to act as we do, begging us with profuse pleadings to grant his desire. How could we have refused him?"

I now implore the God of Truth that He inspire you to grant me satisfaction by fulfilling this request of mine in all its particulars. May He, in His manifold mercies, protect you and all that is yours from every harm, opening to you the gates of mercy and ease, success and prosperity. May He allow you to see His salvation, your eyes to behold the king[6] in his beauty—speedily and soon, amen! And this further do I beg of you: wherever this document may arrive, that you

4. [A standard derogatory term for Sabbatian belief, used by the nonbelievers.]
5. [Describing God's abandonment of His "anointed" messiah.]
6. [The true messiah.]

proclaim it there to the fullest extent both in writing and orally and so disseminate it among all our Jewish brethren.

> *These are my words—I, your servant,
> lowly and insignificant in every way,
> Sabbatai Tsevi*
>
> *Witnessed by: Jacob Najara, Nathan
> Ashkenazi, Benjamin Rejwan, Samuel
> Gandoor, Meir Rofé* [7]
>
> *Translated by David Halperin*

7. [Major figures in Sabbatai Tsevi's circle.]

9

Nathan of Gaza, A Letter on Conversion

Source: Gershom Scholem, "Iggeret Natan ha-Azzati al Shabbatai Tsevi ve-hamarato," in *Mehkarim u-mekorot le-toledot ha-Shabbeta'ut ve-gilgulehah* (Jerusalem: Byalik, 1974), 298–331.

And in that same year, after my spirit was awakened with visions of angels and holy souls, I was engaged in a prolonged fast[1] during the week of the portion of *Va-yakel*, and was secluded in a special room in holiness and purity. After having prayed the silent prayer with great weeping and while reciting supplications, behold "a spirit passed before my face, that made the hair of my flesh to stand up," [Jb 4:15] "and [my] knees smote one against another" [Dn 5:6]. I gazed upon the divine chariot and I beheld visions of God all that day and night, and then I prophesied a perfect prophecy as one of the prophets [with the words]: "Thus saith the Lord, etc." And about whom my prophecy was as well as the necessity that he live and endure forever were inscribed within my heart with perfect clarity.

And I kept the matter hidden until the redeemer proclaimed himself in Gaza and identified himself as the messiah, whereupon I was permitted by the angel of the covenant[2] to reveal what I had beheld. And its veracity was confirmed to me by the proofs given over by the Ari, of blessed memory, according to whom he [i.e., the messiah] will reveal deep matters of the Torah, and nothing of which he informs will fail to pass. And so it was with the above-mentioned angel, who appeared to me while I was awake and revealed to me a number of awesome matters. And among the things he said was that now is the final end regarding which the verse states "for the day of vengeance that was in My heart [and My year of redemption are come]" [Is 63:4].

While no angel informed me of the time when he will be revealed, I did hear a [divine] pronouncement during [the month of] Elul of the year [5]425[3] as follows: "A year and some months from now the messiah the son of David will

---

1. [*Ta'anit Hafsaka* is a period of incessant fasting of more than one day, and often lasting three days or a week.]

2. [I.e., the prophet Elijah.]

3. [August 23–September 21, 1665.]

be revealed to the world." Perhaps this refers to the spread of his name; but although it is possible that there be no substance to this [divine] pronouncement, one cannot deny the clear prophecy, heaven forbid, or the angel whose veracity I had confirmed, for it is a great principle and foundation which all the winds in the world cannot move. As long as the true redeemer lives and endures in the world, no being may deny this prophecy.

And I also received from that angel that even if all the Jews be wicked, heaven forbid, their sins will not impede the redemption, as our Sages of Blessed Memory, have said: "[The son of David will come only] in a generation that is [either altogether righteous] or altogether wicked."[4] I further received from [the angel] that the Jews ought to have faith without any sign or wonder and that if someone does not have faith, this shows that there is an admixture of evil in his soul from the generations that rebelled against the kingdom of heaven and the kingdom of the house of David. And I can [offer] a defense on behalf of this entire generation, since most of the Jews did have faith at first and although they retracted and stopped having faith, it was like that in Egypt [as well,] where nevertheless their [i.e., the Israelites'] initial faith was counted to their merit, so that regarding them it was stated: "[T]hey were redeemed only in merit of their faith."[5] Still, one who remains steadfast in his faith is certainly of greater worth, for this shows that he is of the generation of the King messiah and his soul is a branch of the root of the soul of the King messiah.

For whoever has faith in the redeemer, even if he be wicked he shall live by virtue of the root of the redeemer that is within him. And whoever desires and craves to enter this faith and seeks after it, fulfills the verse that states, "And they shall seek the Lord their God and David their king" [Hos 3:5]. And the term "seeking" refers to something that is devoid of sense and incomprehensible. And this is [the meaning of] the conclusion of the verse: "And they shall come trembling unto the Lord and to His goodness at the end of days" [Hos 3:5]; it is [something that is] rejected in terror for it appears to go against their received law. And I have a great proof as to why it is forbidden to have faith in this because of a sign, and there is confirmation from the Talmud that one ought to have faith without any sign, for we maintain that a person does not lie regarding something that is bound to be revealed.[6]

4. [BT Sanhedrin 98a.]
5. [Mekhilta, Exodus 14:31; Yalkut Shimoni, Josiah, 619.]
6. [BT Berakhot 36a; BT Rosh Ha-shanah 22b.]

For when God shines his light upon that person about whom the prophecy was spoken, he performs various inexplicable and strange deeds in public. And were he not the true redeemer even a single one of the least[7] of [these deeds] he has committed would have already led to his being forgotten. And this is a great confirmation of his messiahship, for we maintain that God does not perform a miracle for a liar.[8]

Whoever says something that cannot be said by [means of] the human mind [alone] this constitutes a sign, and although one may doubt whether there is any truth in him, it is a biblical requirement that one believe in him because of this sign, as Maimonides writes in the "Laws of the Foundations of the Torah." Indeed I have sworn on a number of occasions, before various people, very solemn oaths regarding the truth of this matter and in order to fulfill the verse that states: "And wilt swear: 'As the Lord liveth' in truth, in justice, and in righteousness" [Jer 4:2] and I declared, "I hereby swear in the name of the Lord, God of Israel and his holy Torah that of all that I have said regarding the redemption, I have not fabricated any of it in my heart nor have I added or subtracted from what I have received. And 'may the heavens reveal my iniquity and the earth rise up against me' [Jb 20:27] and may all the curses of the Torah fall upon me if in my mouth there is iniquity and a deceitful tongue." [. . .]

And while I was still in Gaza, at the height of the reports and of the faith, I said to a number of people, know that because of the strangeness of the deeds of the King messiah those who believe will retract and only a select few will remain.

[As Maimonides wrote in his "Epistle to Yemen,"] we will not know the matters relating to the King messiah until he comes . . . , for we do not understand the words of our Sages [about this]. Nevertheless, anyone who wishes to investigate [the matter] thoroughly will find great assistance and support for the substance of his words in the words of our Sages of Blessed Memory, and especially in the words of the Zohar. And since the Talmud does not state explicitly that he will be opposed, we ought to follow the book of Zohar and decide [the matter] according to its words, as the later authorities have explicitly stated regarding various matters, and in particular regarding [the donning of] phylacteries on the intermediate days of a holiday, which, according to the words of the Zohar, we do not don.

Indeed, the matters of the king messiah were not revealed explicitly in the

7. [The term is *kalot*, which could also mean "flippancies."]
8. [BT Berakhot 58a.]

Talmud so that people [would] not come to error, heaven forbid. And it was stated in an obscure manner in the book of the Zohar, which was [then] secreted away, and he [i.e., the author] wrote in his book that it will only be revealed close to the days of the messiah. And it is also written there that in the generation in which the king messiah will be revealed, several books of the Aggadah that reveal these matters will be found. And in several places in the book of the Zohar it is stated, "[People] will be sustained by your book in the last generation." We ought therefore to cite the words of the Zohar as proof in these matters and whatever in the Talmud is found to contradict our presentation we will clarify with God's help.

And if it is stated that the king messiah will be a very wise and righteous man in the eyes of the people, why would he be scorned by the sages? Even if he be poor and inflicted with wounds, that is no reason for the Sages and the masters of Mishnah to scorn him and speak falsely and vilify him. On the contrary, they ought rather to admonish and reprove anyone who would humiliate him. Why, therefore, are so many oaths by the explicit name [of God] required for the sages to recognize him as [the Zohar] states: "Reveal him to all the heads of the masters of Mishnah"?[9] Wouldn't he be recognized and confirmed by his righteousness and wisdom? Rather, it is surely because of the strange deeds he will perform, so that in the eyes of the sages he will seem to be doing things against the law, and so they will scorn him.

They therefore do not recognize me, and among them I am considered as a dead dog for "the wisdom of scribes will rot"[10] and the reason for this is that they do not know the true wisdom [i.e., Kabbalah], which is the soul of the Torah, but the literal meaning [of the Torah] is the body, and the body without the soul rots . . .

Our Sages of Blessed Memory have stated [that in the verse] "I have acquired oxen and asses" [Gn 32:6], "ass" refers to the messiah son of David.[11] And its meaning is that he has entered into the assembly of the Ishmaelites, who are likened to an ass, as it is written "stay here with the ass" [Gn 22:5], until he will rule over them, as it is stated "a poor man riding on an ass" [Jer 31:36].

Therefore whoever has faith in the king messiah ought not to wonder how it is conceivable that he is the messiah since he commits a number of sins and he

9. [Zohar III, 282b.]
10. [Following Mishnah, Sotah 9:15.]
11. [Genesis Rabba 75:6.]

commands a number of other people to commit [them] as well, for it may be countered and said that it is a temporary injunction. And we have heard him say a number of times that all his words in these matters are in the nature of a temporary injunction. And he also wrote a letter in which he interpreted closely the verse that states: "[If these ordinances depart from before me, saith the Lord] then the seed of Israel also shall cease from being a nation before me forever [kol ha-yomim, lit. 'all the days'; Jer 31:36]" [as implying that] all the days will not cease but some of the days will cease. And this [interpretation] resolves the baffling words that Hosea said when God said to him, "Your children have sinned," [and] he replied, "Exchange them with another people."[12] His intention was not that Israel should be eliminated from the earth, heaven forbid, for how can one entertain such an impossibility. Rather, [he meant] that He should pass them through[13] another people so that they [would] become refined and cleansed, for he gazed far [into the future and saw] that this is what the King messiah will do in the end of days. [...]

And another possible way of completing the rectification of the sins of Israel [lies in the fact] that God has exiled us from our land. For it seems difficult to understand why we were exiled from our land and our portion inherited by the nations who offend and constantly rebel against God. Although we had sinned much, God could have punished us within our land in a manner equal to the pain of exile. But this is resolved by the statement of Nahmanides[14] that the primary [obligation] of the Torah and commandments is solely in the land, and we are only obligated outside the land so that they not be novel in our eyes when we come [back] to the land. And this is the reason that Jacob [was permitted to] marry two sisters and Amram [to marry] his aunt, about which we had wondered. For outside the land, even if someone might sin, this does not cause a defect in the supernal luminaries. For although the soul is soiled because of the sin, since it does not cause a defect above, it can purify itself of its filth . . . However, a commandment that is fulfilled outside the land surely rectifies the soul, for [this follows the principle] "the measure in the case of the good is greater [than the measure in the case of punishment,]"[15] since by unifying God with the intentions [associated with the performance] of the commandments, that place

12. [BT Pesahim 87a.]

13. [This is a play on the Hebrew word he'eviram, which can be read as either "exchange them" or "pass them through."]

14. [See Commentary of Nahmanides on Dt 11:18.]

15. [See BT Sotah 11a.]

[wherein they are performed] can be sanctified. And [the Sages] have said, "The synagogues and study halls that are outside the Land [of Israel] are destined to be resituated in the Land of Israel,"[16] for by means of the Torah and prayers that are performed therein, they have become sanctified with the status of the Land of Israel.

Nevertheless, since our Sages have shown us the way of life and the way of death, it is better to choose life, as it is written: "But the righteous shall live by his faith" [Hb 2:4], and they should at least muzzle their mouths until they see how the matter will turn out. For a principle of all who believe in this faith is that it is not possible that the person who is said to be the messiah should die, and there is no reason to be concerned, as they are, about a catastrophe. And we have already proved previously that there is no greater sign than this. In conclusion, I, at present, have been unable to find any justification for [those who] "open their mouths without measure" [Is 5:14] and speak slander "against the Lord and against His anointed" [Ps 2:2].

And it seems to me that with this we may understand what our Sages of Blessed Memory have said: "How is one proved a repentant sinner? [. . .] At the same time, in the same place, etc."[17] And the reason for this is that it is known that by means of sins false and formless firmaments are created, and they [i.e., the sins] are not rectified until these firmaments are all destroyed. And this destruction [is brought about] by drawing down with one's soul a great illumination and breaking and burning all those firmaments [with it]. And one must come to [the point of] committing that prior sin he was seduced to follow, and the Other Side [i.e., the forces of evil], thinking that he will surely commit it [again], will let the soul of that person enter the firmaments he has built, and he will be able to purify and illumine them. And if that person merits it, [then] while remaining there separated from the sin, he will accomplish a great unification, and a great illumination will be drawn down and all those structures [will be] destroyed.

And it is certainly this holy faith in the king messiah Sabbatai Tsevi, may his glory rise, that all who are connected to it are considered to have fulfilled the entire Torah as our Sages of Blessed Memory have said: "Habakuk came and based them all [i.e., the commandments] on one [principle, as it is said] 'But the righteous shall live by his faith,'"[18] as we wrote previously. The foregoing are but

16. [See Yalkut Shimoni, Jeremiah, 331.]
17. [See BT Yoma 86b.]
18. [BT Makot 24a.]

the outskirts of the ways of this holy faith, whose roots were revealed to me by the Angel of the Covenant, and I was told to send them to our master and king, may his glory rise, because of the baseless arguments.

Translated by Chaim Elly Moseson

III | Sabbatianism in the Ottoman Empire

Early Sabbatian thought was deeply concerned with the theological meaning of conversion: was the apostasy of the messiah a subterfuge in his fight against the demonic powers embodied in Islam, or conversely, was it an attempt to bring the gospel of salvation also to people outside of the Jewish fold? Was God's call to the messiah to become a Muslim a "temporary injunction" to be followed by a triumphant return to Judaism, or was it meant as a final and definitive adoption of an alien faith? Were the religious tenets and practices of Islam merely a disguise lacking any real value, or did they possess some intrinsic sense and worth? And these questions left in their wake another: was the messiah the only one to apostatize, or should his actions be imitated by his Jewish followers? Sabbatai Tsevi himself was never consistent on this point: on the one hand, during moments of ecstasy, he called upon Jews (in some cases specific individuals, on other occasions the entire People of Israel) to convert; on the other hand, till the very end of his life he practiced Jewish customs and commandments and lived among disciples who were nominally Jewish. The two main theologians of early Sabbatianism, Nathan of Gaza and Avraham Cardozo, disagreed on many points, but concurred adamantly that the demand to convert was absolutely exclusive. Sabbatai Tsevi was a Jewish messiah in Muslim garb, and his adepts were to remain faithful to their ancestral religion and tradition. Some Sabbatians, however, reckoned otherwise. After the death of Tsevi (1676), his last wife, Jocheved, announced that the soul of the messiah had not abandoned his followers in the material world, but had been reincarnated in her brother, Jacob Querido. Querido received a series of revelations urging him to follow Sabbatai's footsteps and adopt the Muslim religion. Following these revelations, a group of some three hundred Jewish families converted to Islam in 1683 in the city of Salonika, thus founding the Sabbatian-Muslim sect known as the Dönmeh.

The Turkish word *dönmeh* signifies a neophyte, a fresh convert, and has the derogatory connotations of "turncloak" or "renegade." In modern Turkish, the word serves as a colloquial slur for a male-to-female transsexual. The term was originally coined to defame Salonika apostates, who styled themselves the *ma'aminim* (Hebrew for "believers," the standard self-reference of Sabbatians). Despite its strong negative sense, the term *Dönmeh* entered scholarly discourse and is today commonly employed as a standard designation of the group.

Jacob Querido died during a pilgrimage to Mecca in 1690. In line with the principle of leadership among the Dönmeh, which concerned the reincarnation of Sabbatai Tsevi's soul, several pretenders appeared, each claiming to be the new abode of the soul of the messiah. The Salonika group splintered into three principal branches: the Kavalieros, the Jakubis, and the Koniosos. These branches were fairly porous, and on the whole, the Salonika believers came to form a distinctive group shunning exogamous marriage with either Jews or Muslims and practicing a syncretic religion blending Judaism and Islam. They espoused the radical dualism of the Torah of the Created World (*torah de-beri'ah*) and the new spiritual Torah known as the Torah of Emanation (*torah de-atsilut*). With the advent of the messiah, the former—identified with the commandments of Judaism—was abolished and replaced with the latter. Sabbatai Tsevi's "strange deeds" were to be imitated, thus forming a basis for normative behavior. Accordingly, the Dönmeh's brand of Sabbatianism acquired a pronounced antinomian tendency, whereby ritual violations of the principles and rites of Jewish religion became an integral part of religious practice. Since the advent of redemption signified liberation from the yoke of the commandments, their further observance would be blasphemous as well as senseless.

The two most important leaders of the Dönmeh were the leader of the Koniosos, Berukhiah Russo (aka Osman Baba, 1677–1720) and a rather mysterious figure known as Yehudah Levi Tovah (fl. 1750–1800?). Berukhiah, none of whose writings survive but whose ideas are known from numerous contemporary testimonies, was arguably the most radical of all Sabbatian leaders. According to these testimonies, he argued not only that the positive commandments of Judaism had been abrogated, but that the negative commandments had become positive ones. Around 1716, his followers declared him the incarnation not merely of the soul of the human messiah Sabbatai Tsevi, but also of the God of Israel (the idea of the divinity of the messiah or any form of the doctrine of divine incarnation was generally eschewed by Sabbatians). His group propagated this claim among other Sabbatian groups;

and until his death in 1720, Berukhiah was worshipped by some Sabbatians of Salonika as a living God.

Yehudah Levi Tovah is the author of two lengthy Hebrew commentaries on parts of the Book of Genesis, as well as hundreds of poems, songs, and liturgical hymns, composed in Ladino with Turkish and Hebrew interpolations. His works, which were clearly inspired by the Sufi tradition, interweave Kabbalistic concepts and techniques (such as reliance on numerology) with traditional Turkish poetry. Sabbatai Tsevi himself was quite musical and tended to express his religious sentiments in song. Tovah's liturgical poems serve as a key to the teachings of this particular branch of Sabbatianism, but also to the wider world of Sabbatian ritual. Indeed, study of the Dönmeh may unlock the door to the practice of Sabbatian religion at large.

Alone among the branches of Sabbatianism, the Dönmeh to this day are reported to be a functioning group.

10

Israel Hazzan of Kastoria, Commentary on the
Midnight-Vigil Liturgy

Source: Israel Hazzan of Kastoria, *Perush le-Mizmorei Tehillim* [ca. 1677–1680],
MS Kaufmann 255, fols. 90v–91r, Hungarian Academy of Sciences, Budapest.

We have a little sister, and she has no breasts.
What shall we do for our sister on the day she is bespoken?
  Perhaps she is a wall? Then we will build upon her a buttress of silver.
  Or perhaps she is a door? Then we will shape her as a cedar board.
I am a wall, and my breasts are like towers.
Then I was, in his eyes, like her who finds peace.

Sg 8:8–10.

Behold I will send you Elijah the prophet before the coming of the great and terrible day
of the Lord. He will turn the heart of the fathers back toward the sons, and the heart of
the sons back toward their fathers.

Mal 3:23–24.

COMMENTARY

"We have a little sister." These are our brother Israelites, who were small and
meager in their faith, and allowed themselves to be seduced by the Ancient Rabble.

"And she has no breasts." They did not believe in the faith of Moses and Aaron,
who are called breasts. For the Targum[1] interprets your two breasts [Sg 7:4]
as referring to Moses and Aaron, and our Lord King Exalted is called by their
names. He is Moses the Faithful Shepherd; he is [Aaron] the high priest.

"What shall we do for our sister? What can we do for them on the day she is
bespoken," on that great and terrible day when they shall be made to stand in
judgment?

"Perhaps she is a wall." Perhaps they will make for themselves a wall of words,
pleading that they acted as they did only for fear of their leaders' and their scholars' bitter rage. In that case, "we will build upon her a buttress"—not of silver
[*kesef*], but of shame [*kissufa*]. They will be most thoroughly ashamed of what

1. [The ancient Aramaic translation of the Bible.]

they have done and will shed their tears over it. And as our Mishnah teaches, "Whenever anyone commits a sin and is truly ashamed of it, all that person's sins are forgiven."[2]

"Or perhaps she is a door." Perhaps they have locked their heart like a door and have no willingness to hear. Then "we will shape her as a cedar board"; then they shall take on the shape of withered trees, they shall never merit the life that shines from the King's face.

What answer gives the Community of Israel?[3]

She says: "I am a wall, and my breasts are like towers!" Indeed, I did not maintain the faith, but that was out of duress, for I feared their bitter rage. The faith lay deep in my heart. "And my breasts are like towers": shadai, "my breasts," are the divine name Shaddai in its fullness, which is the foundation of faith.[4] They are like towers, for the Lord's name is a tower of strength into which the righteous runs[5] and is lifted up high [Prv 18:10]. And the numerical value of the phrase "and my breasts are like towers" [823] is equivalent to the numerical value of Sabbatai Tsevi [814], once the seven [Hebrew] letters and the two words of his name have been added in [814 + 7 + 2 = 823].

"Then I was, in his eyes, like her who finds peace." I did not find peace myself, but I was like her who finds peace, that is to say, like the Holy Band [of the faithful].

And it is for the sake of this other band, those who acted under duress, that Elijah will come—

"Not to set anyone apart—

Not to bring anyone near—

But to make peace.

For so it is written:

He will turn the heart of the fathers back toward the sons, and the heart of the sons back toward their fathers."[6]

Translated by David Halperin

2. [BT, Berakhot 12b.]

3. [From the Targum to Sg 8:10.]

4. [The "fullness" of the Divine name Shaddai is the combined numerical value of the names of its three letters, shin-dalet-yod (360 + 434 + 92 = 814), which is also the numerical value of Sabbatai Tsevi.]

5. [The initials of the Hebrew words bo yaruts tsaddik, "into which the righteous runs," when rearranged spell the name "Tsevi." Sabbatai's followers understood the "tower of strength" as the fortress at Gallipoli, where he was imprisoned in 1666.]

6. [Mishnah, Eduyot 8:7, abbreviated.]

MEVLLIDI SHERIF OF MI SHEBERAKH
Anonymous

Source: Anonymous, "Mevllidi Sherif[1] of Mi Sheberakh,"[2]
MS 2270/11, Yad Ben-Zvi, Jerusalem.

Sabbatai Tsevi is the redeemer
Beloved Mehmed Tsevi
He is the light of Israel
Sultan Mehmed Tsevi
Truth came to the world
My love Mehmed Tsevi
He is the Shekhinah of Emanation[3]
Beloved Mehmet Tsevi

Shats[4] was born to Mordechai
The Messiah whose secret name is Shadday
Only hear the words of Adonay
Beloved Mehmed Tsevi

Tishbi[5] was born on the ninth of Av
With his force which is the "Vav"[6]

1. [Turkish: the Blessed Birth. This refers to the celebration of the birth of the Prophet Mohammad.]

2. [Hebrew: (May) He who blesses. A traditional Jewish prayer for an individual or a group recited in synagogue.]

3. [Shekhinah is the feminine Divine Presence. "Emanation" is the highest of the four spiritual worlds of Kabbalah.]

4. ["Shats" is the acrostic of the Hebrew letters Shin and Tsaddi, the first letters of the name Sabbatai Tsevi.]

5. [Refers to the birthplace of Elijah the prophet and hence one of his monikers. In Jewish tradition Elijah is the herald of messianic occurrences. The word "Tishbi" is an anagram of Sabbatai.]

6. [The third letter of the Tetragrammaton.]

That is the secret of "Tav"[7]
My love Mehmed Tsevi

The whole world was illuminated
For the ninth of Av was abolished
His name was here discovered
Sultan Mehmed Tsevi

Tsevi Tsaddik[8] brought unification
His deeds are beyond comprehension
Let there be "Hesed,"[9] light of consolation
My love Mehmed Tsevi

Berakha Kedusha Yihud[10]
Their acronym is the name "YaBoK"
Made by the Shekhinah of Emanation
Sultan Mehmed Tsevi

Yud Hey Vav Hey he unified
When to his kingship he arrived
"It is good" to him it was said
Beloved Mehmed Tsevi

Messiah is the light of faces
He opened the Divine Torah
Moshe Shimon Yitshak Hayim[11]
My love Mehmed Tsevi

The congregation shall stand.

He brought us a great joy
Ma'aminim! that you shall know
"Mi She'Berakh" to him we owe.
To Sabbatai Tsevi

7. [Aramaic: good.]
8. [Hebrew: the Righteous. Tsaddik is identified with the *sefirah* Yesod.]
9. [The first of the six lower *sefirot*. In Hebrew: kindness.]
10. [Hebrew: blessing, holiness, unification. In Kabbalah different meanings are attributed to this combination.]
11. [The acrostic of these names is the Hebrew word for messiah.]

Happiness was aroused
And His name is Yahweh
On his crown is the name Teftefya[12]
My love Mehmed Tsevi

Wisdom he gave us
We will sing in our rituals
Zihri and Tovah[13]—your servants
Sultan Mehmed Tsevi

Pleading to you, all your nation
Make apparent your governance
Your hardship makes us moan
Amen

Translated by Hadar Feldman

GAZEL TOVAH
Yehudah Levi Tovah

Source: Yehudah Levi Tovah, "Gazel Tovah," MS 2273/10, Yad Ben-Zvi,
Jerusalem; Harvard Hebrew MS 80/8, Houghton Library, Harvard University.

Acknowledge and Believe, there is nothing but *Hu*[14]
Know of a surety[15]and worship, you will find nothing but *Hu*

Hu and His name are one, there is no other creator
Come and see, understand: there is nothing but *Hu*

With the idea of *Hu* evil will be destroyed, that is Samael Belial
Feel Him and you will see Him, say: there is nothing but *Hu*

Hu is hidden, *Hu* is present, was not created heaven forbid!
Do not ask, do not try, do not think: there is no one but *Hu*

12. [One of the names of Metatron, the angel of Divine Presence.]
13. [Two names of the Sabbatian poets: Yehyah Zihri and R. Yehudah Levi Tovah.]
14. [In Hebrew and Turkish (from Arabic): He. *Hu* is one of the names of God in the
Sufi tradition.]
15. [Gn 15:13.]

Hu said so, *Hu* demanded so, *Hu* decreed so, none other
Do not be weary, do not err, there is no God but *Hu*

Hu is the first, *Hu* is the last, *Hu* is the master of the worlds
Study the Scriptures, you will see: there is nothing but *Hu*

Tovah, a thousand times you speak, the rule is this:
There is no other, you will not find another, LA ILAHA ILLA HU[16]

Translated by Hadar Feldman,
Eliezer Papo, and Katja Šmid

GAZEL ON LOVE
  Yehudah Levi Tovah

Source: Yehudah Levi Tovah, "Gazel on Love," MS 2270/16, Ben Zvi MS 2273/15,
Yad Ben-Zvi, Jerusalem; Harvard Hebrew MS 80/9, Houghton Library, Harvard
University.

My heart is stirred with a good word
It only wishes good and no sorrow to anyone
Filled with the fire of love
Day and night burning for the Faith

The love of my Faith is overwhelming
Like the great and wide ocean
Like a torch, in my heart
Day and night burning for the Faith

The river of Persimmon[17] is my love
Washing over my heart, which is Har Hamor[18]
His fire is like the river Di-Nur[19]
Day and night burning for the Faith

16. [There is no god but *Hu*, a Sufi variation of the Islamic credo "La Ilaha Ila Allah,"
meaning "There is no God but Allah."]
17. [A concept from the Zohar, sometimes invoked as one of the names of Sabbatai
Tsevi.]
18. [The Mount of Myrrh (Sg 4, 6), a common name of the Temple Mount.]
19. [Aramaic: a river of fire, a heavenly river, appearing in various Jewish sources.]

Seven seas and seven rivers
With them also the water of creation
And my love consumes them
Day [and night burning for the Faith]

Silver, gold, pearls, and jewelry
Together with all the riches of the world
My heart despises them
Day [and night burning for the Faith]

Eating, drinking, and pleasures of the world
They are nothing compared to Him
To this love my soul is bound
Day [and night burning for the Faith]

Upon this love my soul sustains
Truly tied with King Solomon
And in my heart it is a flame
Day [and night burning for the Faith]

This world, and the world to come,
On this love leans
Tovah, if they kill you, there will be no other
Day [and night burning for the Faith]

Translated by Hadar Feldman,
Eliezer Papo, and Katja Šmid

GAZEL
Yehudah Levi Tovah

Source: Yehudah Levi Tovah, "Gazel," MS 2270/4, Yad Ben-Zvi, Jerusalem;
Harvard Hebrew MS 80/27, Houghton Library, Harvard University.

The Messiah is the Almighty of souls
Nothing like him exists in the world
He fills the heavenly throne
He is the unity in the faith of God
I stepped out, called his name
I long to see his image

O unknown one, interpret your essence
No one had known your cloth
The Believer shall wait for him,
Life sacrificed on His path
He is the conqueror, king of heaven
I long to see his image

The house of prosperity is like Him
The worlds were suddenly created
No one like him had ever come to the world
He is the hidden heavenly messenger
He shall be praised by the nations
I long to see his image

Translated by Hadar Feldman

12

Yehudah Levi Tovah, Commentary on the Torah Portion Bereshit

Source: Aharon Telenberg, "Sabbatean Theology in Judah Levi Tovah's Commentary to Genesis," *Kabbalah* 8 (2003): 302–6.

"And on the seventh day God ended His work which He had made; and He rested on the seventh day from all His work which He had made" [Gn 2:2].

Rabbi Tovah of blessed memory opened by saying: "[A]nd he finished all his house [1 Kgs 7:1]. Come and see that all things that were fashioned during Creation rested, with each one remaining in its original form.

The *Zohar Hadash* on Genesis[1] states: "As was taught in a Mishnah: those creations that begat their offspring on a daily basis paused and rested, for they were complete." For this reason "on the seventh day God ended His work which He had made" [Gn 2:2], referring to the work performed on each day. Once they were all completed, the verse continues, "He rested on the seventh day from all His work which He had made." That is the rest and completeness of the Sabbath. With regard to this we find that the Song of Songs relates: "Until daybreak, and the shadows flee away, I will get me to the mountain of myrrh and to the hill of frankincense" [Sg 4:6]. And the Sages of Blessed Memory taught: "Until daybreak" refers to the Sabbath; "and the shadows flee away" is the dominion of the *kelippot* that will flee and never know the Sabbath, since the Sabbath contains no evil, as is written "neither shall evil dwell with thee" [Ps 5:5]. "I will get me to the mountain of myrrh" is the World to Come; "the hill of frankincense" is the Garden of Eden, where the Holy One Blessed be He comes to rejoice together with the righteous ones. Furthermore, the Sages of Blessed Memory taught: "The Holy One Blessed be He did not sit on His Throne of Glory until the Sabbath came, lifting up His grandeur."[2] At that time when the Sabbath arrives, that is, our savior Sabbatai Tsevi, about whom it is written "a Sabbath of rest to the Y-H-V-H" [Ex 35:2], it is then that the Holy One Blessed be He will sit on His Throne of Glory and all will be complete.

---

1. [*Zohar Hadash* 9, 9:4.]
2. [*Midrash ha-Ne'elam, Zohar Hadash* 17, 9:2.]

Come and see the verse that reads: "And on the seventh day God ended His work which He had made" [Gn 2:2], meaning the Oral Torah, which is the seventh day, about which is said—according to the mystical sense—"The law of thy mouth is better unto me" [Ps 119:72], and indeed, it is good. Through it the world is ennobled, which is the fulfillment of "from all His work which He had made." "His work" is the Written Torah. Anything whose source is wisdom is taken from the written word.

The Torah repeats the expression "the seventh day" three times:

"And on the seventh day God ended His work" [Gn 2:2].

"And He rested on the seventh day" [ibid.].

"And God blessed the seventh day" [Gn 2:3].

The first appearance relates to the eve of the Sabbath, for it leads up to it, which is why the verse teaches "God ended His work," meaning that He would complete it.

The second relates to the Sabbath day, about which the verse says: "Remember [zakhor] the Sabbath day" [Ex 20:8]. "Remember [zakhor]" is the numerical equivalent of God's Name "A-H-Y-H Y-H-V-H" when it is spelled out letter by letter. Thus, the numerical value of spelling out *alef-hey-yod-hey, yod-hey-vav-hey* is 233, which matches the numerical value of *zakhor*. [. . .]

The third appearance relates to the World to Come, which is the great Sabbath, the secret of the holy Sabbath, about which is written: "And God blessed the seventh day" [Gn 2:3]. This is the intent of the verse that reads: "Until daybreak, and the shadows flee away" [Sg 4:6], referring to the great Sabbath, the secret of the holy Sabbath, about which is written: "And God blessed the seventh day and sanctified it" [Gn 2:3]. Indeed, it is so. This day, blessed by God, is blessed with all things. It is blessed with the four Names, A-B S-G M-H B-N, which add up to the numerical value of "shall be blessed [yevarekh]." It is with these Names that He blessed this day, sanctifying it. The spelling of "And He sanctified it [Vayekadesh]" is lacking a *vav*, indicating that it is a day dedicated entirely to delight. It does not contain prohibition and permission, acceptable and disqualified, ritual defilement and purity, which are the six orders of the Mishnah; neither are any of the mundane activities of the week to be found there. Regarding this day [it] is written: "Eat that today; for today is a Sabbath unto the Lord" [Ex 16:25]. Note an amazing mystery: the opening letters of the words making up this verse, together with the letter *yod* that closes the middle word, come together to cre-

3. [*Berit Menuhah*, 3a.]

ate the Name A-H-Y-H. The *Berit Menuhah*[3] comments that it emanates from the treasuries of wisdom, and blessed is the man who comprehends its secrets. Since the Sabbath has become ennobled, and the Name A-H-Y-H serves to honor it —we can deduce that this Name represents the true delight, and from it the ultimate redemption.

Perhaps you will suggest that this refers to the World to Come, and will ask when the age of the World to Come is to begin? We can understand this from the verse "Until daybreak, and the shadows flee away" [Sg 4:6], whose opening letters spelled out equal a numerical value of 5381, which corresponds to the year of the birth of David son of Jesse, that is our savior, Sabbatai Tsevi. It is about him that the verse "a Sabbath of rest to Y-H-V-H" [Ex 35:2] refers, and that marks the beginning of the World to Come, which is the great Sabbath.[4]

"Until daybreak" [Sg 4:6], indeed, that is so. "And the shadows flee away," which is the dominion of the *kelippot* that were then separated from the holiness. For this reason, all of the restrictions fall away, as is taught in *Idra Zuta*,[5] that when grace is aroused, the grace of all graces in all of the worlds is revealed. All of the prayers of the lower worlds are accepted, and they shed light on the countenance of the *Ze'ir Anpin*, and all of the decrees are preserved and contract on the Sabbath. That is our intent in saying "Until daybreak," about which it says: "And God blessed the seventh day," that is, the day of the great Sabbath, as we have explained [. . .] when all of the decrees are suppressed. This refers to the laws established by the Sages, like the decrees that serve as protective fences, which are not found on the Sabbath. But mercy remains in all of the worlds. The Sabbath, however, has no decrees, neither above nor below, and it is for this reason that the fires of Gehenna die down and remain in their place. Thus, anyone who knows to keep the holy Sabbath will not suffer [in] the fires of Gehenna, much as the fires of the Chaldeans did not affect our father, Abraham. It is for this reason that the soul fills with rejoicing on the Sabbath day. This is the intent of the verse: "And Y-H-V-H shall guide thee continually, and satisfy thy soul in drought [*tsahtsahot*]" [Is 58:12], indicating that on this day the soul fills with joy and is satiated even in dire straits. How is this accomplished? The term *tsahtsahot* used in the verse is made up of the word *TS-H*—meaning "light"—which, together with the letters Y-H-V-H that appear elsewhere in the verse, add up to

4. [With the separation of the *kelippot*, which led to the appearance of Sabbatai Tsevi in 5381, the period of the World to Come is inaugurated.]

5. [*Idra Zuta*, Zohar III, 288b.]

emunah—belief. We can conclude from here that all of these changes are made on the basis of belief in our savior, Sabbatai Tsevi.

Furthermore, we see that removing the final letter *tav* from the word *tsahtsahot* leaves us with the numerical value 204, which corresponds with the value of *tsaddik* and equals *Mehmed Tsevi*. The letter *tav* signifies *tam*—perfection—indicating that in his hands, all becomes perfect. Now we can understand the statement made at the time of Creation: "And on the seventh day God ended His work," meaning that He finished all that needed to be done and it stood at a point of completion. The sin committed by Man, however, caused the weekdays to seize control; and it became necessary to add the Sabbath day to the days of the week.

This was corrected in the time of King Solomon, who reestablished the original order, as we find written: "and he finished all his house" [1 Kgs 7:1]. This refers to King Solomon, who is the purveyor of peace. "His house" is the house of David, the Sabbath Queen. "And he finished all his house" refers to all of the appropriate decorations that were necessary. Nevertheless, his sins and the sins of the Jewish people led to the destruction of this house, and it did not merit to stand for eternity. The messianic king, however, completed the third Temple, establishing Sabbath, and this will stand forever. This is the Sabbath that stands alone, without the mundane days of the week. Regarding this the verse states: "And God blessed the seventh day and sanctified it." Indeed, it was sanctified by Him.

Regarding this, Rabbi Nathan of blessed memory said: "On the holy Sabbath."[6] Note his emphasis on *the* holy Sabbath, which refers to the holy Sabbath on which the hidden light of *yesod abba* is revealed, and emanates from there until the holy oil is wholly consumed, leaving no remnant, because on the Sabbath all is ennobled with holiness. The secret is that *yesod abba* is actually our savior, as is well known. When this holy Sabbath arrives, the oil [*shemen*] emanates and leaves it. This oil [*shemen*] refers to the letters *sh-m-n* according [to] the *at-bash* alphabet, which is the secret of the Sabbath and is equivalent to the letter *b-y-t*, which is the numerical equivalent of *Y-H-V-H*. This holy Name reveals the secret of the ennobling of the Sabbath, as we explained above, which is a delight for all with no remnants, and all is ennobled in holiness.

Blessed is the one who understands these holy secrets, about which the verse relates: "And *Y-H-V-H* shall guide thee continually, and satisfy thy soul in

6. *Zemir Aritsim*, 7.

drought [*tsahtsahot*]" [Is 58:12]. *Tsah* means light; this is the secret of the pure light that is greater than all. "And satisfy thy soul in drought [*tsahtsahot*]," the soul will be satiated in both worlds.

"Because that in it He had rested from all His work which God created and made" [Gn 2:3].

Come and see that which is written in the Zohar on Genesis: "When the day is hallowed at the entrance of Sabbath, a canopy of peace hovers, spreading over the world. Who is the Canopy of Peace? Sabbath, when all spirits, whirlwinds, demons, and the entire dimension of impurity are hidden away within the eye of the millstone of the chasm of the immense abyss."[7] This is, indeed, the case. It is because the Canopy of Peace, which is the great Sabbath, emanates and rests on the world that the verse teaches: "I will cause . . . the unclean spirit to pass out of the land" [Zec 13:2]. "Spirit" refers to Samael, while "unclean" refers to the impure Lilith, who are gathered and removed from the world. The secret of this matter is that the 613 commandments, which are the numerical equivalent of these two who were removed,[8] are collected and annulled. Thus, this Sabbath, which serves as the Canopy of Peace, removed these evil spirits, together with all other destructive forces from the world. The 613 commandments were annulled, together with the days of the week, leaving only peace between those above and those below.

How was this peace established? It is grounded in the verse "Because that [*ki*] in it He had rested [*shavat*]." The letter *yod* in the word *ki* combines with the word *shavat* to create Shabtai. The remaining letters have the numerical value of twenty-eight, which represents *ko'ah*, strength, and together they represent "the strength of Sabbatai." Indeed, it is his strength that accomplished all of this, and it is well known that the numerical equivalent of "the strength of the highest crown" [*koah keter elyon*] is Sabbatai Tsevi. Moreover, an additional secret hidden here is that the words "Because that in it [*ki vo*]," included with the four letters themselves, equals forty-two. The intention of the verse "Because that [*ki*] in it He had rested [*shavat*]" is that with these forty-two, the souls came to rest, both those above and those below.

7. [Zohar I, 48a.]

8. [The numerical values of the names of Samael and Lilith add up to 611. To this, Tovah adds two, representing the number of the words in the *gematriah*. Thus, Samael and Lilith have the same value as the 613 commandments of Judaism.]

"Rested from all His work which God created and made" [Gn 2:3].

God ennobles and repairs on a daily basis by removing spirits and souls—and even spirits and demons. These are activities that serve to repair the world inasmuch as they are used to destroy the evildoers of the world. Nevertheless, there is still more to do since they have not been entirely repaired. Although two elements have been repaired, there are still two elements that remain lacking; for this reason they are constantly attempting to repair themselves.

One may inquire: Where do they look in order to effect this repair? It is regarding this that the Sages of Blessed Memory teach that demons seek out individuals who eat "pairs" and who place themselves in serious danger from demons by doing so. The secret to this is that since their form is that of two elements, they constantly desire to associate and merge with all things that are in pairs. For this reason, when Moses our teacher rose up on Mount Sinai, he taught us that there are three things that are dangerous when eaten in pairs. These three are: nuts, cucumbers, and eggs. Aside from these three, there was a fourth dangerous element, but it was forgotten by the Sages, who therefore decreed that nothing should be eaten in pairs, since we do not know the identity of the thing that was forgotten.[9]

There is a great secret in these three elements.

One is the nut,[10] about which we are taught: "And the earth was without form, and void; and darkness . . . and the spirit . . ." [Gn 1:2], which refers to the four shells [kelippot]. The fourth shell is called Noga, which represents keren, the secret of Ishmael. Since it possesses shells, the demons are desirous of it.

The second is the egg. You should be aware that eggs come from hens that become impregnated asexually without coupling with a male. This hints to the kelippah that is created without the power from above, and without the power of domem and golem. These are the opposite of the straight path, for they do not possess the full and correct balance. It is for this reason that the demons, who desire to reach a state of perfection, crave these things.

The third is the cucumber, which the Sages of Blessed Memory say is an evil food that is powerfully harmful to the body. It is like a sword and hints at the build of the serpent.

Recognize and accept that refraining from the consumption of pairs serves as

9. [On the prohibition against eating pairs, see BT Pesahim 110a-b.]

10. [A nut is encased in several shells. The innermost one represents kelippat noga, which contains the light of the messiah.]

a remedy for all whose souls are insufficiently complete with the full balance of holiness. This refers to anyone who has not yet accepted the belief in the messianic king, about whom the verse teaches: "But the just shall live by his faith" [Hb 2:4], which is the secret of the *kis he-hatum*.[11] Whosoever has not entered here remains incomplete. Anyone who has fully accepted this belief, however, has no connection or union with the *Sitra Ahara*.

From this you can understand a great and deep mystery, which will bring you to accept and encourage this belief. This is the secret of our eating salted fish with cucumber on the holy Sabbath. The salted fish is that which the Holy One Blessed be He killed and salted for the righteous ones in the World to Come,[12] at the time of the arrival of the messianic king. The Mishnah that teaches: "Bread with water shall thee eat"[13] is referring to this, and it is well known that the Ishmaelite kingdom, from its middle and above is called "bread," and it is from here that the repair will emanate. From its middle and below it is Lilith, and for her there is no repair.

This bread is prepared by the messianic king to be eaten, which is the meaning of "killed and salted." Salt [*melah*] shares the same letters as "dreamed" [*halam*], which is a kernel that comes from the mind to the *yesod* that leads to *melah*. "Eating" refers to coupling, and its strength can be eliminated by means of sweetening the salt. Once the bread, together with the salt of the fish, has been sweetened, it can be eaten, and by consuming it we show that it is repaired.

Similarly with regard to the cucumbers that are bad and harmful like a sword to the body, like the build of the serpent. Although they are bad and like the build of the serpent, they have the power to undermine that build and destroy it, changing the bad to good. Thus, the element that was harmful to the body now becomes a lifesaving remedy for it. This is the secret of Rabbi Simon ben Lakish, who headed a band of robbers and, having entered under the wings of the Shekhinah, became head of the Sages, and a savior to the Jewish people.[14]

11. [This should be understood in the context of the abolishment of the prohibitions against sexual impropriety. The final fulfillment of acceptance into the sect was fulfillment of "the commandment of sexual impropriety." Without committing an act of sexual impropriety, there is no release from the *Sitra Ahra*. This is accomplished only with performance of incestuous or adulterous relations.]

12. [BT Bava Batra 74b.]

13. [Pirkei Avot 6:4.]

14. [BT Bava Metzia 84b.]

For this reason, anyone who accepts this belief removes from his soul all foulness. He may consume pairs with no fear. About him our master teaches: "Eat, O friends; drink, yea, drink abundantly, O beloved" [Sng 5:1].

Translated by Shalom Berger of
the Academic Language Experts
team, with Avi Staiman

IV | Avraham Miguel Cardozo

Avraham Miguel Cardozo was born in 1626 in Medina de Rioseco, Spain, to a Converso family. He attended the University of Salamanca, where he received training in medicine, the natural sciences, and theology. In 1648, together with his brother Isaac, Cardozo fled Spain and arrived in Venice, where he openly embraced (according to other sources, converted to) Judaism. The Cardozo brothers joined the Jewish community and studied under the local rabbis. Around 1659, Avraham Miguel left Venice and lived in Cairo and Tripoli. When the news of the advent of Sabbatai Tsevi arrived in the summer of 1665, he became an enthusiastic supporter of the messiah. Following Sabbatai's conversion, Cardozo wrote several epistles defending the apostasy and elucidating its redemptive sense. He also began a correspondence with Nathan of Gaza and other leaders of the movement. Avraham Miguel's enduring and public support for the apostate messiah led to a bitter and protracted quarrel first with his brother Isaac and subsequently also with the Tripoli Jewish community. In 1672, Cardozo penned his first theological tract, *Abraham's Morn*; a year later he was expelled from Tripoli. During the next thirty years, he wrote over sixty epistles and treatises that circulated in numerous manuscripts. These writings caused a storm of controversy with anti-Sabbatian rabbis, but also internecine strife within the Sabbatian camp. These conflicts kept Cardozo from settling down, and he lived in Tunis, Livorno, Smyrna, Constantinople, Rodosto, Gallipoli, Candia, and Alexandria. In 1706, he was murdered by his nephew during a family quarrel. A year later a full account of Cardozo's life, a vitriolic satirical biography titled *The Book of the Sacred Contention*, was published by his opponent, Elijah Kohen.

Nathan of Gaza and Avraham Miguel Cardozo were the two most important—and often competing—theologians of early Sabbatianism. Both were prolific writers who could combine, often in one text, wild visions, brilliant exegesis, and carefully crafted arguments. Nathan's main aim was to integrate Sabbatian theological innovations into the framework of established Jewish discourse; his works put forward novel solutions to traditional problems. Cardozo, by contrast, had little interest in ancient dilemmas. He did not propose new answers to old questions: he posed only one, completely new question. This question, Cardozo's true obsession, concerned the identity of the True God.

Cardozo held that the main religious traditions as well as major philosophical systems are on the most basic level in agreement: they share a conviction about the existence of an omnipotent and omniscient God who is the maker of all being ("the First Cause"). Such a general concept of the Absolute is an innate idea shared by all humans, and no reasonable person can deny it. While serious religious and philosophical debates do not touch upon the existence of God, they concentrate on his attributes and his role in the human world. In particular, the three monotheistic faiths (rabbinic Judaism, Christianity, and Islam) need to solve the fundamental question concerning the relationship between the idea of the First Cause as given to any sentient being and shared by all philosophical and religious systems and the idea of God originating from the revelation(s) that produced particular religious traditions. Despite discrepancies in other areas, Judaism, Christianity, and Islam answer this question in the same fashion: they posit a basic identity between the First Cause, whose concept is known to all, and the God who revealed Himself to Moses on Sinai. (Christians and Muslims additionally believe that the same God further granted other revelations to the founders of their respective religions.) Positioning himself as the ultimate outsider, Cardozo claims that all three religions got it wrong. The God of the Mosaic revelation (the "God of Israel") is not the First Cause. The God of the Bible (and of Midrashim and rabbinic parables) is not omniscient, not omnipotent, and not unqualifiedly good. While ancient Judaism never saw itself as a religion professing a universal Deity common to all humanity, from the Geonic period onward the rabbis and Jewish philosophers made strenuous efforts to reconcile the Jewish concept of God with the idea shared by all peoples. The Jews have "forgotten" the God who made Himself known uniquely to them and replaced His worship with the worship of the First Cause. Having taken a wrong God as an object of its worship, rabbinic Judaism has become a form of idolatry, a religion no better (and in some ways inferior) to the religions of pagans, Christians, and Muslims.

Cardozo's theology of history is the story of God's people forgetting their God. Exile, the central theme of Sabbatian thought, is conceptualized as a cognitive category: "being in exile" means not knowing who the true Deity is. Cardozo's messianism is the story of this Deity's rediscovery. The task of the messiah is also cognitive: he is to find the True God and make him known to the people Israel. Since the true messiah not only strays from the rabbinic mainstream on some points of doctrine or ritual, but also essentially calls for the worship of a God different from the one contemporary Jews worship, his fate is to be rejected and scorned by his people. This messiah is a suffering messiah. In elaborating this concept, Cardozo proposes a creative reading of the fifty-third chapter of the Book of Isaiah and puts forward a concept of the redemptive value of the suffering of the messiah. The messianic reading of this chapter was a centerpiece of Cardozo's thought and a bone of contention for both anti-Sabbatian rabbis and many other Sabbatians. Cardozo's exegesis smacked of Christianity, and he was accused of injecting Christian elements into Judaism. Cardozo retorted that precisely the opposite was the case: it was the rabbis, who mistook the God of Israel for the First Cause, the God of the Christians and other universalistically inclined religions, who were influenced by Christianity. Moreover, Cardozo argued, the rabbis had suppressed the traditional messianic interpretation of the Book of Isaiah. A Judaism freed from alien influences would be a Judaism freed from apologetics: no longer would the rabbis feel the need to keep under wraps doctrines that resemble those of other peoples (the same line of argument would be used by Nehemiah Hayon in claiming that the concept of the Triune God is a legitimate part of the Jewish religion; see the following section).

Yet the messiah was not only to suffer rejection by his people. For Cardozo, Isaiah implied that the messiah was to be profaned. But as no sin removed a Jew from the community of Israel, conversion was the sole path to profanation. Hence, the messiah was to become a forced convert. This motif, the profanation of the messiah by conversion, both accounted for the apostasy of Sabbatai Tsevi and foregrounded Cardozo's own Converso background.

13

Avraham Miguel Cardozo, A Letter to Isaac Cardozo

Source: Jacob Sasportas, *Tsitsat Novel Tsevi*, ed. Isaiah Tishby
(Jerusalem: Mosad Byalik, 1954), 289–97.

Most people, the scholars of our generation included, have supposed that king messiah is to come in power, working signs and miracles and wonders. Thus they have fallen into great error.

Know this: that the sages have said that Israel is destined to utter a song, "but they cannot sing it until the messiah shall have suffered abuse, as it is written, 'Flung abuse, abuse at Your anointed at every step'" [Ps 89:52].[1] Also, they say, the Lord has divided torments into three parts, allotting one part to David and the patriarchs, one part to our generation, and the third part to the messiah, for so it is written, "But he was profaned because of our sins" [Is 53:5].[2]

Commenting on the verse "I will receive him back in love" [Jer 31:19], the sages tell us that the messiah is destined for prison.[3] He is to be the butt of everyone's insults, scorned, a person despised and loathed, many of the Jewish people insulting and abusing him, calling him "plagued, smitten, and afflicted by God" [Is 53:4]. King messiah, in short, is fated to be supreme over the angels, yet brutalized and vilified by all. These two opposites cannot obtain at one and the same time. Rather, he must first be lowly, deemed by the Jews a loathsome villain, suffering torments and all that he was doomed to endure on account of Israel's transgressions; for it was on this condition that he entered the world and for this purpose he was created. Only afterward shall he ascend to lofty rank, fulfilling all the glorious things spoken of him by the prophets and by our ancient Sages of Blessed Memory. [. . .]

One must not fall into the opinion of those who assert that Sabbatai Tsevi cannot be [the] messiah because he did not come in glory, working signs and wonders. Whenever the "true messiah" (as they think [of] him) may come, those

1. [*Midrash on Psalms* 18:5.]

2. [*Yalkut Shimoni* on Ps 2:6 (2, 620). Usually the biblical passage is translated as "wounded because of our sins." The understanding of *meholal*, "wounded," as *mehullal*, "profaned," is key to Cardozo's interpretation of Is 53.]

3. [*Midrash Pesikta Rabbati* 37:2.]

people still will not be able to believe in him. For anyone who comes and is *not* insulted, scorned, and loathed cannot possibly be [the true] messiah.

These points you must retain, from all that I have said: The true messiah is Sabbatai Tsevi. Second, the messiah must be thought to be vile and loathsome. Third, everything that Isaiah the prophet spoke in his fifty-third chapter must be fulfilled in our messiah. For so our sages have learned from tradition and set forth for us plainly.

Now we arrive at the great secret:

True, the Turk threw Sabbatai Tsevi into prison and afterward summoned him. The mufti and his sages took counsel together and decided against killing him, inasmuch as he had a worldwide reputation as messiah. If they were to put him to death, those in distant parts might be misled into creating a new religion, some of the Turks also having been caught up in the uproar. Better to dress him, willing or not, in Turkish garb; and this was precisely what the Turk did.

So king messiah's aim was to undergo a martyrdom, while the Turkish king's was to dress him in garments of shame, as he had been advised. In each and every respect, then, [Sabbatai] was a forced convert,[4] our iniquities being the cause. The crux of the secret: all of us were condemned by the Torah to become forced converts before we might leave exile. For thus it is written in the Torah: "You shall serve other gods, of wood and stone" [Dt 28:36], measure for measure, we having of our own free will violated the Torah and worshipped other gods, inflicting profanation on God's name, such that His blessed Name was profaned among the Gentiles on account of our transgressions. Thus it was an act of justice, explicitly decreed in the Torah, that we should adhere to alien cults and violate the Torah among the Gentiles, this time under compulsion and against our will. Having been ourselves profaned and forced into apostasy, we should then have cried out unto the Lord.

It is a known fact that every one of the kings of Israel worshipped idols, and [was] therefore cast out from God's presence. Even Judah, [who] remained under the kings of the Davidic lineage, forsook the Torah. (So it is written: "Because they forsook the Teaching" [Jer 9:12].)[5] It is also a known fact that kings are considered equivalent to their people and are punished by God for the people's sins, as the Zohar and the Gemara tell us plainly. Thus it was that the Lord ordained

4. [Like the "forced converts" (*anusim*) of Spain, among whom Cardozo's family—and Cardozo himself, in his youth—were numbered.]

5. [Literally, "My Torah."]

that the two messiahs must suffer torments, punishment, and profanation on account of the iniquities of Israel.[6]

Jeroboam the son of Nebat sinned; he caused Israel to sin as well.[7] It was therefore insufficient for messiah ben Joseph to be "profaned because of our sins" [Is 53:5]; no, he must bear upon his shoulders the iniquities of Israel, to be killed by the Gentiles in order to make atonement for us. The people [of Judah] "forsook the Teaching"; therefore, messiah ben David was doomed to profanation, to being made a convert against his will, in such a way that he could no longer carry out the Torah's commands.

You must realize that our ancient Sages, of Blessed Memory, applied Isaiah's "profaned because of our sins" to three individuals. One was Moses, buried outside the Holy Land—at Peor,[8] a profane land, a dry land without any water —on account of Israel's transgressions, so that they might be able to leave their final exile. Similarly messiah ben Ephraim: the Zohar tells us in the name of the prophet Elijah that justice required him and his offspring to be profaned among those of an alien faith, in retribution for the sin of Jeroboam son of Nebat; from having been holy, he must become profane. Justice required, in other words, that the adherents of an alien religion must force him into apostasy, compelling him for this reason—and his offspring as well—to follow that religion. The rabbis applied "profaned because of our sins" also to messiah ben David: from having been holy, he must become profane.

All the Gentiles are called "profane," and also "shell."[9] Israel alone is called "holy," as it is written, "Israel was holy to the Lord" [Jer 2:3]. "For you are a people consecrated to the Lord your God" [Dt 7:6]: you are *consecrated*, the other nations profane. A Jew may sin; he remains *consecrated* as long as he is among the Jews, and is still called "Israelite." (As our ancient sages said of Achan: "Even though he sinned, he was an Israelite.")[10] In consequence, King messiah could not become

6. [Cardozo follows the rabbinic tradition that expects not one but two messiahs: "messiah ben Joseph" (or "ben Ephraim"), who dies in battle against the Gentiles, and "messiah ben David," who completes messiah ben Joseph's work and ushers in the Redemption.]

7. [As described in the Bible, 1 Kgs 12:25–33. Jeroboam was the rebel who established the northern Kingdom of Israel, as opposed to the southern Kingdom of Judah, which remained loyal to David's descendants. Since Ephraim was one of the northern tribes, messiah ben Ephraim suffers for the sins of the northern kingdom, messiah ben David for the sins of the southern kingdom.]

8. [Dt 34:6.]

9. [*Kelippah*, a Kabbalistic term for the demonic.]

10. [BT Sanhedrin, 44a.]

profane without having been brought forth from Israel into another domain, and it is written that he was "profaned because of our sins. . . . The Lord visited upon him the guilt of all of us" [Is 53:6], for we had all been condemned to forced conversion, "and he was numbered among the sinners" [v. 12], for we call those who leave the faith "sinners of Israel"—as it is written, Edom fell away from Israel[11]—and the Jewish people now count him among those sinners. But in fact he "made intercession for sinners," for those who otherwise would have been condemned to abandon faith for Gentile-ness, and "he had done no injustice and had spoken no falsehood" [v. 9]. [. . .]

The case of Esther, through whom the Jewish people experienced a dramatic rescue, is comparable. The bulk of Diaspora Jewry surely detested her for having attached herself to an idolatrous Gentile, an act utterly forbidden by the Torah. But the Sages—who knew this secret, all of whom recognized the truth of the matter—refused to brand her a sinner. Accordingly, they ruled in the Gemara that "Esther was entirely passive,"[12] meaning that without any action on her part she could be compelled against her will, and she could not be held responsible for an action that the doer was able to accomplish without her agreement.[13] That was the case [with Sabbatai Tsevi], whom the Turk, unwilling to execute him, clothed against his will [. . .]

If there is anyone with you who realizes that the words "Awake, awake, clothe yourself with splendor, O arm of the Lord!" [Is 51:9] apply to the Shekhinah, as do the words "Shout, O barren one, you who bore no child!" [54:1]—if he has reached the stage where he can understand on his own who is the subject of the passage from "So marred was his appearance, unlike that of man," as far as "made intercession for sinners" [52:14–53:12]—then that person will be able to grasp the true Kabbalistic significance of this great secret, awe-filled and sealed away: why the messiah had no choice but to undergo a forced conversion to atone for the transgression of Israel; why messiah ben Joseph was irrevocably condemned to profanation among the adherents of an alien faith, yet his violent death was conditional. He will understand also why [messiah ben Joseph] must die.

11. [Presumably, a misquotation of 2 Kgs 8:22, "thus Edom fell away from Judah," possibly influenced by 2 Kgs 1:1. The verb translated "fell away" is *pasha*, the same verb that underlies *poshim*, "sinners." "Edom" is normally used in medieval and later Hebrew literature as a code term for Christendom; the implication is that Christians are, at bottom, "sinful" renegade Jews.]

12. [BT Sanhedrin 74b.]

13. [That is, sex with Ahasuerus.]

Up to this point I have set matters forth truly and clearly. I am confident that very soon the Sun of righteousness will step forth, bringing healing to those who honor his name and yearn for his salvation, which is near at hand. Then will be revealed the righteousness of our messiah, the messiah of the Lord our Righteousness, Sabbatai Tsevi.

Translated by David Halperin

14

Avraham Miguel Cardozo, A Letter to Baruch Enriques

Source: Avraham Miguel Cardozo, "A Letter to Baruch Enriques," MS Opp.
Add. 4° 150 (Neubauer no. 2481), Bodleian Library, University of Oxford.

Tripoli, 29 October 1668

[...]

I received, and I see the publication, which my brother [Isaac] makes of my ingeniousness, sending his writings but neglecting to send mine. I wrote him my first letter informing him of my illness; and while giving him the good news of my spiritual joy, I warned him, that even if he heard the most extravagant [things about] Sabbatai Tsevi, he should not vilify him, because he is the [true] messiah. He answered: "What you see is what you see." I answered him [in an] extensive and satisfactory [letter], and he replied to the second one without refuting many of my arguments. Rather, he reiterates his own, in a disorderly way, and answers those that he wants to pretend I had posited. I assure you that I consider him to be misguided [. . .] and so I am thinking of not answering him, since I already responded to the important points. I also notice the uproar [that] my letters on this issue, which you again ask to see in Spanish, caused. And to satisfy your request, I will begin by saying that our brethren, who came from Spain, are classified into three types: some are doctors, philosophers and scientists; others are naturally wise men and some scholars; and [the third group are] those who cling to everything the Sages say, because they do not consider themselves to be such. Of the first group, most are philosophers and metaphysicians, who attend to the sayings of the Sages of Israel; and [because these are] not dealing in proofs or demonstrations, deprecate them, and that is the fundamental reason for their not trying to achieve understanding. Since the Law is translated and explained by the Sages, and they do not honor the Sages, they end up being bad Jews, but not Christians. Some, who take upon themselves the yoke of commandments, through study end up being wise and obedient. Others take the middle ground and end up being neither Jews nor Christians but Naturalists, against whom I have been a most severe fighter; and were it not that the time of salvation is near, it would have been necessary to print a book showing their theses to be the most vile and them to be the greatest ignoramuses—all of that with effective arguments. Even recently I convinced one of them who had come from those parts "drunk" with Naturalism.

The second group, being proud, asks for a biblical source for everything, which has not been, up to today, well understood or explained by any Sage of Israel, and they want there to be a proper sign. Inasmuch as the particulars of the messiah's comings are not literally described in the Scripture, each verse can be expounded in a different [contradictory] sense by those who deny the Sages. It is necessary to clarify that I do not speak about the messiah except with the Jews, who are perfect in their obedient observance—according to the Law—to the prophets and the ancient Sages of Israel, whose water we drink and in whose light we walk. Consequently, I do not speak about Dr. Cardozo's or Dr. Orobio's or anybody else's imaginary messiah, but about the messiah of Israel as portrayed by the true sages and prophets. One must be aware that ignorance, once it finds shelter in which it feels comfortable, does not know how to leave for any reason. And it is also to be known that the Sages of Israel, seeking the meaning of several secrets, proposed different explanations about the person of the messiah: in one place [they say that] he was born the day the Temple was destroyed; in another, that in every generation there is someone who could be revealed as the messiah should Israel merit it; in another, that he is sitting near the gates of Rome; in another, that he is in Paradise; in yet another, that he is in the yeshivah on high, yet, for someone who knows the secret, in no way are all of these sentences contradictory.

And whoever says that he wants to know [the secret]—I will tell him either to study, or to believe without proof, or to leave this matter. [. . .] [The secret is the following:] that the messiah has to be born, like Moses, from a man and a woman. And the Sages of Israel say that the messiah has to be revealed in the Holy Land, and [they say] that he has to be hurt and profaned for Israel's sins, with reference to the verse in Isaiah chapter 53 [which] they received and taught, that the whole chapter speaks about the messiah. The Christians obtained this [interpretation] from them [the Sages of Israel], and more recent [Jewish] commentators, [. . .] in order to deflect the arguments the Christians adduce [from other sources] [. . .]. This is the true messiah according to the Sages of Israel; the Christians, making use of this, say that he has to be humble, and since at the same time he has to be triumphant, they affirm that all the prophesies have not yet [been] fulfilled in [Jesus] until the second coming, in which he will come triumphant upon the clouds of the heavens. [. . .] Isaiah chapter 49, clearly speaking about him, says: "Thus said the Lord, the Redeemer of Israel, his Holy One, to him who is despised of men, to him who is loathed by the nation, to a servant of rulers: kings shall see and arise, princes also shall prostrate themselves" [Is 49:7]. The prophet gives three sure signs by which we are to know him: "Despised of men": this is because of the acts of his soul, as it is said in [chapter] 53, "and if he places guilt on his soul" [Is 53:10], even if that "despising" that is called sin is [considered] forgiveness of sin—this means that when he placed sin on his soul in apprehension and [asking for] true forgiveness—he will see the fruit [of his repentance] and prosper. "Loathed by the nation": "the nation" and not "nations" because neither the Turk nor the Christian loathe him, only Israel. And it also says about him: "I will also make you a light for the Gentiles" [Is 49:6]: because through him the Lord's and the Law's truth will be known. Finally, that he will have to be "a servant of rulers": being a servant, and in this place it cannot be understood literally to refer to Israel, because the prophet goes on to say that he will free the prisoners. [...]

I answer that, for mysterious reasons, it is impossible to convince one that [Sabbatai Tsevi] is the messiah and none other, but one is forced to concede that he can be: there is no way that one will prove that it is impossible for Sabbatai Tsevi to be the messiah. [...]

Let us now discuss [the following questions]—must one believe according to the Law, and must one believe that Sabbatai Tsevi is the promised messiah. The name of Nathan the prophet was revealed to the world by trustworthy persons from Gaza, Jerusalem, Cairo, and Alexandria. I wrote to these important persons, and they answered me [that] were he to be a true prophet, I should announce: "Thus says so and so: 'Our redeemer has come, Sabbatai Tsevi is his name'"; and to this announcement, so qualified, the whole of Israel, [even] those from afar, would be obliged to give credit. Because the Law commands one to believe in a true prophet, [or face] a death sentence. And he does not have to walk all over the world claiming to be a prophet. A testimony of some [people] in a certain place obligates those in a distant land. And if those virtuous men, versed in Law, lie to us, they will have to answer to God, and we will have fulfilled our obligation just like a judge who sentences on the basis of two credible witnesses—if they lie, the judge is free [from blame]. Likewise, even [if] the case were that the prophet Nathan was not examined, or that underneath this there was something [that stood in] contradiction—we have no other option but to believe it—and anyone who, out of pure stubbornness, does not believe in the good news of the prophet and the redemption, sins against God and his Law as an infidel to this precept. And if Nathan is a prophet as defined by the Law, anyone who denies him deserves the death penalty from heaven. And if it turns out that he is not a prophet, as defined by the Law, whoever did not believe him, sinned, just as the one who eats nonkosher fat thinking that it is kosher fat sins. Because having been informed that he was a prophet, and not knowing that he was not qualified as a prophet, he stopped believing him; [and] because of the fact that Rabbi Sabbatai Tsevi was dressed as or became a Muslim, he turned away from the faith he had had before, that the prophet Nathan was a true prophet—he sinned either from pride or because of error or mortal sin—because God is not below the Law or nature—He is the absolute Lord over everything and He could have wanted or ordered that the messiah do that [become a Muslim], just as He ordered Abraham to sacrifice Isaac; Isaiah, to walk naked; Hosea, to marry a prostitute; Ezekiel, to cook his food with human excrement—His paths and thoughts are not the same as ours. [. . .]

Let us now consider what obligation exists today to believe or not to believe, after having already demonstrated that anyone who says that he cannot be the messiah is either crazy, lacking in knowledge of the Law, or a heretic. [. . .]

Dr. Cardozo of Verona, Dr. Orobio of Amsterdam, and many others say that the messiah must be a saint and not an apostate; must be Jewish, and not Muslim. It is well known that all who convert because they fear for their lives are considered Jews by the Law—and it is clearer than the sun, that the Turkish king forced Sabbatai Tsevi to put on a turban—therefore, according to the Divine Law, he is perfectly Jewish, and according to Christian and Muslim law, he has not yet left Judaism because both consider that one who converts out of fear or under duress does not immediately enter into their fold. Therefore, what they say about his not being a Jew is a new law. I ask those gentlemen and the others who have come from Spain, who while they were there humbled themselves before alien gods, were not circumcised, lived without Law nor performed Jewish commandments: were they Jewish or Christian? If they were not [Jewish] in Spain neither will they be in Flanders. There, they are neither Jews nor Christians; because whoever is not Jewish, as long as he does not circumcise himself and does not go to the ritual bath, remains a complete Gentile—and they do not do it—therefore they neither were nor are Jews. I do not speak about the messiah [with non-Jews]. And if they tell me that we were Jews in Spain and that all the *marranos* who remain there are Jews—which I myself admit—they should be ashamed to open their mouths to call Sabbatai Tsevi an unfaithful apostate. The conclusion is the following: they and their fathers, those who left the faith, some having been forced to do so and others through their own choice, and lived 180 years amid the Gentiles without being circumcised, without being married [in a Jewish ceremony], without [observing the laws of] menstrual purity, without the Torah—to satisfy their worldly interests and for the sake of their great vanity. Thus those, who come fleeing the whip, call themselves perfect Spanish Jews and a Holy Nation, while Sabbatai Tsevi, who since his childhood has dedicated his soul to God through continuous study, mortification, and sanctity, and was forced to put on a turban, does not deserve to be called a Jew.

Translated by David Markovits Farkas
and Katja Šmid

| # Avraham Miguel Cardozo, Abraham's Morn

Source: Avraham Miguel Cardozo, *Drush Boker de-Avraham* [ca. 1670–1672], MS Ginzburg 660, fol. 1r, Russian State Library, Moscow.

I propose to set forth the faith of our ancestors—our prophets, our sages—forgotten by us these thousand years, because of the long duration of our exile. This faith was known to the Tannaim and most of the Talmudic Sages; many of the Geonim, too, had it by tradition.[1] Afterward the directors of the Academies may possibly have kept it hidden in their hearts, or it is possible they no longer knew it, for not one of the books of the Kabbalists from Geonic days to the present speaks a whisper of it.

The Kabbalistic teachings of Rabbi Moses Nachmanides and Rabbi Abraham ben David are indeed true in their entirety, as Rabbi Isaac Luria of blessed memory has said.[2] But their accuracy is limited to matters of *sefirot*, of [divine] unification and governance, for without the Zohar no scholar could possibly arrive at this faith through his own researches, and these men had no access to the Zohar, for it came to light only afterward. No student of Kabbalah, moreover, could have achieved knowledge of this faith without prior awareness of the World of the Mending and the nature of the Five Persons, which Luria was the first to uncover.

It does not appear from Luria's writings that [the prophet] Elijah revealed to him the secret of the faith with any specificity or clarity. Perhaps, if he did grasp it, he was given no permission to circulate the knowledge. It seems more likely, however, that he simply did not have time to search out and expound the

1. [The Tannaim were the first generations of the ancient rabbis, active from the first century CE to about 230. Their successors the Amoraim ("Talmudic sages") lived to the end of the sixth century; the Geonim were the Iraqi Jewish scholars of the seventh through early eleventh centuries, directors of the "Academies" mentioned in the next sentence (from whom Cardozo seems to distinguish them).]

2. [Nachmanides (1194–1270) and Abraham ben David (1125–1198) were for Cardozo the outstanding Kabbalists of the Middle Ages, although from the perspective of modern scholarship the latter's Kabbalistic credentials are somewhat ambiguous. Isaac Luria (1534–1572) was the great giant of the "modern" Kabbalah, who developed from hints in earlier sources an elaborate mythos of the "Shattering" of the primordial *sefirot*, followed by their "Mending" into the humanlike shapes of the "Five Persons."]

faith, continually occupied as he was with writing down those things that he did receive. Constructing long treatises, as he did for his students and particularly for Rabbi Hayyim Vital, was a time-consuming labor.[3] Add to this that (for our multitudinous sins) he died young, not reaching the age of forty, while even Father Abraham, who struggled with all his might and mind to know the blessed Creator, did not fully recognize Him until he was ninety years old, having begun at age fifty and finished forty years later.

We know what has been said: the Jewish people will leave their exile through the Zohar's merit, inasmuch as the secret of the faith written throughout the Zohar and *Tikkunim* by Rabbi Shimon ben Yohai and his associates will be revealed at exile's end.[4] Yet even Rabbi Moses Cordovero, the great systematizer of all Kabbalists ancient and modern, whose massive labors of scholarship culminated in his commentary on the Zohar[5]—even he found himself baffled by a multitude of problems, without the smallest grasp of this faith, lacking as he did any knowledge of the World of Mending. When all is said and done, both he and the Rabbi of blessed memory [Luria] lived at a time when the Final End was still remote, whereas at the present time, God has illumined our mind and the secret of this faith has begun to be revealed.

I myself did not attain it until I had labored twenty-two years over it. Innumerable spiritual torments, born of doubts and misapprehensions, did I suffer. Time after time was I put to the test. For no reasonable person could possibly accept this faith on anyone's say-so, unless that instructor were to work signs and wonders in his presence, as Moses did for our ancestors when he revealed to them the God of their patriarchs. For they also had forgotten Him, so long had their exile dragged on . . .

Translated by David Halperin

3. [Hayyim Vital (1542–1620) was Luria's most prominent student. Cardozo is wrong to speak of Luria as "constructing long treatises." In fact, he wrote very little, leaving others such as Vital to set down on paper their understandings of his ideas.]

4. [The Zohar and *Tikkunei Zohar*, though actually written at the end of the thirteenth century by Rabbi Moses de Leon and his circle, were long believed to be the work of mystically inclined Tannaim, of whom Rabbi Shimon ben Yohai was the central figure. Cardozo takes this for granted, supposing that the thirteenth century was the time of the *rediscovery* of the long-lost ancient Zohar.]

5. [Moses Cordovero (1522–1570) represents for Cardozo the culmination of the pre-Lurianic Kabbalistic tradition. His Zohar commentary *Or Yakar*, which remained in manuscript for more than four centuries, has recently been published in twenty-three volumes (1962–1995).]

Source: Aharon Freimann, *Inyanei Shabbetai Tsevi* (Jerusalem, 1968), 9–10, 37.

There was a man in the kingdom of Portugal, one of the New Christians, descended from the Jews forced into apostasy, from the Thorn-and-Thistle[1] family of dignitaries and judges. He made the journey to Venice and there converted to Judaism. Fornication and liquor, with their attendant vices, were his main interest, and to write love poetry stuffed with lies; yet he pursued an education as well. Among decent folk he feigned decency, but with the willful he was sly, washed in trickery water inside and out. His brazen flesh rock solid, he played shepherd for the whores.

He gained a reputation as a physician, and in Livorno found his great opportunity through the Duke [of Tuscany's] patronage, the latter dispatching him to Tripoli as doctor for the city's ruler Osman Pasha and equipping the devil-goat [Cardozo] with his recommendation. Some of the merchants, too, provided him with a quantity of their wares, assuming he would do honest business and take his commission from the profits. Thus he made for himself in Tripoli an easy and pleasant berth, settling in, siring sons and daughters, never quite getting around to remitting the money for the merchandise with which he had been entrusted.

It was there that he got hold of certain writings of Rabbi Isaac Luria, which he proceeded to ascribe to himself, strutting them like a soldier his weaponry, all rush and commotion with no substance. There, too, he encountered apostate disciples of Sabbatai Tsevi and engaged them in debate on sundry topics, exploring with them the proofs they invoked for their heresies. There he invented his flimsy "faith"—fit only to be flung far away—founded on Sabbatai Tsevi's God-denying fabrications, which the apostate Jacob Palache[2] had brought him, a gift from Sabbatai Tsevi's own lips. Thus he wrote in a letter he sent by special courier to Nathan of Gaza: "Long have I known the God of Truth and taught the

---

1. [I.e., "Cardozo." (*Cardo* is Spanish for "thistle.") Kohen habitually refers to Cardozo as "Bramblebush" (*ha-atad*, from Jgs 9:14–15).]

2. [A rabbi of Marrakesh, singled out by one of the movement's enemies at the end of 1666 as a chief ringleader along with Nathan of Gaza.]

multitudes the Mystery of Divinity; and by the Temple! the God of our exalted Lord and King Sabbatai Tsevi and the God of Abraham Michael are one and the same."

In those days he also wrote fraudulent epistles to the rabbis in Izmir and everywhere else, in defense of believing in Sabbatai Tsevi even after his wrecking the Torah of Moses, on the strength of arguments whose stupidity would have embarrassed Bigtha, Abagtha, and Zethar.[3] Never, [Cardozo] wrote, did Sabbatai Tsevi utter a word of apostasy. No; it was the king who imposed his [Muslim] clothing upon him, a matter filled with lofty hidden mysteries which [Cardozo] decided might be recorded in writing inasmuch as most people do not know Kabbalah: the "mystery of the turban" with which Sabbatai Tsevi was crowned. All [Sabbatai's] repellent acts were ordained by divine providence, performed as a sort of incense offering for the Deity's sake. For if Sabbatai Tsevi were really a scoundrel, he would not have done forbidden deeds; someone out to deceive, after all, will hide his cunning beneath a mask of innocence like a burglar under cover of darkness. [...]

Afterward "Ephraim" offended with poisonous expositions, tailored to suit their wish to fix the Redemption for the year of "He keeps *faith with His anointed* [5466 = 1706]."[4] Basing himself on the words of our ancient Sages, he argued from the First Redeemer to the Last: at age forty, Moses fled from Pharaoh; at age eighty, he stood before the king of Egypt to liberate the children of Israel. Just so, the Last Redeemer Sabbatai Tsevi was born in the year of "His bones are *rubbed away*" [5386 = 1626];[5] in the year of "Why do you *seek further beatings*, that you continue to offend" [5426 = 1666][6] came the apostasy, which [Cardozo] liked to imagine as an "occultation."[7] Q.E.D.: in the year of "He redeems them *from fraud* and lawlessness" [5466 = 1706][8] he [Sabbatai] would stand up for his poor downtrodden folk and become their savior.

3. ["Angels of Confusion," their names taken from Est 1:10.]

4. [Ps 18:50. The last two words of the Hebrew phrase have the numerical value 466, indicating the year 5466 = 1705–6. The name "Ephraim" is taken from Hos 12:15 and applied to Cardozo.]

5. [Jb 33:21. The verb "rubbed away" has the value of [5]386.]

6. [Is 1:5. "Seek further beatings" (*tukku*) = [5]426. In contrast with the use of Ps 18:50, presumably taken from a Sabbatian source, Kohen picks out the most disparaging biblical verses to designate the turning points of Sabbatai's life.]

7. [*Hitallemut*, a standard Sabbatian term for the phase of Sabbatai's career that followed the apostasy.]

8. [Ps 72:14. "From fraud" (*mi-tokh*) = [5]466.]

His emissaries fanned out in all directions. The fraudulent Deathdevil,[9] too, went from province to province and from town to town proclaiming the same glad tidings. Bramblebush had no idea that his day of doom was near, his time of reckoning at hand, when his sins would be lined up in a row and the storm wind marked out. Shall he die a fool's death? Wounds shall wipe the scoundrel away—blows to the inside of his gut—on that day, known to God, when He avenges Himself and His unity.

God raised up the evil from his own household so that it was Shalom, his closest relation, who put his snowy hairs underground. He was [Cardozo's] nephew, whom he had brought up like a son from his very birth, nurturing him at the family table like a rose among thorns. Right properly did he teach him his letters and his craft, and the boy became his apprentice.[10]

One day they set forth in the company of Palmbranch,[11] to pay a house call on a certain Egyptian official and judge. They took their pay in gold florins, and the three headed homeward. [Cardozo] tried as usual to get another's services for free, paying him nothing, and so gave Shalom only a pittance while being doubly generous to Palmbranch, for he was his bloodstained son-in-law.[12]

"Squeeze out anger, and you get a quarrel" [Prv 30:33]—and they did quarrel over it. Bramblebush spoke high and mighty, with haughty arrogance. "Damn you, robber!" the other retorted. "You'll be the one robbed! When you're finished robbing, you'll be robbed. When you're done cheating, you'll be cheated." His hand went to his knife, and he thrust it into his belly and fled from the house.

"O Shalom!" Bramblebush screamed. "How bitter it is!"

His entire household hurried to see what might be done for him, to give him medicine and bandage his wound. While they were thus occupied, [Shalom] made his escape, passing the carved statuary[13] until he reached the Mosque of al-Azhar, the great Islamic shrine where a murderer might find asylum from any revenge seeker. (For it was a law laid down by Pharaoh: that anyone who

---

9. [Kohen's name for the Sabbatian preacher Hayyim Malakh, whose name literally means "Life Angel."]

10. [In the practice of medicine.]

11. [A disciple of Cardozo's who became his son-in-law when he married Cardozo's allegedly promiscuous daughter Zilpah.]

12. [*Hatan damim*, from Ex 4:25–26, where the phrase is translated "bridegroom of blood."]

13. [*Ha-pesilim*, from Jgs 3:26. The reference is probably to the ancient monuments at Giza, just outside Cairo.]

entered there, having killed some person in the land of Egypt, would be absolved of the crime.)

On the third day Bramblebush died, thanks to his treachery against God, his claiming that God is something other than Himself. His fate became proverbial. Whenever some matter was ambiguous, [people would say,] "Is it 'Shalom-Zimri, his master's murderer'? Or 'Zimri son of Salu, the nobleman who was killed'?"[14]

And now, all you who see a vision of well-being when there is no well-being, for the days grow many and every vision comes to naught—every false vision and soothing divination, that is—it was false visions you prophesied and lying divination you uttered![15] May you all end up just as [Cardozo] did!—Dovesdung and Cursed-evilday,[16] Deathdevil and Palmbranch, and the rest of their cronies. He will annihilate them; the Lord our God enthroned in heaven will annihilate them.[17]

Translated by David Halperin

14. [Allusions to 2 Kgs 9:31, Nm 25:14. The Bible knows two men named Zimri, one of whom died from being stabbed through the belly like Cardozo (Nm 25:6–15), the other of whom murdered his master like Shalom (1 Kgs 16:8–20). The "proverbial" saying evidently asks which of the two "Zimris" is relevant to an ambiguous situation.]

15. [A combination of Ez 13:16, 12:22, 24, 13:17.]

16. [Two more of Cardozo's disciples. "Dovesdung" (from 2 Kgs 6:25) is Daniel Bonafoux, while "Cursed-evilday" is Yom Tov Mevorakh, whose name literally means "blessed good-day."]

17. [Combining Ps 94:23 and 123:1.]

V | The Hayon Controversy

Nehemiah Hiyya ben Moses Hayon was a Kabbalist and the author of the only indisputably Sabbatian work to be printed by the Sabbatians themselves. Hayon was born around 1650 in Sarajevo and grew up in the Land of Israel, receiving his education in the Hebron yeshivah. He briefly held the rabbinate of the city of Uskup (Skopje) in Macedonia, but mostly lived an itinerant life traveling between Kabbalistic centers in the Land of Israel and Europe. In the early seventeenth century, Hayon met Avraham Cardozo in Safed and received from him a manuscript titled *Raza de-Meheimenuta* (The Mystery of Faith), a tract attributed by contemporaries to Sabbatai Tsevi (modern scholarship holds it to be the work of Cardozo himself). In 1711, in Venice, Hayon published his first book, a small treatise titled *Raza di-Yihudah* (The Mystery of Unity). Two years later, in Berlin, two more books appeared. The first one was a collection of sermons entitled *Divrei Nehemiah* (The Words of Nehemiah), while the other one was Hayon's main work, *Oz le-Elohim* (Power to the Lord). The book consisted of a lengthy introduction, a full text of *Raza de-Meheimenuta* (renamed by Hayon *Meheimenuta de-Khola* [The All-Encompassing Faith]) and his two running commentaries on the Cardozo/Sabbatai tract. Hayon made no mention of the authorship of the tract he was expounding. Both *Divrei Nehemiah* and *Oz le-Elohim* were printed with approbations of several important rabbinic authorities.

In June 1713, Hayon arrived in Amsterdam and presented his books to the leadership of the Portuguese community, seeking permission to sell them in the city. The chief Portuguese rabbi, Solomon Ayllon (himself a suspected Sabbatian), established a committee to decide on the matter. Some members of the community also sought the opinion of Rabbi Moses Hagiz, an emissary from Jerusalem temporarily living in Amsterdam as well as of the chief rabbi of the city's Ashkenazic community, Tsevi Hirsch ben Yaakov Ashkenazi (Hakham Tsevi). Hagiz and Hakham Tsevi instantly realized that the main text printed and explicated in *Oz le-Elohim* was in fact a notorious heretical tract held to be the work of Sabbatai Tsevi. Although Hagiz advised caution, Hakham Tsevi immediately excommunicated Hayon. He also published a broadside, *In the Sight of All the House of Israel*, in which he attacked what he regarded as the most contentious aspects of Hayon's doctrines. The disregard for the Ayallon committee proceedings and interference of an Ashkenazic rabbi in the internal affairs of the Sephardic community was seen as an affront and an open breach of jurisdiction. While some committee members harbored doubts, the body decided to fully exonerate Hayon. Feeling the support of the rich and powerful community, Hayon began to publish pamphlets denigrating his detractors. Hagiz and Hakham Tsevi were placed under a ban and forced to flee Amsterdam. They arrived in London, where Hagiz penned his main anti-Hayon work, *The Destruction of the Wrongdoers*. The Hayon controversy quickly turned into a battle of books—in the form of broadsides, newspaper articles, and tracts. Christian civil authorities were called in to intervene, and Christian scholars were asked to provide expert opinions. Excommunications and counter-excommunications were issued. While officially supporting Hayon, the Amsterdam Portuguese community grew increasingly uncomfortable with the public nature of the affair, and the Kabbalist was paid to leave the city. Wandering from country to country and finding little support for his views, he died in relative obscurity in North Africa in 1730.

The Hayon controversy raged around three main points. First was the printing of a tract that was not only Sabbatian in nature, but attributed to Sabbatai Tsevi himself. Hakham Tsevi and Hagiz's familiarity with the text suggests they had read it before Hayon showed it to them. During the first stage of polemics, it was not the actual ideas put forward in the treatise, but the fact that Hayon dared to make it public, that was targeted. By printing the words of the messiah, Hayon introduced Sabbatian Kabbalah to open debate. Hagiz and Hakham Tsevi positioned themselves not only as opponents of Sabbatian heresy, but as guardians of the time-honored boundaries of esoteric tradition: secret teachings, in their view, should be kept secret by restricting access to texts containing them. The second issue was the Trinitarian character of Hayon's concept of the Godhead and the real or alleged similarities between Sabbatianism and Christianity. This aspect of the controversy did not emerge until relatively late, at which point the polemicists merely rehashed the claims made earlier for and against Cardozo. The third facet of the controversy touched on ideas presented in the introduction to *Oz le-Elohim*. This introduction, by far the most original text penned by Hayon, was intended as a kind of manifesto. In *Oz le-Elohim* Hayon did not merely print, for the first time, a secret Sabbatical tract; he also formulated an ideological basis for his actions. Hayon held that Kabbalistic texts should be printed and made available to all, even those studying esoteric lore without an authorized teacher. Indeed, he understood Kabbalah as best studied on one's own: he interpreted the traditional admonition to transfer esoteric teachings only "in a whisper," "to one person," as a call for the solitary silent reading of a printed book. Most radically, Hayon claimed that misunderstandings stemming from such a mode of study were in fact necessary (and praiseworthy) elements of religious praxis: nothing pleased God more, according to Hayon, than mistakes made in the search for Him.

In Hayon, the radically individualistic and experiential character of the Sabbatian religion was translated into the language of hermeneutics. Sabbatianism blurred the boundaries between the esoteric and the exoteric and—even more radically—between reading and misreading. God was indeed hidden in the sacred texts, but there was to be no monopoly on their access. Religious tradition was infinitely fluid, brooking no privileged authorities, texts, or interpretations. The quest for the True God was the individual's quest for meaning.

Nehemiah Hiyya Hayon, Power to the Lord

Source: Nehemiah Hiyya Hayon, *Oz le-Elohim* (Berlin, 1713), fols. 1r–5r.

"Whosoever speculates on four things, a pity for him! He is as though he had not come into the world, [to wit], what is above, what is beneath, what before, what after, etc."[1] And the Gemara teaches: "Nor [the Work of] the Chariot in [the presence of] a single individual. R. Hiyya taught: But the headings of chapters may be transmitted to him. R. Zeira said: The headings of chapters may be transmitted only to the head of a court and to one whose heart is anxious within him. Others say: Only if his heart is anxious within him. R. Ami said: The mysteries of the Torah may be transmitted only to one who possesses five attributes, [namely] the captain of fifty, and the man of rank, and the counselor, and the cunning charmer, and the skillful enchanter."[2] Clearly this Gemara proves that the Work of the Chariot cannot be passed on to any individual unless he possesses the qualities that are mentioned.

I, in turn, say that it is well known throughout the Gemara that in every matter there are those who forbid and those who permit, and it is impossible to fulfill both opinions. In a case where no final decision is reached in the Gemara, those who rule in these matters closely examine the connotation of the Gemara and decide either toward leniency or toward stringency.

We therefore find that the greatest of the authorities, Maimonides of blessed memory, rules in the fourth chapter of the Laws of the Fundaments of the Torah in a lenient manner—according to Rabbi Hiyya—saying: "What is the difference between the Work of the Chariot and the Work of Creation? The Work of the Chariot cannot be expounded even in the presence of one, unless he is a sage who can understand of his own knowledge, to whom the headings of chapters may be transmitted."[3] Thus, he rules according to the opinion of Rabbi Hiyya that we do transmit to him the headings of chapters. He does not accept the positions of Rabbi Zeira or Rabbi Ami, and it is logical to conclude that were

1. [Mishnah Hagigah 2:1.]
2. [BT Hagigah 13a.]
3. [Mishnah Torah, Hilkhot Yesodei ha-Torah, 4:11.]

the law to follow the opinion of Rabbi Ami, the Torah would be forgotten by the people of Israel.

Even though it appears that Maimonides rules according to Rabbi Hiyya, it is still worthwhile to examine and discuss this Mishnah, for clearly this Mishnah is difficult to comprehend and can be understood in a variety of different ways. Although the Talmud questions the language of the Mishnah and replies with definitive answers, nevertheless, "They left room for us to distinguish ourselves,"[4] for the language of the Mishnah is unclear and can be interpreted in two ways:

When the Tanna teaches: "Nor the [Work of the] Chariot in [the presence of] a single individual, unless he is a sage and understands of his own knowledge,"[5] the simple meaning appears to be that we do not expound the Work of the Chariot to any individual unless he is a sage who understands of his own knowledge. This can be seen from the fact that each of the three clauses of the Mishnah includes what is forbidden to expound and what is permissible to expound. For example, the Mishnah teaches: "The subject of forbidden relations may not be expounded in [the presence of] three," indicating that it can be expounded in the presence of two. Similarly: "nor the Work of Creation in [the presence of] two" indicates that it can be expounded before one. Therefore, the third clause —that is, the Work of the Chariot—must also consider both the possibility that expounding is permitted, as well as the possibility that it is forbidden. Ordinarily, the Work of the Chariot cannot be expounded in the presence of one, but it can be expounded to an individual who is a sage and can understand of his own knowledge. This is one approach to understanding the language of the Mishnah.

But there is another approach, a more stringent one. Perhaps when the Tanna taught: "Nor the Work of the Chariot in [the presence of] a single individual," his intention is to say that the Work of the Chariot cannot be expounded under any circumstances to anyone, neither to an ordinary person nor to an exceptional person, that is, not even to "a sage who understands of his own knowledge." According to this approach, when the Tanna teaches "unless he is a sage and understands of his own knowledge," it is a separate teaching, whose meaning is: Given that the Wisdom of the Chariot cannot be expounded under any circumstances to any individual, then the Torah will be forgotten, since according to this ruling it is forbidden for anyone to study the books of Kabbalah. In response to this, the Mishnah concludes: "Unless he is a sage who understands of his own

4. [BT Hullin 7a.]
5. [Mishnah Hagigah 2:1.]

knowledge"—only such a person may read such works, for he will come to understand the Work of the Chariot on his own.

What is clear is that according to both of these approaches there is no prohibition against printing the teachings of the Kabbalah. In fact, each of the two approaches offers good reason to permit their publication. According to the first approach, the Mishnah forbids expounding the Work of the Chariot except to an individual who is a sage and understands of his own knowledge. It appears that he must be taught silently, lest another person who may be standing behind the doorway hear his voice outside, causing the Work of the Chariot to be expounded before two. Similarly we find in the Midrash: "Rabbi Joshua the son of Yehotsadak said: '[A]s it was told to me in a whisper, that is how I told it to you.'"[6] Accordingly, speaking in a whisper is no worse than printing a book, which will be read by an individual on his own. Nevertheless, not too many should be printed since "wisdom . . . is more precious than rubies,"[7] nor should they be freely distributed, for if they are distributed for free, it is possible that the book will be given to someone "whose heart is not anxious within him." Having such a volume available, however, would allow him to transmit the hidden secrets of the Torah to someone who desires to possess it by dint of his wisdom, or someone "whose heart is anxious within him." This is supported by the Gemara: "R. Zeira said: The headings of chapters may be transmitted only to the head of a court and to one whose heart is anxious within him."[8] Thus, publishing the book has two advantages: The Rabbi who authored it is speaking silently, and the individual who comes to acquire it will be someone "whose heart is anxious within him."

According to the second approach, the intent of the Mishnah is to prohibit expounding to anyone, whether he has the ability to understand of his own knowledge or not, and when the Mishnah teaches "unless he is a sage who understands of his own knowledge," it permits an individual to study and understand on his own. In that case, apply the statement: "If Rabbi has not taught it, whence would Rabbi Hiyya know it?"[9] If no books can be found, and it is forbidden to teach to anyone, how can the sage understand of his own knowledge something that he can neither see nor hear? We are forced to conclude that it is permissible to publish works of Kabbalah. And the individual "whose heart is anxious within

6. [Yalkut Shimoni, Bereshit 1:4.]
7. [Prv 3:13–15.]
8. [BT Hagigah 13a.]
9. [BT Yevamot 43a; BT Eruvin 92b.]

him," can go and acquire them and understand of his own knowledge with "no utterance and no words."[10]

[...]

If so, we are faced with a severe difficulty with the Mishnah. For in the Mishnah it says that is permissible to teach the Work of the Chariot to a sage who understands of his own knowledge, after which the Mishnah teaches: "Whosoever speculates on four things, a pity for him! He is as though he had not come into the world, [to wit], what is above, what is beneath, what before, what after."[11] The term "speculates" means that he understands of his own knowledge, without the direction of a teacher. But if he is permitted to expound, how much more so he should be allowed to speculate! Given that the Work of the Chariot is what is above, as is the implication of the Gemara, and as Rashi explains the language of the Mishnah: "What is above—the firmament that is above the heads of the creatures."[12] We can conclude that when the Mishnah says "what is above," it is referring to what is above the firmament of the creatures, which must be the Work of the Chariot, etc.

As appears in the Gemara (13a): R. Joseph was studying the Work of the Chariot; the elders of Pumbedita were studying the Work of Creation. The latter said to the former: Let the master teach us the Work of the Chariot. He replied: Teach me the Work of Creation. After they had taught him, they said to him: Let the master instruct us in the Work of the Chariot. He replied: We have learnt concerning it: Honey and milk are under thy tongue. The things that are sweeter than honey and milk should be under thy tongue. R. Abbahu said: [It is inferred] from this verse: The lambs [kebasim] will be for thy clothing. The things that are the mystery [kibshono] of the world should be under thy clothing. They [then] said to him: We have already studied therein as far as, "And He said unto me: Son of man."[13] He replied: This is the very [portion of the] Work of the Chariot.[14]

Rashi explains: "This is the very [portion of the] Work of the Chariot—If you have studied this far, then you have studied much, for these two verses 'I looked ... a gleam as of amber, etc.'[15] and 'like the appearance of a bow,' etc.,[16] are the

10. [Ps 19:4.]
11. [Mishnah Hagigah 2:1.]
12. [BT Hagigah 11b.]
13. [Ez 2:1.]
14. [Cf. BT Hagigah 13a.]
15. [Ez 1:4.]
16. [Ez 1:27–28.]

ones that the sages insisted could not be expounded, since they discuss the form and appearance of the Divine Presence."[17] Clearly the Work of the Chariot is the very portion of what is above. And if it is forbidden to speculate on them with a mindful eye, how much more so to expound on them. So how could the Mishnah say that it is permitted to expound to a sage who understands of his own knowledge? For if he is permitted to expound, surely he should be permitted to speculate! And how did the Tanna say: "Whosoever speculates on four things, a pity for him! He is as though he had not come into the world?"[18] This implies that he may not speculate in order to understand what is above. Thus, we have a contradiction between the earlier clause and the latter clause of the Mishnah.

And furthermore, immediately following the Gemara brings: "An objection was raised: How far does [the portion of] the 'Work of the Chariot' extend? Rabbi said: As far as the second 'And I saw.'[19] R. Isaac said: As far as 'Hashmal'[20] —As far as 'I saw' may be taught; thenceforward, [only] the heads of chapters may be transmitted. Some, however, say: As far as 'I saw,' the heads of chapters may be transmitted; thenceforward, if he is a sage able to speculate by himself, Yes; if not, No."[21]

It is therefore clear that according to everyone, speculation regarding the Work of the Chariot—that is to say, what is above—is permissible. In that case, how does the Tanna say: "Whosoever speculates on what is above, a pity for him! He is as though he had not come into the world," contradicting his earlier words? Rather we are forced to conclude that when the Tanna said: "A pity for him! He is as though he had not come into the world," it is not to denounce the individual who speculates, rather it is to praise the one who speculates on what is above. For the Zohar teaches with regard to those who do not speculate in the glory of their Master: "How obtuse are human beings, totally unaware of the glory of their Lord."[22] And it is true that they are obtuse, since they see the Mishnah that forbids expounding and they read the Gemara, but they do not read it in a precise manner.

And now I will explain the intention of the latter clause of the Mishnah: "Whosoever speculates on four things, a pity [ratuy] for him! He is as though

17. [BT Hagigah 13a.]
18. [Mishnah Hagigah 2:1.]
19. [Ez 1:27.]
20. [Ibid.]
21. [BT Hagigah 13a.]
22. [Zohar I, 58, 68a.]

he had not come into the world, [to wit], what is above, what is beneath, what before, etc."[23] Rashi explains that the word *ratuy* is an expression meaning "pity," and he brings a parallel usage from the *Midrash Torat Kohanim*: "to his remaining sons, Eleazar and Ithamar"—they deserved to have been burned,[24] but scripture had pity [*ritah*] on Aaron. But before we come to explain the Mishnah, we must be precise in explaining the expression: "He is as though he had not come into the world." It should have said, "It were a mercy if he had not come into the world," just as the continuation of the Mishnah says: "Whosoever takes no thought for the honor of his maker, it were a mercy [*ratuy*] if he had not come into the world."[25] Why, when discussing "whosoever speculates on four things" does the Mishnah say: "A pity [*Ratuy*] for him! He is as though he had not come into the world," which is an excessively wordy expression? For this is what is found in the Amsterdam printing of the Gemara.

And we must investigate what is brought in the Gemara Eiruvin regarding the dispute between Shammai and Hillel on the question of the creation of man: "For two-and-a-half years were Bet Shammai and Bet Hillel in dispute, the former asserting that it would have been better for man not to have been created than to have been created, and the latter maintaining that it is better for man to have been created than not to have been created. They finally took a vote and decided that it would have been better for man not to have been created than to have been created, but now that he has been created, let him investigate his past deeds."[26]

The language used in the dispute is redundant both for Bet Shammai and Bet Hillel. Why is it necessary to say "than to be created," which is certainly understood once the position is taken that it would have been better for man not to have been created. And for Bet Hillel, as well—once he declares that it is better for man to have been created, why is it necessary to say "than not to have been created"?

It appears that Bet Shammai recognizes that every man who is created must accomplish something in this world, for he certainly fulfills some of the commandments. Nevertheless, he cannot possibly rise to the foundational level that he was at prior to his creation if he does not fulfill all of the 613 commandments in a positive manner. It turns out that this unfortunate soul toils his entire life,

23. [Mishnah Hagigah 2:1.]
24. [Lv 10: 6–7.]
25. [Mishnah Hagigah 2:1.]
26. [BT Eruvin 13b.]

yet it is doubtful if he will succeed in returning to his original condition. For this reason, it would have been better for him, and greater comfort, had he never entered this world. This is what Bet Shammai means in saying that "it would have been better for man not to have been created than to have been created," i.e., there would have been greater pleasure for him to have remained in his original situation, before he was created, than the pleasure that he attains from his toil after he is created. That is why they repeat: "It would have been better for man not to have been created than to have been created."

Bet Hillel believed that in the end someone who benefits from what does not belong to him is embarrassed to look his provider in the face.[27] It is, therefore, better to have been created and enjoy the fruits of one's own labor, rather than not have been created and benefit from that which is not his own. This is the intent of the repetition: "it is better for man to have been created than not to have been created." In the end, however, Bet Hillel examined the matter closely and understood that [man] may not attain his original position. They took a vote and decided that it would have been better for man not to have been created than to have been created. The intent of the statement: "But now that he has been created, let him investigate his past deeds,"[28] is so that he will not lose his original position, and perhaps he will succeed in returning to that place. Thus we learn that man's entire purpose is to attain the position that he had previously so that it will be as if he never entered this world; that he is untainted of all the sin that he committed in this world.

[...]

And this was the intent of the Tanna who taught: "Whosoever speculates on four things, [to wit], etc. A pity [*Ratuy*] for him!" That is to say, God should have mercy on him for what he did, and it is as though he had not come into the world, that is to say that he is entirely faultless. And you will see if you examine this matter that the attribute of mercy only applies to the individual who is liable according to the letter of the law, and the heavens showed him mercy by refraining from carrying out the judgment. That is what is meant when it says: "A pity [*Ratuy*] for him! He is as though he had not come into the world." And this answers all of the questions that we posed. For the Tanna is not criticizing the one who speculates on what is above, rather he is praising him, for he reaches the highest level, as though he had not come into the world.

27. [Yerushalmi, Orlah 1:3.].
28. [BT Eruvin 13b.]

[…]

To those who say "Incline your ear,"[29] and pay no attention to "empty folly,"[30] arguing that we have no business with hidden things and may not investigate them, for the individual who pursues such an investigation will forfeit his soul, "and the foul smell rise and the stench shall be great."[31] All who say this, "Their eyes are smeared and they see not; their minds, and they cannot think."[32]

[…]

And if one attempts to make each thing stand on its essence for the sake of Heaven, there is nothing damaging about investigating. As we find in the *Sefer ha-Bahir* attributed to Rabbi Nehunya ben Ha-Kanah: "The students asked Rabbi Rehumi—What is the intent of the verse 'A prayer of the prophet Habakuk for errors?'[33] It should say a song of praise! Rather, when anyone turns his heart from worldly affairs and speculates on the Work of the Chariot, it is accepted by God as if he prayed the entire day, for it says 'a prayer.' What is the meaning of 'for errors'? As it is written, 'With its love you shall always err.'[34] And to what does this refer? To the Work of the Chariot."[35]

The above-mentioned book also teaches: "Rabbi Rehumi said: What is the meaning of the verse 'And the way to life is the rebuke that disciplines'?[36] This teaches us that when a person accustoms himself to study the Work of Creation and the Work of the Chariot, it is impossible that he not stumble. It is therefore written 'Let this stumbling be under your hand.'[37] This refers to things that a person cannot understand unless they cause him to stumble. The Torah calls it 'the rebuke that disciplines,' but actually it makes one worthy of the way of life."[38] It is clearly proven from this teaching that even if he errs, since it is done out of love, God responds by crediting him as if he prayed the entire day. Furthermore, it says that it makes one worthy of the way of life. But if a person only has the traditions that he received from his teacher, why would he experience stum-

---

29. [Is 58:3; Ps 78:1.]
30. [Ps 31:7.]
31. [Jl 2:20.]
32. [Is 44:18.]
33. [Hb 3:1.]
34. [Prov 5:19.]
35. [Bahir 68.]
36. [Prv 6:23.]
37. [Is 3:6.]
38. [Bahir 140.]

bling? Rather we must conclude that the student has received a tradition from his teacher and desires to investigate the inner sanctum. When doing so there is no doubt that he will occasionally stumble, as is written: "Let this stumbling be under your hand." Even so, the verse teaches: "With its love you shall always err." From everything that I have said we can conclude that it is permissible to investigate and expound in order to reach the wondrous things and those things that are hidden.

[. . .]

And if one were to ask: why is it that in our generation—and even in the time of the ARI of blessed memory (who successfully revealed many higher secrets) —neither fire nor angels appear, as they did in the time of the Tannaim of the Mishnah, when the angels would come to hear the original teachings? It must be that all contemporary teachings are worthless and are not deserving of such appearances! I will answer that in the earlier generations the original teachings were new thoughts and ideas, and those attracted the angels. But in later generations, "the souls are old," as the ARI has written, for we find that for all that people expound—both in revealed Torah and in hidden Torah—most of those teachings can be found in earlier sources. How did the sage, who had not seen those works, come to know them? Rather we must explain that he was born under the same sign as the original author, and he intuited his thoughts since their souls share a common root. That is why he is able to teach ideas that he had never seen, since his soul had already taught them in a previous incarnation.

Similarly with regard to the Work of the Chariot. From the time that the Talmud was canonized, all revelation has been sealed, and in particular, the wisdom of Kabbalah, which has only begun to be revealed in recent times. All that can be found in the books of Kabbalah are teachings that were revealed in the time of the Mishnah, which were sealed and hidden, and in every generation they are taught and revealed. This is why we no longer see angels, and they no longer come to hear these teachings. For all of these teachings are known to them, having been taught in the times of the tanna'im when the Work of the Chariot was expounded. The appearance of the fire and the angels when Rabbi Eleazar expounded proves that he was teaching an idea that he had not received from his teachers.

[. . .]

For this reason an individual must practice investigation in order to understand the essence of everything, even if he did not receive a tradition from his teachers who only transmitted chapter headings, like the ten *sefirot*. For he did not study his teachers' words in order to remain in place without adding or taking away from them. If that is what he does, his intentions are mistaken, since his own knowledge does not establish this decisively. If, however, he does attain the matter by means of investigation, or if he has a deep-seated belief that this is the truth, then even if he is mistaken, as long as the intent of his investigation is to attain its essence, his error is not considered to be an intentional sin, about which is written "unwitting errors are accounted as intentional sin."[39] On the contrary! This error is one with which God is pleased, as is written: "With its love you shall always err." And it was regarding this that King David taught: "Happy the man who God does not impute of intentional sin."[40]

[…]

By way of example: When a king decrees that his subjects serve him, if they make mistakes when fulfilling any of the commands they will be subject to lashes, since the path of service was short and clearly laid out. The subject is blamed for not paying attention to the command and for making a mistake. The king does not desire such service, and the error is accounted as intentional sin. However, if the king decreed that his subjects should comprehend him, and he places himself in the midst of a great ocean, his subjects will come to seek him in order to call on him. Since the subject had never before traveled these waters —as he had no need to do so until he desired to search for the king—and there is no set path in the ocean, for it is water with no end, we can be certain that he will lose his way. Will the king demand to know why he did not come in the most direct path, and went "hither and yon"? Given that there was no established path, will he ask, "[W]hy did you falsify the path?" On the contrary! It is "a path not known to the bird of prey." The more that the subject toils and searches, the more pain that he suffers in his search for the place, the greater the reward that the king must give him. This is the intention of the verse: "With its love you should always err," for you will receive a reward for the errors, aside from the reward that you will receive in discovering Him and seeing the King's face.

[…]

As you can see, it is permissible to study the Torah of truth, and to investigate, even if errors will be made. This stands in opposition to those with hearts of stone who are mistaken in their beliefs and do not wish to investigate or to expound issues of Kabbalah beyond what is found in books, fearing that they will

39. [Mishnah Avot 4:13; BT Baba Metzia 33b.]
40. [Ps 32:2.]

make mistakes. But "Once an error has entered, it remains."[41] This is a tremendous mistake, an error for which they will be punished, not rewarded. Someone who refrains from investigation will be unable to attain true understanding of God's holiness. What will such a person respond on the Day of Judgment when he is asked: "Did you engage in the study of My stature?" They do not say "Did you study?" but "Did you engage?" meaning that he should have engaged in dialogue and debate in order to understand the essence of the matter. And if mistakes are made—he will receive a reward even for the errors, as is written: "With its love you shall always err," as we explained above.

Translated by Shalom Berger of the
Academic Language Experts team,
with Avi Staiman

41. [BT Pesahim 112a; Baba Batrha 21a.]

18

Tsevi Hirsch ben Yaakov Ashkenazi (Hakham Tsevi), In the Sight of All the House of Israel

Source: Tsevi Hirsch ben Yaakov Ashkenazi, "Le-Einei Kol Yisrael," in Aharon Freiman, *Inyanei Shabtai Zevi* (Berlin, 5673 [1912]), 118, 121–22.

They distort the words of the living God. It is a clear Torah lesson, as the sages have taught: "Whosoever speculates on four things, a pity for him! He is as though he had not come into the world."

This quarrelsome individual raised his hand against the King of the world, and the King commanded that he be split in two. Half to be consumed by fire; an unfanned fire will consume him to the point of destruction. His remaining part will reek and be condemned to boiling excrement; he will melt away as water. Yet he says: No! For our lips are our own. We will rise and fight—not only against Rashi, Light of the Exile, who serves as eyes for us, but against the sages of the Talmud who have stated clearly that investigating these four matters is forbidden. For these are the words of the Talmud regarding the above-mentioned passage: "Granted as regards what is above, what is beneath, what [will be] after, that is well. But as regards what was before—what happened, happened!—Both R. Johanan and Resh Lakish say: It is like a human king who said to his servants: Build for me a great palace upon the dunghill. They went and built it for him. It is not the king's wish [thenceforth] to have the name of the dunghill mentioned."[1]

Thus, it is perfectly clear that examining these four matters is forbidden. And that the expression "a pity [*ratuy*] on him—it is as if he never came to this world" means, as Rashi taught, that it would have been better for him had he never entered the world. He also deigned to say that "when the Sages taught: 'If your teacher is comparable to a Godly angel, only then can you seek Torah from him,' this refers only to legal rulings of things that are prohibited or permitted, but with regard to celestial matters, even an evil person can serve as a teacher." Come and see the extent of his foolishness and the evil ways of this author who argues against axiomatic principles. For surely if it is forbidden to learn simple positive or negative commandments that relate only to individual sin, whether purpose-

---

1. [BT Hagigah 16a.]

ful or accidental, from a teacher who is not comparable to a Godly angel, how much more so those subjects that are the basis of religious belief and the tenets of our religion, with which most people are unfamiliar and whose prohibition is severe, must be studied only with the supremely holy ones.

Anyone who examines his writings will recognize and know that he has spoken against his own life. Who has ever seen an author [who] opens his work by stating that anyone can study from it even though the author is an evildoer. But he was undermined by his own tongue to publicize himself in a place where he was unknown so that others will not follow him. [. . .] Behold and see: is there any pain like this [Lam 1:12], that the sages of the Talmud taught regarding the Mishnah, that it is forbidden to examine these four things. [. . .] Also, throughout the Talmud it is clear that an individual who exhibits impudence toward the Torah has not a share in the life of the World to Come [Mishnah Avot 3:11.], and surely there is no greater impudence worse than this. [. . .] And his punishment is stated clearly in the Talmud: he is to be boiled in excrement, as is the ruling for any individual who mocks the words of the Sages.

[. . .]

And he went on at length with his repulsive tongue, speaking blasphemy and cursing all of the sages who rule that Kabbalah can only be studied from a teacher who is comparable to a Godly angel. [. . .] Be astonished, O ye heavens, at this, and be horribly afraid, be ye very desolate [Jer 2:12], for has risen an insignificant mocker, an evil and worthless denier to taunt the ranks of the living God [1 Sm 17:26], to uproot the foundations of the entire Torah and to curse all those who study and support it. [. . .] And since the aforementioned accursed book where all of these revolting statements are found is not in our hands, I find myself obligated by the power of my beliefs and the beliefs of all the children of Israel throughout their dispersion, to stir their hearts with these short words.

Translated by Shimon Altshul of the
Academic Language Experts team,
with Avi Staiman

19

Moses Hagiz, Destruction of the Wrongdoers

Source: Moses Hagiz, *Shever Posheim* (London, 5474 [1719]),
10, 13, 15–17, 20–21, 24–25, 65–67, 74.

These are the words that Moses addressed to all Israel:[1]

Hear, O Israel! You are about to join battle with your enemy:[2]

"There is never any dispute regarding matters of tradition [Kabbalah], and it is known that any matter where a dispute is found cannot be a tradition handed over from Moses our teacher." So writes Maimonides of blessed memory in the first chapter of the Laws of Rebellious Ones. Similarly, we have a tradition from our forefathers, that there is no doubt that matters of mystical teachings [Kabbalah], referred to by the Jewish people as the Wisdom of Truth, were also received from Moses our teacher who transmitted them to Joshua and the Elders, who handed them down to the Members of the Great Assembly.

[...]

Examine and understand these Godly words, so many of his superior statements agree with our position—which is the position of the Torah—that the true wisdom referred to as the wisdom of Kabbalah is not given to empty and frivolous people, and that we cannot believe anyone who comes and says "I am a master of Kabbalah. Come and I will teach you the secrets of the Torah, for they are hidden." This cannot be believed unless the individual can produce a sign and a marvel in the miraculous ways of wisdom. Furthermore, his words must stand in agreement with the words of the Kabbalistic works that do not conflict with the written Torah.

[...]

This is what the Sages taught: "Seek not things that are too hard for thee, and search not things that are hidden from thee. The things that have been permitted thee, think thereupon; thou hast no business with the things that are secret."[3] Examine, you will find and understand that it is regarding those things that are too hard and hidden that the Sages say "from thee," since it is possible that it is

---

1. [Dt 1:1.]
2. [Dt 20:3.]
3. [BT Hagigah 13a.]

because of you, that the preparation of your matter and form does not allow your intellect to be on a level to expound and investigate these matters. An individual may involve himself in profound books containing Torah secrets that are beyond his ability to understand and grasp, both because of a deficiency in his intellect and because of the profundity of the material. For these two reasons not only won't he gain from his efforts, but he will become confused and will regress from his earlier state.

[…]

An individual who undergoes mental preparation and strives to understand heavenly matters, may, in fact, succeed in comprehending matters that are beyond the ken of others. It is for this reason that regarding things that are beyond and hidden the sages taught "from thee," that is to say, it is because of you. Regarding that which is above and below, however, the expression "from thee" does not appear, since these are matters that are hidden from every living being. It is for this reason that the sages taught in the Mishnah: "Whosoever speculates on four things, a pity for him! He is as though he had not come into the world,"[4] meaning that all the sages of Israel conclude that these are forbidden.

[…]

For in accordance with these commandments I make a covenant with you and with Israel.[5] For this Evil Snake[6] who is well-known as a heretic and an apostate, together with his worthless companion the defiant rebel who supported him and approved of his book, which are volumes of heresy and divination printed in Venice, Berlin, and Amsterdam. Even if one were to argue—something that is not true—that the words of the repugnant Hayon are—as the apostate claims—wondrous secrets, as is claimed by the empty and frivolous fools who are seduced by their words, nevertheless, they and their followers are liable as those who are despised by God, as in the above-mentioned teaching of Rabbi Simeon bar Yohai. They are excommunicated for transgressing his words and commandment at the time of his passing, by publicizing these secrets. In fact, the truth lies with us, that neither this repugnant individual [Hayon] nor his promiscuous friend [Ayllon] have anything but devastation and destruction in their borders,[7]

4. [Mishnah Hagigah 2:1.]

5. [Ex 34:27.]

6. [A play on the phonetic resemblance of Hayon's second name, Hiyya, and the Aramaic word for snake, *hivya*.]

7. [Cf. Is 60:18.]

together with heresy and denial and ruin of the Torah in their falsification, which can be shown and proven.

[...]

And let us see if we, the Children of Israel, should believe that the hand of God appeared specifically to the revolting Hayon and Ayllon—their names should be blotted out—and that with them the wisdom of Kabbalah will expire. [...] And he added sin upon iniquity when in his introduction he repeatedly cursed the leadership of the holy people, the holy rabbis of our generation, in a frivolous manner by calling them members of the mixed multitude. [...] And this did not satisfy him, until in the above-mentioned apology he wrote: "And not for the honor of my father's house, but for that of God, etc.," that I should not arrive in the World to Come in embarrassment having been unable to proclaim His Godliness in this world. [...] Ah, this is the day I hoped for, [for] I have lived[8] to uphold my failed belief before all of Israel. In order to succeed I will include [the words of] those ignorant elders and moneyed ones, and through them I will engage in this battle that is not for the sake of Heaven, for it is not only against the sages of Israel, but against the general principles of faith that were received at Sinai. Our experience has proven his audacity up to and including today when he remains rebellious and upholds his heresy in a revolting manner. For there is no greater sign or proof than that he dares to dispute all of the sages of Israel regarding belief in Unity that even the non-Jewish sages do not deny. [...] Regarding him and Ayllon and anyone who believes that on such an unclean one such as him—heaven forfend—the Hand of God has been revealed, they should be cursed unto God and removed from the community of Israel. I said: Behold I have come in writing to reveal their shame in a public forum so that a future generation might know[9] as well as the children who succeed you,[10] the identity of the repulsive author as well as the apostate who supported his words and the ignorant elders who were drawn to follow him.

[...]

And they permitted themselves to place a blemish in the holiness of heaven and the holiness of the study of the holy Torah, to place the filth of the primeval serpent, behaving according to their foolishness, allowing every leper and every

---

8. [Cf. Lam 2:16.]
9. [Cf. Ps 78:6.]
10. [Cf. Dt 29:21.]

afflicted one and everyone who is unclean[11]—Call out: Unclean! Unclean![12]—to enter into the innermost of the holies, bursting though the fence establish by the sages, something that is profane for us. [. . .] Moreover, when he heard and saw that the community leaders handed the book over to us and that we offered our opinion that it was to be rejected from its very inception, he certainly should have fulfilled and accepted our opinion, which was true and just. We never could have imagined the severe insolence and audacity with which he would argue and confuse the community leaders to seduce and entice them from the beliefs of their fathers.

Furthermore, he wrote on page five of his introduction to the first knowledge regarding the question of whether it is permissible to understand and delve into the mystic speculations of the divine chariot: "Your eyes clearly see that one can read the True Torah. Even if one errs it is not the error of those with a stone heart, etc. And if he does make a mistake, he will receive reward for that." See there where he also wrote that when the sages say "be careful in study, for an error in study amounts to presumption,"[13] they are referring only to questions of what is forbidden or permitted or with regard to monetary matters. Regarding issues of Kabbalah, however, God enjoys the individual who is out of the ordinary. Can one believe what is related, casuistry that is against all human and Godly intelligence!? All are in agreement—those who approach the text in a simple manner together with Kabbalists, both early and late—accepting upon themselves and their descendants that these words must be understood according to their simple meaning, to prohibit themselves the second part of the first knowledge. This prohibition was taken lest they break through to God[14] by means of their inquiries and investigation. It was forbidden in order to spare the honor of the Creator of heaven and earth.

[. . .]

Therefore, you people of Amsterdam who love God and hate evil—men, women, and children—hearken, comprehend and gather to defend the belief of our forefathers for it is the basis of our existence, and by doing so you will merit long lives. [. . .] However, you, the Children of Israel must know the truth, that if you do not offer a clear public sign and indication—as you have failed

11. [Cf. Nm 5:2.]
12. [Cf. Lv 13:45.]
13. [Mishnah Avot 4:13.]
14.]Cf. Ex 19:21.]

to do publicly in the past—that your hearts are true to the God of Israel, by eradicating the evil from your midst so that you will be holy, all of the sages of the Diaspora will be forced to separate you. No longer will they be able to protect your honor, since the honor of God is greater than all else in the world. [. . .] I was therefore zealous on behalf of the God of Israel, with the strength of my father and my father's father going back twenty-eight generations, during which time, thank God, neither the crown of Torah nor the crown of a good name went missing from my family pedigree, which originates with the scholars and leaders of Castile. Also with the strength of my mother's father and her father's father, whose pedigree in the Galante family goes back eighteen generations. But most of all my strength stems from the truth. When God directed matters so that the community leaders, with the agreement of the Gaon, our teacher and rabbi, Rabbi Tsevi (The Merciful One should protect and save him) arranged for the sexton to hand me the book so that I should inform them of my opinion so that the students should not mistakenly establish the law and allow many of the general populace to stumble, I hastened and did not delay and I performed my duty.

[. . .]

I therefore inform you and warn you, once, twice, three times, that this ass (his name should be blotted out) has responded in falsehood in this matter, as well. For we are all in accord that even in matters less essential than this all of Israel is obligated to compel and coerce one another so that he will uphold truth and justice, the laws of God and His Torah. [. . .] Our responsibility to one another that has been passed onto us from our fathers is what leads us to be called the congregation of Israel, for we are a unified congregation, the only one of her mother, the delight of her who bore her.[15] And all of the holy Diaspora communities are considered to be a single, unified community, and your community as well as all similar communities are obligated in this, and all have a single law. [. . .] And I am fulfilling the commandment of expounding as well as the commandment to obliterate evil from the midst of the Israelite settlement when I publicize the defilement that can be seen hidden beneath their wings, and with the assistance of the true Helper in the years to come—as many as God will grant me in His mercy—I will strive to fulfill my obligation, as it is my desire to be true to the God of Israel, and I will not return empty-handed from whence I came. And God will assist me to perform His will and to serve Him with a perfect heart, etc.

15. [Sng 6:9.]

Let us return to the matter at hand. I am committed to this battle, an obligatory war about which the Torah commands: Fear no man, for judgment is God's,[16] according to its simple, straightforward meaning. [. . .] And I will raise my voice as a shofar regarding the commandment: Gather the people—men, women, children, and the strangers in your communities—that they may hear and so learn to revere the Lord your God,[17] etc., etc. It was for this ultimate purpose that I began these words to you with the verse Hear, O Israel! You are about to join battle with your enemy,[18] as intimated by the man of God, Rabbi Simeon bar Yohai.

Translated by Shimon Altshul of the
Academic Language Experts team,
with Avi Staiman

16. [Dt 1:17.]
17. [Dt 31:12.]
18. [Dt 20:3.]

Source: Unsigned review of *Oz le-Elohim*, by Nehemiah Hiyya Hayon, *Bibliothèque raisonnée des ouvrages des savans de l'Europe* (July–September 1728): 335–52.

Concerning a new Hebrew book published in Berlin. The book is in rabbinic characters [i.e., in Rashi script], *without punctuation, and is entitled* Mehemuta de Cola [Meheimenuta de-Khola], *which means* "The Belief of All." It is a quarto; the first part of it has eighty-eight half-sheets and the second one only sixteen, which are numbered only on one side with the letters of the Hebrew alphabet, so that in all this volume has 416 pages.

Rabbi Nunes Torres of The Hague [. . .] gave this work to one of the contributors to this journal together with a historical note to inform the scholars [. . .]. We thought it would please curious readers presenting them [with] a few excerpts from this book and some remarks that serve as an introduction and inform them of different opinions and huge schisms among many famous rabbis. Christian debaters do not know these issues and do not even know how to read such rabbinical writings, which not only have uncommon letters but also are completely lacking the punctuation of the *Massore* [Masorah], which is necessary for many Christian scholars to understand the meaning of the Hebrew words. Therefore, they are not aware of this book, which has become very popular among the rabbis.

In the beginning of July 1713 a rabbi called Nehemiah Hiyya Hayon came to Amsterdam bringing with him a book that he had published under the title that we mentioned at the beginning of this article. The book was divided into two columns; the first of these consisted of the text of his work full of deviations and was entitled *Beth Codesch a Codaschim* [Bet Kodesh ha-Kodashim], meaning "Home of Sanctity of the Sanctities." This is what the Latins call "Sancta Sanctorum," and the French "the very Holy Place," which was once in the inner part of the Jerusalem Temple that the high priest entered only once per year. The second column of the same book was the commentary called *Hos l'Elohim* [Oz le-Elohim], which means "The effort for God" [*sic!*]. The text explained by this commentary also contains notes and proofs taken from the most famous Kabbalistic books, by which the author endeavors to show the truthfulness of his argument, which touches on the essence and the attributes of God, that he imagines consisting of five personas, which he had organized in the strangest system, of which we had never heard, as we'll see in the excerpt of it that we present.

Immediately upon publication of the book, it was condemned by two [Ashkenazic] rabbis in Amsterdam, who also published letters of other rabbis from Germany and Italy who condemned this book and its author as heretical and very dangerous; however, the Portuguese Jews of Amsterdam established a committee of seven rabbis to examine this book; they didn't find anything censurable, and approved it. This was the reason for the strife and discontent among the Jews of that great city, but since the Portuguese party was stronger, the [Ashkenazic] rabbis were terribly persecuted by it and forced to move elsewhere in order not to be exposed to bigotry.

Since their departure, this quarrel has continued to smolder, and from time to time, new comments are made on the heresies of this book. The book is condemned and cursed in a low voice in order not to invite bad behavior on the part of the opposing side; for this reason Christian scholars who do not know this work or many others of this kind will be able to satisfy their curiosity concerning the new theological system or perhaps, the fanatical system of this rabbi. It is surprising that many of his colleagues wanted to adopt his extravagances, which are not only ridiculous in what he says about the essence and nature of God, but also horrifying because of the inconstancy and imperfections that he attributes to Him, as may be seen from what we reproduce here from this strange work.

First, he promises to show "who is, how is, and what is the 'God very-High,'"[1] and assures us that those who will read his treatise "will understand immediately and without difficulty the Essence of Divinity."[2] [...]

He posits that the Infinite cannot be the source and the Creator of the World, because the Infinite is a simple being that cannot possess any diversity of thought or will that makes it do something, or choose something at a certain time rather than at another. From this, he argues that it can have neither the idea to create the world, nor a motive for forming it in a finite period of time in a particular way that is preferable from the other options that the Infinite Reason[3] could think of had it thought eternally.[4] [...]

1. [Hayon, Oz le-Elohim (Berlin, 1713), 1r.]
2. [Ibid., 1v.]
3. [Mahshavah Illa'ah.]
4. [Hayon, Oz le-Elohim, 2r.]

In the same section of the book, he posits that there is a God that has proportions and is confined by certain limits, from which he necessarily concludes that He is corporal in His nature. He calls this God "the Ancient Holy of Holies,"[5] and attributes to Him a soul, which he says is the soul of the souls of all who lived[6] in the previous centuries, live in the present one, and will live till the end of the world. He adds that mountains, hills, and rocks and [even] all things have souls that make up a part of the soul of the supreme God, in a way that His power and domination extend everywhere.[7] [...]

Also, he tries to prove in various sections of his book that this Ancient Holy of Holies not only has dimensions since it is surrounded by the Light of Infinity, but also has body parts, proportioned according to His greatness, and that He has all the parts that make up the human body; for this reason, he says, those who "take the Infinite for the Substance of the Divinity err."[8] [...]

He imagines that God engages in movement, agitation, and even passions, such as envy, anger, boredom, and all other sentiments that a soul may have, because he attributes a soul to this Divinity as well as to the Holy of Holies. He considers the difference between these two to be in the function that he attributes to them. His overactive imagination even comes up with the idea that the Divinity has its defects and that its knowledge is not eternal.

Then, turning to some of arguments to support his idea that the Infinite cannot be the maker of this world, he proposes the following claim: everything that has an end and limits must also have a beginning. The concept of creation presupposes an end of the execution, and therefore the idea itself had to have a beginning, from which he argues that this idea or knowledge once had to be new to the Creator. Therefore, the Infinite cannot be the Creator, since being simple and eternal, the Infinite cannot discover or form in itself new thoughts or knowledge.[9]

[...]

It is even more amazing to see that at the end of the first chapter he argues that the Ancient Holy of the Holies, which is the principle and source of everything, had created himself, and that this mystery which seems impossible, is hidden in the fifteenth verse of Psalm 139.[10]

5. [*Atika Kadisha de-khol kadishayya.*]
6. [*Nishmata de-khol hay.*]
7. [Hayon, *Oz le-Elohim*, 2v.]
8. [Ibid., 26v.]
9. [Ibid., 4v.]
10. [Ibid., 5r.]

Yet the only thing mentioned there is the wonderful structure of human em-
bryos that are secretly formed in the wombs of their mothers according to the
provisions of the mysterious Divine Providence. However, he also quite incorrectly supports his hypothesis about the formation of the First Principle of all
things by recalling that the wicked Pharaoh said: "My river [is] mine own, and
I made [it] for myself" [Ez 29:3], to express that it was God [who] had created
Himself. From this we gather that the Pharaoh imagined himself a Creator God
who is not at all eternal. He even argues that from the moment that there appeared the Creator, he created the world and one cannot ask why he had not
created it before, as he could not create it before he existed himself.[11] He does
not stop there and posits dogmas of polytheism and supposes the existence of
several divinities to whom he attributes various functions, from which often
come very controversial effects.

[. . .] These are weird and extravagant opinions of Rabbi Nehemiah Hiyya
Hayon. They might be called wicked, yet they were truly approved by the seven
Portuguese rabbis who had assembled [to discuss] this topic in Amsterdam and
who persecuted those among their German colleagues who disapproved of the
dogmas contained in the book of the rabbi. The book became very famous by
virtue of the quarrels and divisions that it caused among the Jewish scholars and
leaders of their nation who are still troubled now in a similar way that we see
troubled the prelates of Christendom divided by the famous Papal Constitution
of *Unigenitus*.

Yet to give the justice due to both Rabbi Nehemiah Hiyya Hayon and the seven
approvers of his book, we have to note here that the very renowned Jewish Kabbalists who have written upon this matter are of the same opinion as the author
and approvers of the book and the commentary to it which is now discussed
among them, and that some Kabbalists even hold opinions much more extravagant and obscene on the supposed origin of four hypostases of their Divinity.
They expressed these [opinions] in terms so contrary to the provisions of sexual
morality that modesty prevents us from expounding it here. It would also make
this article too long.

Translated by Paweł Maciejko

11. [Ibid., 62v.]

VI | The Eibeschütz Controversy

Rabbi Jonathan Eibeschütz (1690–1764) is the greatest riddle in the history of Sabbatianism. A towering figure in a period that constituted the apex of Torah scholarship in Ashkenazic countries, author of two halakhic masterpieces that to this day are part of the standard curriculum of rabbinic scholars, head of the most important yeshivot in Europe, admired teacher whose students flocked to him from distant countries, and a charismatic preacher whose sermons entered the golden canon of Jewish homiletics. And simultaneously: a suspected heretic, alleged collaborator with Christians against the Jewish community, trailed from early youth by rumors of misconduct and misbelief, and excommunicated by some of his most revered colleagues. Other Sabbatian strife concerned mavericks and individuals from the fringes of Jewish society. Eibeschütz, in stark contrast, belonged to the innermost elite of the rabbinic establishment. While the heterodox worldviews of Nathan of Gaza, Cardozo, or Hayon are undeniable, to this day Rabbi Jonathan Eibeschütz remains one of the most revered figures within the Orthodox Jewish world. While most scholars do consider him a Sabbatian, a minority opinion holds that such charges were unfounded. Among all the Sabbatian controversies, the debate about Eibeschütz is the only one that is still alive today. Despite considerable consensus on certain points of this debate, overall, the jury is still out.

In truth, the Eibeschütz controversy was actually three controversies. The first one concerned whether the rabbi was indeed a heretic. Rumors of Eibeschütz's Sabbatian leanings had circulated at least since 1725, when he served as a preacher in the Jewish community of Prague. At that time, the dispute centered on a Kabbalistic manuscript entitled *And I Came This day unto the Fountain* (*Va-Avo ha-Yom el ha-Ayyin*). The manuscript, which enjoyed a wide circulation in Europe, was distributed anonymously, yet popular opinion had it that it was Eibeschütz's work. Faced with charges of heresy, the rabbi publicly distanced himself from the Sabbatians and signed a ban condemning them. The matter died down temporarily. However, the accusations returned, and with a vengeance, in 1751, when Eibeschütz was charged with having distributed amulets during his tenure as a rabbi of Metz (1741–1749) and of Altona-Hamburg-Wandsbeck (since 1750) that contained ciphered allusions to Sabbatai Tsevi. The charges were first lodged by Rabbi Jacob Emden, an Altona resident and an important rabbinic authority in his own right. Emden claimed to have been approached by several members of the community with a request to interpret an amulet given by Eibeschütz to women for use in childbirth. Although he recognized the Sabbatian character of the amulet immediately, Emden was at first reluctant to enter the fray. Before long, however, the quarrel spiraled out of control. Faced with attacks by Eibeschütz's allies among the community leaders, Emden attempted to mobilize his own supporters. Expelled from Altona, he began to build a power base across Europe. The amulet controversy (often referred to as the Emden-Eibeschütz controversy) quickly wracked the major Jewish communities, with leading rabbinic authorities choosing sides. Excommunications and counter-excommunications were issued, scores of pamphlets in several languages were printed, non-Jewish authorities and intellectuals were called in to adjudicate. Rabbinic courts issued contradictory rulings, and two separate legal cases were launched before the Hamburg Senate and the Royal Court of Denmark. Attempts to broker a compromise allowed Emden to return home to Altona, yet the strife did not subside. Emden collected voluminous testimony and legal rulings documenting Eibeschütz's real and alleged misdeeds and analyzing his purportedly heretical views. A prolific writer and a printing press owner, he released this documentation in the form of books and brochures, thus raising the public profile of the debate yet again. Eibeschütz responded with an apologetic book of his own; letters calling for support of friends, former disciples, and Christian notables; as well as behind-the-scenes machinations to silence Emden and his allies. The quarrel turned into the most contentious public affair to involve eighteenth-century Jews.

Archival evidence evinced by modern scholars demonstrates that contemporary rabbis generally concurred with Emden on the question of Eibeschütz's heterodoxy. However, this state of affairs only prompted additional dissension and led to the second controversy: those rabbinic authorities who privately agreed with Emden were reluctant (or in some cases, vehemently opposed) to join his public crusade against an important Jewish communal leader and one of the greatest scholars of the time. Thus, the discord on whether a prominent rabbi was indeed a heretic became, to a large extent, discord concerning what to do with a heretical prominent rabbi. Combating heresy had to be balanced against combating centrifugal forces threatening the internal cohesion of the Jewish religion and community. Unlike earlier anti-Sabbatian battles, whence the rabbinic establishment closed ranks to hunt down and expose the sectarians, in the case of Eibeschütz this same group went to great lengths to hush up the affair. Indeed, opinion had it that the damage caused by the controversy to rabbinic authority (and arguably the very unity of Judaism as a whole) by far outweighed any gain from defeating the heresy.

Below the surface of these two layers, the factual question of Eibeschütz's belief and the political question of how to handle a heretic occupying a position of power and respect lay a further, and much more subdued, question. This third and final controversy entailed how to grasp the nature of Eibeschütz's worldview and conceptualize his position. Eibeschütz never openly mentioned Sabbatai Tsevi by name, yet hints and allusions to the messiah in his writings and amulets seemed clear enough. He also publicly denounced Sabbatians, yet the phrasing of these denouncements was peculiar and purposely ambiguous—on closer look they might have been read as their endorsements. *And I Came This Day unto the Fountain* drew on Sabbatian imagery and utilized conceptual apparatus developed by Nathan of Gaza, Cardozo, and Hayon. Since he referred to Sabbatai Tsevi in a seemingly positive (and possibly messianic) fashion, Eibeschütz was automatically subsumed under the seemingly familiar and well-defined category of Sabbatianism. Still, more sophisticated protagonists in the drama knew full well that Eibeschütz's ideas were so singular that they escaped easy classification. While these notions certainly strayed from what might be considered mainstream Judaism, they also burst the limits of earlier Sabbatianism. *And I Came This Day unto the Fountain* stood out by its sheer weirdness and open pornography. The cosmology (creation as a sexual act performed by a God suffering from erectile dysfunction) and soteriology (redemption as a homoerotic union between the messiah and the God of Israel, raising the feminine aspect of God above the masculine) propounded by this tract would shock Nathan of Gaza no less than they shocked Emden and his party. The name of Sabbatai Tsevi might have been embedded in Eibeschütz's amulets, but this did not say much about the theology driving the amulets themselves; the very idea that a consistent theological position might be articulated in amulets and not in treatises or learned commentaries was tantalizing to many. Pigeonholing Eibeschütz as a Sabbatian might have been useful for polemical purposes, but it glossed over some of the deepest issues raised by the multivalent controversy. Some of the key players of the Eibeschütz debate proposed alternative conceptualizations, the most notable being those of complete atheism (i.e., Eibeschütz's references to Sabbatai Tsevi were yet an additional layer of smokescreen masking his mockery of all religiosity) and crypto-Christianity (i.e., Eibeschütz's messianic intuitions pointed at Jesus as much as they did at Sabbatai Tsevi).

21

Jonathan Eibeschütz, And I Came This Day
unto the Fountain

Source: Paweł Maciejko, ed., *R. Jonathan Eibeschütz, And I Came This
Day unto the Fountain* (Los Angeles: Cherub Press, 2014), 157–60.

In time of exile, we must not dedicate our intention and prayer to the God of
Israel and His Shekhinah in the manner previously set forth.[1] [. . .] He does not
pour His effluence into the Shekhinah; "a heaven's distance separates Her from
Him"[2]; and consequently when we set our intention to bring down the effluence
it all has the quality of uncontained ejaculate,[3] not received within the Female.
It thus brings about devastation, Shattering of the Vessels in all the worlds, for
inasmuch as He does not couple with His Female, He is precisely like the Ancient
One to whom prayer must not be directed. [. . .]

[The Bible] gives the reason why we must pray neither to [the God of Israel]
when He is not coupling with the Shekhinah, nor to the Ancient One who is
Holy of all the holy, Concealed of all the concealed. "That the rushing mighty
waters not overtake Him [Ps 32:6]," meaning that He must not again undergo a
Flood and a Shattering of Vessels, which is "rushing mighty waters," for when
[the effluence] has the quality of uncontained ejaculate, its nature is that of
"rushing mighty waters." Understand.

All this is the evident lesson of the Shattering of the Vessels, which were shat-

1. [The God of Israel, the biblical YHVH, is the central male potentiality (or deity), by
whom the created universe is guided and ruled. The Shekhinah—the highest of a number
of Shekhinahs in this complex system—is the central female potentiality, currently alien-
ated from the God of Israel and therefore unable to transmit His "effluence" to the lower
realms. Superior to them both is the Holy Ancient One, a being of pure Grace unmixed
with Judgment—not a wholly desirable trait, since the unbounded expansion of Grace is
a threat to all existence unless Judgment is on hand to circumscribe it. For our author, the
"God of Israel" is the God of Judaism, while the Holy Ancient One is the God of Christianity, superior to Judaism but in the present state of things less capable of nurturing the
universe and its dwellers.]

2. [An expression for a wife's alienation from her husband, based on the Mishnah,
Nedarim 11:12.]

3. [Literally "wasted seed," a rabbinic expression for semen ejaculated somewhere
other than into a woman's body.]

tered because they received their effluence in the quality of uncontained ejaculate: [. . .] that we must not pray to the Ancient One or even the God of Israel when He is not coupling with His Shekhinah, for world-destroying ejaculate would be the result. [. . .]

This is why the Bible says: "Israel shall go many days without the True God" [2 Chr 15:3]. They cannot pray to the God of Israel who is the True God, in view of the profundity of their exile and of His concealment and obscuration, even though—when things are working as they ought and the effluence descends from the God of Israel into the Shekhinah—He is the one to whom prayer and intention ought to be directed, for He is our God and we His servants. And so it is written: "They cried out, but there was none to deliver; cried to the Lord, but He did not answer them" [Ps 18:42].

But know this: the true messiah[4] couples with the Ancient One (who is the Shekhinah's "head"),[5] so that with Him as well there is no uncontained ejaculate, and in His presence does [the messiah] pray [. . .] functioning as Shekhinah. He then "pours forth his plea before the Lord" [Ps 102:1], which is to say, prays to the Ancient One who is called "before the Lord." [. . .]

Know that the Ancient One consists of pure Mercy without any Judgment whatever, even for those who violate the Torah. This is significance of the "Af," which is the Holy Ancient One . . . [who] "loves the nations" [Dt 33:3],[6] even the Gentiles, since He is altogether without Judgment. This is why on the Purim festival, over which the Ancient One holds sway, "It is the duty of a man to mellow himself with wine until he cannot tell the difference between 'cursed be Haman' and 'blessed be Mordecai'" [BT Megillah 7b]—for [the Ancient One] is pure Mercy. [. . .]

Know: a time will come when the Shekhinah will be sexually opened.[7] So the Bible says: "Fallen, not to rise again is Virgin Israel" [Am 5:2]—meaning, no lon-

4. [*Mashiah ha-amitti*, which in one possible spelling has the same numerical value as "Sabbatai Tsevi."]

5. [The Ancient One is regularly represented in this text as the "head" of divinity, as opposed to the God of Israel who is divinity's "heart."]

6. [*Af hovev ammim*; new JPS, "lover, indeed, of the people." The author understands the word *af*, literally "indeed" or "even," as a title for the Holy Ancient One in His character of pure Mercy. *Af loves the nations*: the God of Israel is bound up with Judaism and the Jewish people, but the Holy Ancient One loves all nations.]

7. [*Be'ulah*, the passive feminine of the verb meaning "to copulate with"; as opposed to Her current status as *betulah*, "virgin."]

ger shall She stand as a virgin, for at that time there will be no fear of the Insolent Waters since they will all have been mended.[8] She will be sexually opened; to Her will apply the verse, "Spread wide the place of Your tent" [Is 54:2]; and so the Bible says, "The moon will be dug" [Is 24:23],[9] "dug" as in "the well which the chieftains dug," and so forth [Nm 21:18]:[10] she will be sexually opened. "And the sun will linger." At present their coupling is intermittent; but a time will come when it will be continual [. . .] with Him perpetually erect. The Bible goes on to explain: "For the Lord rules in Zion," referring to the God of Israel, and "in the presence of His elders He is a Glory"[11] [. . .] i.e., that it is He who is called His Female's "Glory."[12]

A time will come when the Higher Shekhinah will be above the God of Israel, in Her quality as "a capable wife, crown for her husband" [Prv 12:4]. This is the significance of "then Moses shall sing" [Ex 15:1]. As matters now stand, the Shekhinah does the serenading whenever She wants sex, as in "I am a rose of Sharon" [Sng 2:1].[13] But a time will come when the God of Israel will serenade Her, and this is what is meant by "then shall sing Moses," who is the God of Israel.

This is the inner meaning of the verse, "The light of the moon shall become like the light of the sun" [Is 30:26], conveying that the Shekhinah will be in a lofty place like the God of Israel, who is symbolized by the "sun," while the sun's light will take the place of the moon. And thus "the light of the sun shall become like the light of the seven days" [Is 30:26], i.e., like the light of the Shekhinah, who is called "Seven Days," not meaning of course that His light will be diminished, but rather that the Shekhinah will be elevated until the God of Israel will be in comparison to Her as the Shekhinah is now in comparison to Him. Then "the Lord shall be One and His name One" [Zec 14:9]. Blessed be He forever! Amen!

8. [The "Insolent Waters" are the forces of chaos and destruction (Ps 124:5), from whose penetration the Shekhinah's virginity has until now protected Her.]

9. [The author understands Isaiah's "moon" and "sun" as the Shekhinah and the God of Israel.]

10. [The verse continues: "which the nobles of the people hewed out with a rod and with their staffs."]

11. [The continuation of Isaiah 24:23, its first part slightly abridged.]

12. [As opposed to the present, when it is the Shekhinah who is *kavod*, "Glory," to the male God. In this golden future, not only do the Shekhinah and the God of Israel engage in unending sex, but their roles are reversed, with Her as the dominant figure.]

13. [Interpreted as in the Zohar I, 221a (= III, 107a), which derives "Sharon" from *sharah*, "she sings."]

This is why David,[14] when "he came to the Head" (symbolizing the Ancient One),[15] "where he was to prostrate himself for God" (indicating sexual coupling) [2 Sm 15:32],[16] "sought to engage in alien worship" [BT Sanhedrin 107a] in accord with "*Af* loves the nations" [Dt 33:3].[17] Understand.

Translated by David Halperin

14. [Sabbatai Tsevi, the Davidic messiah.]

15. [In its biblical context *rosh* obviously means a mountaintop. The author finds it convenient, however, to take the word in its more common meaning of "head."]

16. [That is, offer his back parts for penetration, thereby stepping into the role of the Ancient One's missing female and making it possible for the world to receive the Ancient One's effluence.]

17. [The strange Talmudic passage, which understands "head" in 2 Sm 15:32 to hint at idolatrous worship, is taken by our author to speak of Sabbatai Tsevi's transition to an alien religion, in this case Islam. He understands Sabbatai's conversion as a passage from the domain of the "God of Israel" to the judgment- and distinction-free realm of the higher deity who "loves the nations," that is, all humanity.]

22

Jacob Emden, Purim's Letter[1]

Source: Jacob Emden, *Iggeret Purim*, 1751, MS Mich. 618 (Neubauer no. 2109), Bodleian Library, University of Oxford.

Assorted strange letters of correspondence with the wicked heretics of the sect of Sabbatai Tsevi, may his name be obliterated, were found in his [Rabbi Jonathan Eibeschütz's] possession. In particular, he corresponded with the accursed Liebele Prostitz,[2] who circulated among all of the synagogues in Moravia. He wandered through the land [Gn 4:12], and none among the Jews provided him with lodging, until he died in his youth and his life was as that of the depraved [Jb 36:14]. For he prophesized that he would rule in place of Sabbatai Tsevi, may the name of the wicked rot; that he would take his place and lead his followers. These letters testify to his evil, which has become clear since his connection with that sect of impure and corrupt individuals. Impurity creates impurity such as itself,[3] and anything that is attached to impurity is referred to as impure.[4] Nonetheless, the work of Satan was successful at that time, and he misled the hearts of the sages of that generation. Although they initially attacked him with the sword of excommunication, intending to destroy him; they then accepted his patently false apology. They vindicated him from [the charge of] other gods [Jb 32:2], based merely on his deception and seductive words, his fawning submission and denial of that which is known by means of oaths. At that point, the spirit of the rabbis who were pursuing him softened [Jgs 8:3]; and his comrades were able to treacherously appease and convince them by means of falsehood and deception, to cover up for him, for the sake of the honor of his family and that of his wife's family. [...] Additionally, they forgave him that time, and hid him like the night,[5] as he was still of tender age and this was his first offence. Despite the fact that they knew the truth, namely, that he had sworn falsely, they believed that he would now abandon his ways and thoughts, and cast the vermin (i.e., the evil of

---

1. [The word "Purim" is the numerical equivalent of Emden's name, "Ya'akov ben Tsevi."]
2. [The Sabbatian prophet Judah Leib Prossnitz.]
3. [BT Pesahim 18b.]
4. [BT Bava Kama 92b.]
5. [BT Moed Katan 17a.]

Sabbatai Tsevi, may the name of the wicked rot) from his grasp, purify himself and change his clothing [Gen 41:14], and return to the Lord, and He will have compassion on him [Is 55:7], before darkness overcomes him and his thoughts perish [Ps 146:4]. But he once again confounded the Jewish people. [...] And he is like a tree that causes damage to the public and was designated to be cut down[6] many years ago, and should have fallen from its root. [...]

At this time, they [the members of the Altona community] returned, and brought me a copy of an amulet that contained a drawing of a Star of David. These people did not know what it was, for [its author] hid and obscured [its meaning] under the wings of [1 Kgs 8:6] various exchanges of letters of the alphabet. [...] When he heard about this, the heretic also sent [a messenger] to the owner to request a copy of this amulet (which he had given to his wife, and was in her possession). It was given to him, and he promised to interpret it properly. They were waiting for a very long time for its interpretation to be given over to them, and they tarried until they were ashamed [see Jgs 3:25]. Only after several weeks during which he sat and interpreted in a flawed homiletical fashion (as if amulets are subject to various infuriating interpretations, replacing beauty with vomit); and turned it into a sort of "astonishing Midrash," which is interpreted and resolved based on several introductions, without regard to whether or not the author of the statement intended them. The homiletical interpretation was offered regardless, and one does not refute a homily. He treated this in the same manner, to explain it away by means of a work of delusion [Jer 10:15], to reveal in it nonexistent depth and cleverness, which all who see and hear will laugh at. His interpretation, which is intrinsically falsified, is impure, and it is clear to any intelligent person that his efforts are for naught [Is 49:4; 65:23]; and that he broke his head over a far-fetched and polished [Is 18:2, 7] interpretation, unheard of in the history of writing amulets. Why didn't he know how to read it and reveal its meaning publicly right away, without delay and hesitation. Since he was the author who produced it, he should have shown his innocence, rather than endure disgrace for no reason. Rather, he should have answered those who questioned him immediately: "Such and such is its meaning, and what iniquity is there to be found in it?" [...] In any case, he was forced to claim that others tampered with it, and forged letters in it; because he was unable to fit [his interpretation to the text as it was]. And he was unable to explain many of its words. Even the long delay did not suffice to produce a cover-up for them, however false. After he won them

6. [There is a halakhic principle of cutting down a tree that causes public damage.]

over and misled [Jb 12:24] the leaders of the people, he then demanded that the members of the communities prosecute those who slandered him. [. . .]

Nonetheless, I held out hope that our hopes and visions for him not be lost, and I always prayed on his behalf, as follows: "Please, Lord, remove the heart of stone [Ez 11:19] from the midst of this coarse person who is evil in his doings: the villain Jonathan Eibeschütz, who spoke ill of you and your messiah. He taunted the armies of the living God [1 Sm 17:26], and discouraged the Jewish people regarding the redemption, caused many to sin with respect to the Torah, and caused grave harm to the entire Diaspora. Open his eyes and cause him to see [2 Sm 6:17], embrace the truth, and correct that which he corrupted, in order that he not die in his ignorance and perish without knowledge [Jb 36:12]. Soften, please, his uncircumcised heart, which is hard as iron, to confess to his sins, and to give honor and acknowledgment to your name. In order that he not go to Hell, and that your name be sanctified because of him. May you send a cure to him, and make his heart understand, so he repents and be healed" [Is 6:10]. I pleaded in this fashion on his behalf and on behalf of all of those who attached themselves to Baal [Nm 25:5] and are drawn after his slaughter; that the Lord turn their hearts to Him, to serve Him with their whole hearts. And thus I continued and did not cease praying on their behalf. Until he added sin to his rebellion [Jb 34:37], iniquity and guilt and evil; to draw iniquity with cords of vanity, and sin with a cart rope [see Is 5:18], to rob the living and the dead [Ru 2:20], as will be clarified below, with the help of God. I then said that his hope is lost, and [he will not repent during] his lifetime. About such is said: Return wayward children [Jer 3:14], with the exception of this heretic who is devoted to his idolatry and attached to it like a dog. Before this, I would always affix a prayer for him at the conclusion of my prayers, beseeching the Lord to transform his heart to truly return to Him, and to correct his corruption, such that one who is banished be not an outcast from him [2 Sm 14:14]. [. . .]

I found no other way than this, namely, that I go to the great synagogue and stand on the platform on the day on which the people congregate, holding the small amulet that I was given by those who asked me concerning it (it being the source of all of the commotion, and the cause of all of the confusion). I would then curse and excommunicate whoever created it. And all the congregation would then answer Amen. For everyone agrees that it is unworthy, and it is the work of a total heretic, a believer in Sabbatai Tsevi, may the name of the wicked rot. It is just that some suspect that unworthy people deliberately produced it in order to slander and defame an innocent and righteous person, by accusing him of writing it. Therefore, it is necessary to clear them and myself (as either he or I are suspect, and only in this way can these thoughts be put to rest) of people's suspicions. And by personally cursing whoever wrote it, I will uproot entirely the stain of this slander. It follows that whoever forged it and slandered, falsely and deceitfully hanging it on a tall tree, will certainly bear his punishment, will certainly not be cleared, and all of the curses will come to rest on his head. And then the slander will be removed, and suspicion will be eliminated from all sides, and this entire nation will arrive at its place in peace [Ex 18:23]. And if he were to do this, I would place my hand over my mouth, cover up the shame and forgo the suspicion, not hold a grudge, and pay no attention to any possible gain. However, he and his group did not wish to act in this manner. Rather, he said that he has no need to exonerate himself; neither personally nor by means of another. [. . .]

[Even in the case of] one of the proper Jewish sages, about whom there is testimony that he saw signs of success in his learning; his actions would have caused him to be rejected once [he acted in a wicked way], and no one from the sages of the previous generations would have truly spared him. And this one, for whom no one testified concerning his Torah, for it is totally faulty and an infamous heresy, and his words of wisdom and Torah novella (which his disciples laud) should be lost forever and shall never see the light [Ps 49:20]. Even all his writings that are in the hands of his disciples, even the simple interpretations and sermons—on which he grew up and were his profession from youth—are all filled with nonsense and are made up. There is nothing good in them to make one wise [Prv 16:20] or desirable; they are not sweet to the palate [Prv 24:13] of one who understands, nor acceptable to the healthy ear nor [do they have a pleasant] fragrance. His halakhic rulings and verdicts also demonstrate that they are all erroneous and putrid. And even if we granted their contention that he is great in Torah, there are greater than he whose wisdom only caused harm both for themselves and for others. And if, in fact, they said that he is a sage in terms of evildoing,[7] then there is none to be found who is his equal; he is unique in his generation. For here they call him the master of the robbers, a destructive villain who is called the son of a thief and a miser; and his soul has collected all of the negative character traits. In the final analysis, he does not fear God. Behold, he has despised the word of the Lord! In truth, he is insane, a total fool, who reigned on his own by means of his foolish disciples who supported him. It was

7. [See BT Sanhedrin 21a.]

they who empowered him, and he rested his hands on them. Establish the man in accordance with his presumptive status, the appearance of an imbecile. [...] I would put one question to his disciples: "Answer honestly. Do you have any sign of being of Jewish lineage or not?" [...] One who blesses him is blaspheming. He seeks only evil [1 Kgs 20:7]. [...]

Ungodly people went out from our midst to draw away the inhabitants of the lands, and sent their deceitful letters upon the fields, in four ways. First, they testified falsely against me, as if I forged the famous amulets, and fabricated all of the defamation, because of the jealousy of the despicable Eibeschütz; and the sages of the generation also helped me to do this evil, because of their jealousy of him and his honor, which greatly outstripped their own. They vilified the righteous and exonerated the one who [was] guilty from the beginning, and testified about his integrity and faithfulness. Woe to their souls, for they have wrought evil onto themselves [Is 3:9]. Second, they prepared themselves to give a gift in order to bribe those who stray after falsehood. They filled their hands with fistfuls of toil and despair [Eccl 4:6], to commission letters for themselves, and regarding the rabbis supporting me. Third, they prepared themselves for war, by sending letters to the rabbis and sages of all of the communities, instructing them not to enter the fray (which is the Lord's fray). So they wrote to all of Persia and Medes, to each and every community [see Est 1:22], to cry out how I and my supporters wronged their master. They pleaded with them in this way, and protested and prevented them from harming their interests, causing them to avoid dealing with this [quarrel]; tying their hands and feet so that they do not write and sign anything against him—as they have already agreed to lay down their lives for their master, and to attack anyone who opposes him, and to harass such a person in all aspects of his life. Fourth, it was not enough for them that they slandered me and to contradict me at the time of the judgment, for the dead to contradict the living [see BT Berakhot 36a]. They further plotted to deceive and to lend credence to the rumors how I have always been a contentious man, all the time that I resided with them as a guest. They also gave their words standing [by] mixing bits of truth into the lies, as is the way of a liar. And in this deceptive way they persuaded the common people who did not know their right from their left [...] However, they did not succeed in convincing even one of the rabbis of the generation in Germany. And in Poland, there is no one [who would listen] to their antics and plots; as they all know as well as we do that the truth is on our side. All is known from the earliest times, and this heretic's corruption notorious. Also, I am known in the gates [Prv 31:23] as a man of truth. Therefore, they dove in mighty waters, and only ended up with a shard in their possession. Their only gain was that the majority of the rabbis of the generation became deaf and dumb, out of fear of the enemy that fell upon them when they saw the strong arm which was on his side. In particular, the work [of Satan] in terms of this, because those who were distant were not familiar with the signatories of those letters, and did not know who the leaders (the primary judges and teachers) of the three communities are. They thought that these signatories are the leaders and elite of the nation. But, in fact, they were marginal members of the camp. They are the rejects of the nation, who rebel through their speech and are contentious. Not one of the authoritative teachers signed; they did not agree to testify falsely, even if they pleaded extensively with them and offered them much payment and gifts. Rather, they sacrificed their livelihood. But they took some of the poorest sort of the people of the land and instructed them to sign as judges. Those from afar who saw the plethora of signatures thought that the signatories were the pillars of these three communities and these people signed on their orders. Therefore, they were afraid and the plan of the wicked succeeded, since many people in other communities are allies of this heretic, by virtue of family relationships and friendships with some of the signatories.

Thus, heads of many communities, particularly of Germany, were persuaded. This is especially so because the evil inclination will reply to them, misleading them by means of falsehood: "Even if we accept the claims of those accusing the heretic and defaming him, still he is a scholar before ignoramuses and the other nations." Many have been ensnared in this net of deviousness and were snared in their traps; to turn to their deceitful words and listen to their cries. They protested and warned their rabbis and the heads of their court not to involve themselves in the matter. Woe to a generation that judged its judges, and said to the seers: "See not" [Is 30:6].

Translated by Shalom Berger of the
Academic Language Experts team,
with Avi Staiman

23

Jonathan Eibeschütz, A Letter to Rabbi Jacob Yehoshuah Falk

Source: David Leyb Zinz, *Gedulat Yehonatan* (Piotrków Trybunalski: DL Cinc, 5690 [1930]), 129–35.

1. Praise the Lord, from my youth until I have grown old [see Ru 1:12], I have learned much wisdom. I have searched and inquired thoroughly [see Dt 13:15], and all can testify and declare, praise the Lord, that I am no less [a scholar] than he is.[1] What does he know that I do not know? What concealed wisdom is there with which he can enlighten me? Show me, I beseech you, where is the place of understanding? [see Jb 28:12].

Where is the home of the seer of knowledge which is beyond me that I am not able to master? And therefore why are you here [See I Kgs 19:9]? If indeed I have erred, then my error will remain with me [Jb 19:4]. I will not allow myself [literally, "my corpse"] to stay the night [Jb 21:23] on the tree of knowledge, good and evil, [guarded by] the flame of the whirling sword [see Gn 3:24].

2. What does he want with me [literally, "my name"], for it is unknowable [Jgs 13:18], I beg you to investigate between the two of us. Who bears more [responsibility] for the dispute, and from whose belly did this quarrel [literally, "Korach"][2] come from [regarding] our true faith?

For my way has always been the one of holiness, and my words are friendly to those who walk in rectitude [Mi 2:7], "I am filled with strength by the spirit of the Lord, and with judgment and courage, to declare to Jacob his transgressions and to Israel his sin" [Mi 3:8].

I healed the lame and the strayed [see Zep 3:19]; my words have kept him who stumbled in the fear [of God] from falling [see Jb 4:4] and strengthened the knees that are slack [Is 35:3]. Now his words come and make us weary, asking: "Who conceived [this]? Who bore [these] [Is 49:21], and who carries [them] in his bosom?" [Is 40:11].

---

1. [Throughout the letter, Eibeschütz addresses Falk in the third person, as is common in rabbinic writings.]

2. [A reference to the biblical figure Korach, who engaged in a dispute with Moses. See Nm 14.]

3. Therefore what does he seek, if not to arrogantly cause one to decide before he hears [both sides of the dispute], as if he possesses some extraordinary spirit [Dn 5:12] or as if God anointed him with the ability to sense the truth by his reverence for the Lord,[3] and [enables him] to be a teacher and judge for innermost thoughts and to decipher the concealed.

4. Show me the way of the ARI[4] in the first chapter of *Ets Hayyim*, regarding the question posed by those who believe in the eternity [of the universe]. Why was the world not created ex nihilo in completely good state, in such a way that the good not tarry? The ARI explained it.

Tell me, how does his answer suffice, for creation ex nihilo is an accepted premise and a foundational belief? If I could hear a clear explanation [from someone], I would wash the dust off his feet. On the other hand, if the power of speech is closed to him and the reigning spirit possessed him to properly understand the principles of faith, then he should walk with his staff and his satchel[5] in order to breathe in the shelter of [my] wisdom [Eccl 7:12] and hear it from me.

5. I know that he lacks wisdom and his hands are weak. And the Lord has favored me [see Gn 34:11] to prevail over him with clear philosophic proofs. I [expect to] know my father's God [see 1 Chr 28:9] in [His] absolute unity, and all the attributes of the ARI will not affect change in His true and absolute unity, [for] wisdom is with those who are unassuming [Prv 11:2].

6. What of spirits that take hold of men and women [to cause them] pain and a despondent spirit? [Dt 28:65]. They rise up like ghosts from the earth [See 1 Sm 28] with the sound of the tune of defeat [Ex 32:18]. Pray tell, if this is the soul of a wicked person who introduces himself, then how does he escape from Sheol and the sufferings of the wicked? Is it possible for an evil person to flee Sheol? Or can he leave for a short time to roam over the earth [Jb 1:7] [. . .] how does he come and go? When he leaves he will shake the earth [Jb 9:6] never to return again. Even though man can go to and fro [Ez 1:14] which can be proven both empirically and logically, pray tell, what is this all about and how can one tell the difference between this and a demon disguised [as a human being]?

7. The Lord has wondrously graced me [with knowledge] without anyone knowing or understanding [see Is 43:10]. I have many such explanations, and

3. [Like the Messiah in Is 11:3.]

4. [ARI = Rabbi Isaac Luria.]

5. [See BT Shabbat 31a. This also alludes to Rabbi Gamaliel's demand of Rabbi Joshua in the Mishnah Rosh Hashanah 2:8.]

if so, anyone who hears [them] will wonder, "How can you [mean to] rule over us?"[6]

8. Remove the beam from between your eyes; why are [you] concerned with the slivers in my hand,[7] for thanks to the Lord, I have tasted the milk and honey [Sng 4:11] of Torah which have enlightened Jonathan's eyes, my feet are on level ground, in assemblies I will bless the Lord [Ps 26:12]. I have removed from the heart of all unwitting and ignorant persons [Ez 42:20] [all heretical beliefs] and have excommunicated and banished all those who follow the abominable Sh[abbatai] Ts[evi].

9. All this would be worth it [Est 5:13] to me if I saw that he acted toward me ethically and with courtesy, and he wrote useful and truthful statements [about me] [see Ecc 12:10] without publically [Sng 7:5] revealing what he wrote about me. [It is appropriate to] reprove your kinsman [Lv 19:17] when one speaks with loving words behind closed doors where no strangers may come near.

10. But I waited for naught, because before I finished speaking and he circulated a letter and sent representatives far and wide and they degraded me with passion as mighty as Sheol [Sg 8:6], he sent written copies to show in every city and town [Est 3:14], there was no city that was too mighty (to be excluded) and under every verdant tree [Jer 2:20] my name has become an abomination, from north and south, and from different countries, this heart [. . .] was presented as a despised one [see Is 49:7], a child's plaything.[8]

11. They gnash [Ps 35:16] a tattoo, [in order] to demolish the entire building, [see BT Gittin 55a] my study house, which is open to the public for everyone to drink the water from my well.

12. And in particular, for the last ten years he has spread lies about me saying that I do not wear phylacteries on the intermediate days of the festivals, let all those on the face of the earth see, as if I violated a negative commandment that is a capital crime, and he was told that his claim was false. In fact, Rabbi Jacob of Emden himself does not wear phylacteries on the intermediate days of the festivals, and no one says a word and he was never reproached for it [see 1 Kgs 1:6].

6. [Referring to Jacob Emden, see Gn 37:8.]

7. [BT Arakhin 16b discusses the requirement of reproving one's fellow: "It was taught [in a Baraitha]: Rabbi Tarfon said, I wonder whether there is anyone in this generation who accepts reproof, for if one says to him: Remove the sliver from between your eyes (i.e., a minor transgression), he would answer: Remove the beam from between your eyes."]

8. [See the Mishnah in Baba Kamma 2:4.]

13. It is as if all say let "Glory be unto him" [see Ps 29:9] — to increase his honor, but to belittle my honor [together with] the honor of Heaven, and he does not renounce the evil that he perpetrates [Jl 2:13].

14. The God who has been my shepherd from my birth [Gn 48:15] and seated me among the princes of wisdom, [and blessed me] with boundless numbers of students, He will not leave or abandon me, no weapon formed against me will succeed, and I will defeat every tongue that contends with me at law [Is 54:17].

15. Nevertheless, I will not reveal his weakness to vilify him, [literally, make him smell putrid] even though there are many things to be said when you examine them [. . .] for his book [*Pney Yehoshuah*] is full of errors and mistakes and could have been written by a child. My students have already compiled a booklet to refute "the stone of errors."[9] But I will curb my tongue [so as] not to cause a desecration of God's name, so the masses do not say that the rabbis are quarreling with each other like enemies at the gate [Ps 127:5]. But there is yet a prophecy for a set term, [Hb 2:3] God willing, if He does not silence me [Ps 22:3]. And with this I will take leave and say, "It shall be well, well with the far and near" [Is 57:19], as is the desire of this writer who waits for God's salvation.

Translated by Shalom Berger of the
Academic Language Experts team,
with Avi Staiman

9. [A wordplay on the "a stone of the losers": a stone in Jerusalem from which announcements of property lost and found were made. See Mishnah Taanit 3:8.]

24

David Friedrich Megerlin, Hidden Testimonies for the Truth of the Christian Religion Deduced from Twenty-Four New and Rare Jewish Amulets

Source: David Friedrich Megerlin, *Geheime Zeugnisse vor die Wahrheit der christlichen Religion, aus vier und zwanzig neuen und selten jüdischen Amuleten oder Anhang-Zetteln gezogen* (Frankfurt am Main and Leipzig, 1756), 8–23.

With Your Royal Majesty's permission I will lay bare my thoughts on the severity of this litigation [. . .]. It is not about a mere amulet quarrel. Nor is it about the justification of vain Kabbalistic quibble and divination. [. . .] The very essence of the Christian religion is impugned. The most Holy Trinity, the name of the only true messiah Jesus Christ, and His fully valid merit, as well as the honor of His worship and hence the Christian creed and divine service of worshipping the Father together with the Son and the Holy Spirit [. . .] along with ancient Kabbalah [. . .] are declared to be impure and idolatrous [. . .] under the mere pretext and in the borrowed beggar's cloak of Sabbatai-Tsevism.

[. . .]

The false pretext of belonging to the cult of Sabbatai Tsevi [. . .] ceases to apply, for the attributes ascribed here [i.e., in the amulets] by no means befit him. Consequently, Rabbi Jonathan was accused of practicing Christianity by his adversaries, and furthermore to be quite in accordance with the basic tenets of the Trinity, the messiah Jesus Christ and His suffering, His merit, His spiritual kingdom and glory [. . .]. After correctly deciphering the amulets, together with the attached shields of David according to Kabbalistic precepts, no one [. . .] can claim that said Rabbi Jonathan has been wronged. [. . .] If, however, the Jews justifiably judge in this vein, should not the Christians pass judgment thus, yet even more so?

[. . .]

Man must leave aside the two words Sabbatai Tsevi [. . .]. Consider solely the featured *prædicata* [i.e., the things said about an object] or undeniable expressions that are often arranged according to the doctrinal concepts of the Christians. And the said Jonathan seems to have been a crypto-Christian at least in writing. [. . .] [T]his commonsense rule is to be applied: *Qualia prædicata sunt, tale subjectum poni debet*: The name and essence of a thing must reflect the object's manifestation and attributes; from whence one sees the proper criteria for the truth. Only Jesus Christ, the true messiah, has to be put in the stead of Sabbatai Tsevi in the said [...] amulets.

[...]

Finally, may Your Majesty grant me permission to present a single testimony of recent date [...] wherefore Jonathan's own admission on the bottom of page twelve of his *Tablets of Testimony* [...] will serve as proof. For there he himself explains the ... amulet that he had given to a child in Hannover. [...] [On it is written] "May the God of Israel, the God of all spirits, the God of *Peloni Almoni*, the Unnamed One, save this child from all evil hazards." This (he claims) is, according to the Kabbalistic books that he cites, one of the names of Metatron and a means of protection for children. Whereas he invokes the name of God and the Messiah at the beginning of most of the other amulets, here he invokes Metatron, who is called in the Zohar messiah, firstborn, Shekhinah, the beginning of God's creation, the servant of God, the Lord of the world, the prince of God's host, the mediator, the likeness, the word of God, the angel of the countenance, the angel, the savior, the angel (Ex 23:20–21) in whom the Name Jehovah rests, whose name is like the name of the Lord, Shaddai, etc. Hence, if these names [...] and attributes befit the messiah, whom Jonathan invokes in all amulets, and since only the messiah of the Christians bears them in accordance with Scripture, the other name too must and can only be Jesus Christ, and by no means Sabbatai Tsevi. Thus it becomes apparent [...] that he is a crypto-Christian and that he follows the way of the Christian messiah. He is a good Kabbalist at heart even though he seems to present himself differently to the outside world for the time being, namely, as an outwardly coerced Rabbanite and Talmudist.

[...]

The fifth amulet against difficulties in childbirth, which was given to the wife of R. Mordechai:

[...] This is one of the smallest and shortest amulets, but at the same time also one of the most important and most substantial ones. [...] (I) A child (II) is born (III) unto us (according to Is 9:5; Mt 1:21–23), (IV) a son (according to Ps 2:7 and 12; Heb 1:5; Acts 13:33) (V) was given (according to Jn 3:16 and 4:10; Rom 8:32) (VI) to us (i.e., the long promised messiah, the son of David (2 Sm 7:19 and Prv 30:4), the son of God, Jesus, in agreement with the following attributes) (VII) What about this son? Prv 30:4. (VIII) He came with water (according to Ez 36:25, Zec 13:1, in order to raise disciples through baptism) (IX) and with blood (in order to bring reconciliation for sins with the exemplary high-priestly blood) (according to

Lv 16:14 and 27; Heb 9:13 and 10:14; 1 Jn 5:6), (X) to judge the snake (i.e., he came in order to destroy this ill will and the works of the devil, Gn 3:15; Jn 3:14; 1 Jn 3:5 and 8). Now this is the seal (XI) (of the covenant with God; Cant 8:6; Neh 10:1; Jn 3:33; Rom 4:11; Rv 7:3). Whoever accepts the testimony of the messiah seals it in spirit as well. Finally (XII) the prayer follows, which is based on this creed of faith and arranged in accordance with the order of salvation (Ps 2:7–8; 2 Tm 2:19), in the symbolic Kabbalistic word *Yabok* no. 12, 13, 14, i.e., three words according to the three letters that originate in the story of Jacob (Gn 32:23; Hos 12: 4–6) when he fought, prayed, and triumphed. These three words are found in the prayer books of the Jews; they are taken from Ps 20:10 in the three last expressions: (1) May He answer us (2) on the day (3) we call. YBK, i.e., (1) *Yah yaanenu:* may the Lord, our God, the Lord (Dt 6:4), Yah, i.e., Jehovah, the God of Abraham, Isaac, and Jacob (Ex 3:6; Mt 22:32) answer us, when we observe the time of prayer. (2) *Beyom,* on the day of salvation (2 Cor 6:2; Ps 95:7) in the name of the Messiah, the son of God, *ben* or *bar* according to Ps 2:7 and 12; Jn 16:23–24; Ps 80:16–17 [...] at the time of righteous invocation according to the word. (3) *Korenu,* i.e., when we pray to him in the truth of the faith (Ps 145:18–19; Jn 4:23–24) through the power of the Holy Spirit, the *Ruakh Hakkodesh,* who makes us pleasant to God with the help of the Shekhinah, that is the messiah (Ps 51:13–14; Rom 8:9 and 15). [...] This wishful word YBK embodies *Yah,* the Father; B—*Ben,* the Son; K—*Kadosh,* the Holy Spirit, i.e., the Three Persons of the Deity. [...] That is how I understood and interpreted the [...] figures of this [...] amulet back then and therefore [...] addressed Rabbi Jonathan himself: Instead of being a secret, Zoharic, and plain Kabbalistic half-Christian, he should become an overt, evangelical, and purely New-Testament-based Christian [...].

Translated by Niels Eggerz

Source: Jacob Emden, Sefer Shimush (Altona, 1762), 64v–66v.

They [the Sabbatians] only wanted to flatter the Christians and find favor in their eyes, to show that they shared some of the beliefs of some Christian sects who maintain that their God took upon Himself human flesh to atone for their sins. One who knows that these two elements characterize the belief in Sabbatai Tsevi, may the name of the wicked rot, the false messiah of the rebellious sect that made him a god, who suffers to atone for the sins on their bones, will immediately understand two well-known amulets, one for a newly born child [. . .] and the other one given to a pregnant woman and whose false explanation he [Eibeschütz] presented [. . .] in print for all eyes to see in an act of deception. Yet he merely fooled the Christians, for he concealed his true intention, which is undoubtedly as we understood it.

It is not wrong of us to be involved with another's beliefs. We wouldn't protest at all, just as we can't protest apostates, since each person has freedom of choice, and especially now, in our exile, we are not responsible to do this, and he who wishes to separate himself from us may do what he wishes, and we are not responsible for him. However, he causes us ill by fooling us and others, because in the eyes of the public, he is connected to the Jews and acts in accordance with their customs, so that he can have the honor of the rabbinate among the Jews, honor which he wouldn't be able to receive from the Christians, and his mouth doesn't speak what his heart feels, for he is completely separated from Jewish beliefs, nor does he go wholeheartedly with the Christians, for he doesn't follow their practices, nor does he worship or call out in the name of their messiah or their God publicly. So he loses on both ends; he is no longer a Jew, but he's not really a Christian. Since these wicked ones who rise up against us do not explicitly mention the Nazarene's name in any of their words, their true thoughts can be discerned. They established a new faith made up from all other faiths and beliefs, according to their whims (from Christians, Muslims, and even cooperation with a sect of heretics in order to find favor in the eyes of all of the opposing opinions so that they will let them continue as they wish). And they worship Sabbatai Tsevi, may the name of the wicked rot, they place their faith in him, and therefore we needed to make his [Eibeschütz's] character known, so that people could guard themselves against the hypocritical charlatans, for no nation or culture can tolerate a person who is two-faced.

[. . .] The true intention of the author of the amulet was to his belief in Sabbatai Tsevi, may the name of the wicked rot, which is exactly the same as the beliefs of the Christians in our country. It can immediately be discerned in all of the amulets of the well-known author that they all attest, using similar language and formulations, to the fact that he believed in a physical messiah with literally divine properties, who clothed himself in flesh to atone for sins. All this is in accordance with the foolish beliefs of the Christians, as you were shown with the arguments that were presented here, but "their souls loathed" [Zec 11:8] the old, crucified [god], so they instead chose for themselves a "new god, nearer to them" [Dt 32:17]. But they didn't announce whom they were worshipping with such descriptions; they kept their intentions a secret, intending to fool the Christians into joyfully thinking: "Look, members of the Jewish people have found confirmation of our beliefs, they say that it says so in Kabbalah." [. . .] Therefore, the essence is missing from the words of our adversaries; they didn't mention the name of the Nazarene, for their hearts are not with him, only his qualities, characteristics, and deeds were appropriate for these fools, seeing that they are fit to praise their messiah, especially since they are particularly in need of atonement, for the load of their sins is too great for a goat to bear, so they needed to invent something even more harsh, worthy of hell. Therefore, they created a god who can bear sin, for the beast of burden to match the load [BT Ketubot 67a], but they had a temporary need, in order to fool the priests, to hide the name of the one they worshipped. [. . .] They pretended to be righteous and upright, and pretended that their god was wicked and traitorous, as it is written: "The wicked is atonement for the righteous, and the traitor is in place of the upright" [Prv 21]. Once they did not announce that they worship the Christian messiah equally, it is clear that they are being deceptive, and that they don't believe in their New Testament. Who is so foolish as not to detect their trickery? For they should have first clearly explained all of their claims, to lay a firm foundation upon which they could base all of the assumptions of the Christians whose path they chose. But their silence proves that their intentions are undoubtedly toward a different messiah or god, as has been indisputably proven, that they are referring to Sabbatai Tsevi, may the name of the wicked rot, and it is he whom they describe with the physical descriptions [. . .] and they paid him homage in the way of the apostates, who say that all of their sins are placed on their God's head, to atone every iniquity and give respite and balm to every sin.

Jacob Emden, A Whip on the Fool's Back | 137

[...]

Did you think this was justice, to decide in favor of the man of words [i.e., Eibeschütz; cf. Jb 11:2]? Or, did you hope in this way to gain honor and a good name in the eyes of the Christians, with words absent any reason, naked any grace or pleasantness? We were, indeed, very surprised at the Christian priests in Poland. How could they let such cursed ignoramuses invent a new religion for themselves, especially when it infringes on their own religion, by means of tremendous fraud and deception? Not only to misrepresent us to them with empty, false, dark words, and faulty foundations, but they mock them as they do us. They are not Christians, just as they are not Jews, but rather their own foolish, boorish nation, a non-nation, they fear people, and do their deeds in the dark. They have betrayed God, given birth to strange children, the bastardly offspring of incest. Praise God, our offspring is known to the nations, that we are careful regarding forbidden sexual relations even of the second degree. All who see us recognize that we are a seed blessed by God, guardians of His covenant who remember His commands and do them, who tremble at His word; our soul's desire is for the sake of His name and his remembrance. And if we suffer the burden of the long exile readily, and our hearts do not retreat from keeping what we are required, every refined word of God [Ps 18:31], then an eye will see and attest, and an ear will hear and confirm that we have not despaired, and we don't deny God's word in the Torah and in the mouths of all his prophets, whose truth all of the major nations that control the world agree upon. Our straight and proper path—it's simplicity will not be stripped, that which is sensed will not be denied, that which is understood will not be considered foolish. (The path of the righteous is smooth [Prv 15:19], and the path of the wicked is in darkness, so that they do not know what makes them stumble—intellect, feelings, text are all like night. They make what is impossible possible, and what is possible impossible. They ruin the foundations of the fences of our ancestors, which is understood through logical reasoning, as well as from the texts, and from tradition. The return to Zion, the rebuilding of Jerusalem and the revelation of a human redeemer for Israel at the end of days, which is not impossible, and which all the prophets as one attest to, are denied by these stubborn sinners without compunction or shame or reason.) We will not destroy the borders set by humanity, and by keeping the Torah, the political landscape will be repaired in the best possible way, and what is better and preferable is without a doubt possible. If this is so, who can condemn us for the honesty of our hearts, the conviction of our opinions, the purity of our thoughts, the bravery of our hearts, and our great faith in God [...]. Terrible tragedies did not deter us, all of the many terrible events and difficult, bitter occurrences did not tire us, we did not cast our Torah behind our backs, rather we increased our nerve, to hold on with even greater strength and greater power [Gn 49:3], to guard and do all that is written with all our hearts and all our souls and all our might. [...] Anyone who is honest, from every people, nation, and tongue, can attest and say what the people of the world lose because of our holy faith, the good and straight aspect. Or would they receive physical or spiritual gain from words of foolishness and evil debauchery invented and fabricated by unfaithful, evil seed, the children of incest, the sect of the abominable Sabbatai Tsevi [...].

Thus ends the answers to evil people, who shepherd lies, children of the dark who don't bring the morning, and the words of those who see the light of morning have been explained and clarified.

Translated by Shalom Berger of the
Academic Language Experts team,
with Avi Staiman

VII | Jacob Frank and the Frankists

Jacob Frank (1726–1791) stands on the opposite pole to Rabbi Jonathan Eibe-schütz. The latter was the scion of illustrious rabbinic lineage, a widely ac-knowledged master of Jewish learning, respected community leader, and one of the most sophisticated minds of his time. The former was a man from nowhere; a gratified ignoramus, apostle of brute force. The Polish-born Frank was taken by his parents from the country as an infant to grow up among the Sabbatian communities of the Balkan provinces of the Ottoman Empire. In 1755, he returned to Poland as an emissary of the Dönmeh of Salonika. A man of singular personal charisma, he managed to unify splintered Polish Sabbatian groups under his leadership. Publicly violating commandments and engaging in bizarre ceremonies, he openly threw down the gauntlet to the regional Jewish leaders. Faced with the most brazen challenges to their authority, Polish rabbis decided to take the unprecedented step of reporting Frank and his followers to the local bishop. The heretics, opined the rabbis, simultaneously offended Judaism, Christianity, and universally human moral norms, and should be burned at the stake. Frank turned the tables on his op-ponents, claiming that the real reason for the Sabbatians' persecution by the rabbinate was the proximity of their belief to that of the Christians. This led to the staging of two public disputations (1757 and 1759) between the followers of Frank and the representatives of the rabbinate; in the wake of the second disputation, Frank and several thousand of his disciples converted to Roman Catholicism. Shortly after the conversion, Frank was imprisoned, this time as a *Christian* heretic. He spent thirteen years in the monastery-fortress in Częstochowa, where he developed his own teachings, later recorded by his disciples in a large manuscript titled *The Words of the Lord*. Released in 1773, Frank left Poland and settled in the Habsburg monarchy, drawing a substan-tial following among the Jews of Moravia, and later, Prague. He died in Offen-bach am Main in 1791. Frankist communities consisting of his believers, some nominally Jewish, most Christian, survived till the mid-nineteenth century.

While loosely drawing on earlier Sabbatian ideas, Frank's doctrines are highly idiosyncratic and feature his role as destroyer of all established religions, customs, and mores. This destruction was to pave the way for unconstrained humanity liberated from the oppression of gender, class, and religion. Generally, Frank characterized himself as a *prostak* (simpleton, boor) and made out that he lacked even the most basic of religious training. Of course, Frank was never as uneducated as he claimed: *The Words of the Lord* reveal substantial, if not systematic, knowledge of the fundamental texts of Judaism. This apotheosis of unlearning and even foolishness is rooted in the fundamental Sabbatian belief that nonmediated religious experience was superior to any learned knowledge. Sabbatai Tsevi heralded an existential religiosity of personal encounter with God. Some of his disciples were simple people with little or no formal Jewish education or rabbinic training who received private revelations, experienced ecstatic trances and visions, and performed unheard-of miracles. Unlettered charismatics challenged members of the official religious establishment, which responded with claims that Sabbatian leaders were madmen, dunces, and fools and that their teachings were a mumbo jumbo for the ignorant masses. Sabbatai Tsevi took rabbinic dysphemisms directed against him as positive characterizations and signed several letters as "Utter Fool." Yet there was a fundamental difference between seventeenth-century Sabbatianism during its heyday and eighteenth-century Frankism. Frank's *prostak* was not a Sabbatian mystic who worshipped the True God in the depths of his soul, but one who rejected wholesale religious teachings and revelations, including those of the innermost kind. Frank took great pains to stamp as superfluous any religious experience and to articulate his conviction that religious knowledge (including the mystical knowledge based on existential experience as well as esoteric knowledge based on Kabbalah) is harmful. The revelation of the *prostak* signified the imminent collapse of all religious traditions, doctrines, and customs: "You see me as a *prostak*; it follows that all the religions, Laws, and Teachings will collapse." Whereas Sabbatai Tsevi was given special personal revelations that permitted him to expound the mysteries of the Torah, Frank denied it all: revelations, the mysteries of the Torah, and the Torah itself.

Sabbatai Tsevi's move against the religious establishment was made in the name of the spiritual experience of an individual. Frank, for his part, viewed the problem through a political lens: the world of normative religion was the world of endless division, contention, and strife. In Frank's view, the world would be far better off stripped of any vestige of religion. From this perspective, Sabbatianism a hundred years after the advent of Sabbatai Tsevi was for him as petrified and void of content as rabbinic Judaism, institutional Christianity, or Islam. Calling his followers "soldiers," Frank proclaimed: "Soldiers must not have a religion." Accordingly, the Frankists redefined Sabbatian conversionary theology, replacing Sabbatai Tsevi's paradoxical, yet ultimately optimistic, quest for the True God in the realm of Ishmael with a much darker and much more destructive vision. Frank did not seek God; rather, Frank sought the obliteration of God's name in the world.

Source: Jacob Emden, *Sefer Shimush* (Altona, 1760), fols. 16r–21r.

Now scoundrels have come out of the dwellings of heretics. They have dismantled the yoke of Torah and commandments with an upraised arm and have rejected religion in public. And this too is for the best, for God desired to make known their iniquity and to separate these accursed people from the holy seed, the righteous people of Israel, so that they would not be mixed in with us anymore, and we won't marry them as before, and they will be distanced from all the holiness of the people delivered by the Lord who suffer the yoke of bitter exile for their observance of the Torah and keeping of their faith. Therefore the rabbis of Poland who are faithful to God, as it says "It is not an orphan generation" [BT Hagigah 3b], girded themselves with strength. Blessed is He who gave his world to the guardians, "posted guards in the vineyard" [Sng 8:11], since these aforementioned righteous sages stood in the breach; and they excommunicated and separated all this rabble from Israel, and they sentenced these heretical books of theirs and the writings of heresy that they held, even if they contained mentions of the Name of God. But the disgusting heretics behaved brazen-facedly, like dogs; they went to the bishop of Kamieniec and some priests and deceived them by saying that they too believe in the Nazarene or are close to them in their beliefs and opinions, and that that is why they are persecuted by the Jews. And they stole the hearts of those priests for a time, "a lying tongue for but a moment" [Prv 12:19], and they purchased their freedom from this aforementioned bishop and [permission] to practice and keep their aforementioned false new religion, "and truth was hurled to the ground" and the wicked sect "prospered in what it did" [Dn 8:12]. In this year[1] (mentioned previously), perhaps the influence of Saturn,[2] as mentioned above, caused this. However, we are secure in God, that they will

1. [1757.]

2. ["Sabbatai" is the Hebrew name of the planet Saturn, and the Jewish tradition often linked "the reign of Sabbatai" (the astrologically elevated position of the planet Saturn) with the coming of the messiah. Sabbatai Tsevi's messianic convictions were shaped by the deep awareness of the astrological meaning of his name, and the nexus between the advent of Saturn the planet and Sabbatai the messiah was elaborated between his followers and many contemporary observers.]

not prosper, even if [God] should place Saturn in the center of the Sun's sky. Israel will pay no heed to false prophets, since God is testing us, and they will not learn from the omens of the sky and they will not turn from them.

[...]

A wondrous thing [occurred,] the like of which has not occurred to this day and whose like has not been heard of [since]. For the Christians sentenced the members of Sabbatai Tsevi's sect, may the names of the wicked rot, [to death] by fire. Since this is a fabricated faith, newly invented by empty and irresponsible people, who have no right to practice it openly anywhere, even in the countries which give freedom to all of the ancient beliefs, such as in the lands of Ishmael and in Holland and England, [even there] they do not allow the establishment of a new faith. But we have heard that all of the priests and bishops in Poland, together with the rulers and their deputies, have opened their eyes, and they know clearly that the accursed evildoers, the ousted sect of Sabbatai Tsevi, may the names of the wicked rot, have deceived them, and they will shortly be sentenced to death by burning at the command of the Pope in Rome.

[...]

And [they are suspected] even of sleeping with cattle and wild animals. Everything is in their eyes as plains and valleys. Not only [do they act as if] all of the grievous sins have been permitted to them, rather they have turned them into obligations. Although the nations of the world even erected for themselves a fence [in this matter] after the Flood, and one need not mention the nation of the Christians, which added for itself additional fences in order to distance themselves from even those things that are permitted to Israel. Even that which is not forbidden [sexually] to us, and that which the Torah has permitted, since they do not permit a man even to take two wives as one; and the sister of a woman, even after the death of her sister, as well as additional kinships are forbidden to them. And they are admonished regarding [even] truthful oaths and the hint of theft. And they have several praiseworthy attributes and honorable morals. And they abstain from revenge and hatred, and even from doing evil to those who hate their adherents; fortunate are they and fortunate are we if they act toward our nation according to their own religion ... and according to the practice of their pious kings and their honorable ministers, [who are] righteous and cautious, far be it from them to allow the heretics of Sabbatai Tsevi, may the names of the wicked rot, to intermingle with them. [For they are] worse than the animals of the forest. Therefore, be strong and become brave men, and stand before the wise and quick-witted rulers, the bishops, who have a monument and a name [after Is 56:5] in the kingdom of Poland, [exhorting them] to flog these afore-mentioned foolish and deviant heretics with whips and scorpions [after 1 Kgs 12:11] and to chastise them. And reveal their treachery and their vileness, their deceptions and ruses, [so that] they will [be] undressed, in the full gaze of the sun, of the clothes of treacherousness and the coats of sacrilege with which they adorn themselves,[3] and will no longer keep hopping between the two lies [after 1 Kgs 18:21], telling the nations that they believe in the messiah of the Christians, and saying to the Jews: "We are friends together with you" (in the manner of the Cutites to those who returned from the Exile), in order to cause their hearts to lose courage and many to fall [Ez 21:20] from both camps.

For it is a well-known fact that even the Nazarene and his pupils, particularly Paul, warned [their disciples] that they must keep the Israelites' Torah, and said that all of the circumcised are bound by it. And if they are true Christians, and their mouths and hearts are one, they will act like them without any lies or treachery and will not encroach upon them with their false messiah, Sabbatai Tsevi, may the names of the wicked rot, a new [messiah] who came but lately [after Dt 32:17], to make the world a desolation [after Jer 18:16].

However, truthfully, even according to the words of the authors of the Gospels, no Jew is permitted to leave his faith, since Paul, when writing to the Galatians, wrote in this language: "Behold I, Paul, say to you that if you receive circumcision, Christ will be of no benefit to you. And I testify again to every man who receives circumcision, that he is under obligation to keep the whole Law" (Gal 5:2–3). And thus, for this reason he warned in one of his epistles to the Corinthians, that he who is circumcised should not make himself uncircumcised (i.e., he should not attempt to restore his foreskin), and that he who is uncircumcised should not be circumcised (1 Cor 7:18).

And here some raise questions regarding Paul's statements from others of his statements. For in the Acts of the Apostles it is mentioned that he circumcised his student, Timothy (who was the son of a Greek man) (Acts 17:3), and they were extremely confused by this, for this action of his was in contradiction to his statements, which supposedly prove that, in his opinion, circumcision was a temporary obligation, valid only until the arrival of their messiah, and this story took place after the coming of the Nazarene.

But knowest thou and accept the truth from those who have stated it. For from this it is clearly evidenced that the Nazarene and his Apostles did not come

3. [This is a double play on the Hebrew words for clothing and coats.]

to eradicate the Torah from Israel, God forbid. Since it says in Matthew that the Nazarene said, "Do not think that I came to abolish the Law, I did not come to abolish but to fulfill. For truly I say to you, until heaven and earth pass away, not the smallest letter or stroke shall pass from the Law until all is accomplished. Whoever then annuls one of the least of these commandments, and teaches others to do the same, shall be called least in the kingdom of heaven; but whoever keeps and teaches them, he shall be called great in the kingdom of heaven" (Mt 5:17–19), and thus it says in Luke (Lk 16:17). Therefore, the matter is very clear, that the Nazarene had no idea of abolishing. And thus he commanded the leper who was healed from his leprosy to go to the Temple and bring sacrifices as it says in the Torah of Moses, in addition to the fact that he admonished regarding observing the Ten Commandments, and it is known that they include all of the obligations. And thus can be found in the words of his student, Paul, in his writings to the Corinthians, that he accuses them of the sin of incest, and sentenced one of them, who had married his father's wife, to death (1 Cor 5:1–5).

[...]

And thus will be revealed, further, the intentions of the Nazarene and his students, that they did not do all this but in order to show affection for the nations of the world, in order to bring them closer to the Torah. For it is because of this that they did not want to burden them with the acceptance of the yoke of the 613 obligations, which they are not obligated in at all, and therefore they allowed them to eat forbidden foods, as was their former practice, in order that they not think that they are thereby worse than Jews who keep the Torah faithfully (and therefore come to envy the Jews and not want to accept the new ways of behavior, since they would think that it makes them of lesser value than the Jews). Therefore they were devious and gave an interpretation of the Torah not according to the halakhah,[4] as if no food appropriate for man was forbidden in the Torah, as Paul wrote: "Eat anything that is sold in the meat market" (1 Cor 10:25), whether it be pure or impure, they need not distinguish, and thus also told them the Nazarene taught that what enters one's mouth does not make a man impure (Mt 15:11). And you should wonder regarding your own [opinion]: Who would believe his words, if not one who had witnessed the lights of the divine Torah, and who didn't know of Israel, His chosen nation, the keepers of His commandments and His covenant. For from the day the Torah was given, until our time, the entirety of Israel (and even the Sadducees, the Boethusians, and

4. [According to BT Sanhedrin 99a-b.]

the Karaites, who withdrew from the majority of the Jewish people) has been careful to abstain from the forbidden foods clearly mentioned as forbidden in the Torah, and the admonishments regarding them have been multiplied several times, with many threats and excessive vigilance.

And [it has been repeatedly mentioned] that they cause abomination and defile the soul and dull the heart. (And if they say, regarding all of this, that it is but the use of an allegory, they upturn the words of the Living God, and turn all of the Torah, in its entirety, into a proverb and a byword [after Dt 28:37], they will not leave of themselves neither stock nor boughs [after Mal 3:19] to keep any of its commandments, or to safeguard themselves from the grievous sins of the Torah, of any kind. If they do not say such an unfounded thing, [that one should] not accept the clear, revealed meaning of the Torah, then how are these different from others, what reason is there to separate different groups within them?!) And Adam's first commandment was abstaining from eating, and its reason is known to God, Blessed be He. And for the transgression of this commandment he and his descendants were punished with mortality, and he caused the destruction of this little world in its entirety, which has no full redemption until the Holy One, Blessed be He, renews his world; all this evil was caused by one act of eating that entered [Adam's] mouth without permission.

[. . .]

However, the nation of Israel is a different matter, since they were obligated in the Torah because God removed them from the iron-blast furnace to be His very own people.[5] Therefore they and their descendants and their descendants' descendants, forevermore, became enslaved to the Torah. This is their covenant, which will not be forgotten from their mouths and will not perish among their descendants [Est 9:28]; they give their lives for it throughout all of the generations. And when, in times past, the poet informed us that "all this has come upon us, yet we have not forgotten You or been false to Your covenant" [Ps 44:18], in any event I have no doubt that anyone who admits the truth will admit [the truth of] these words, that the Christian and his apostles did not intend to abolish the Torah of Moses from an Israelite who was born a Jew. And thus wrote Paul in his letter to the Corinthians that everyone must persist in the religion that he practices (1 Cor 7:17) (and we have already revealed his intentions, that he didn't intend to exclude one who truly converts [to Judaism]), and therefore they acted according to the Torah when they forbade circumcision to the nations of the

5. [Dt 3:20.]

world, according to the law and the halakhah formulated by the rabbis, that [circumcision] is forbidden to one who does not accept the yoke of the commandments in general. And they knew that the observance of the Torah of Moses our Rabbi, may he rest in peace, would be too weighty for the nations, and they therefore warned them of this, that they should not circumcise themselves.

[...]

O generation [Jer 2:31], Jews, Christians, and Ishmaelites, three central nations of the world that have erected their fortress on the foundations of the Torah of Moses our Rabbi, may he rest in peace, and have spread throughout the world. Open your eyes, will you not be in fear or in dread? [after Dt 31:6]. I call even upon the idolaters who reside in the far reaches [of the earth], look about and see: Is there any agony like this agony of ours? [after Lam 1:12]. Linger and wonder. Is there a terrible sect and an evil group and a wicked company like this accursed sect of Sabbatai Tsevi, may the name of the wicked rot (who proceed to defile the virgin Israel with these abominations, [the like of which] were not, to this day, known in the world). For even the ancient idolaters, their sons and descendants were attributed to them, and thus said our rabbis of blessed memory: "The Gentile's son is called his son, and Scripture ascribed him to his father and his father's father, as it is written, 'Ben-hadad, the son of Tabrimmon, the son of Hezion'" [BT Yebamot 62a]. And they said: "They certainly gave no license to their wives" [BT Sanhedrin 82a], and these accursed ones forfeit their wives, and do not recognize their offspring. Their sons are not theirs (but rather the sons of a hundred fathers and one mother).[6] [...] Shall God not punish such deeds? Shall He not bring retribution on a nation such as this? [Jer 5:9]. And if we are silent our sin will find us out, if God arises and calls us to account what shall we answer him [Jb 31:14], since all of Israel are accountable [for] one [another], even in such a matter, which touches upon the entire world, since they will destroy the land and all in it.

Translated by Sara Tova Brody

6. [See other interpretations of this expression in the commentators on BT Sotah 42b.]

27

Jacob Frank, The Words of the Lord Spoken in Brünn

Source: Jakub Frank, *Zbiór Słów Pańskich w Brunnie mówionych*, MSS 6968, 6969, Biblioteka Jagiellońska, Kraków.

1. I had a vision in Salonika. The following words were spoken to somebody: "Go lead the wise Jacob into the chambers. When you come with him to the first chamber, I admonish you that all the doors and gates be opened to him." When I entered the first chamber, a rose was given to me as a sign by which I could go on to the next and so on *consequenter* from one room to the next. And so I flew in the air in the company of two maidens the beauty of whom the world has never seen. In these chambers I saw mainly women and young ladies. In some, however, there were groups of students and teachers, and the moment the first word was spoken to me, I immediately grasped the whole matter and the full meaning. The number of these rooms was innumerable; in the final one I saw the First [Sabbatai Tsevi] who also sat as a teacher with his students, dressed in *frenkish*[1] clothing. He immediately asked me: "Are you the wise Jacob? I have heard that you are strong and bravehearted. I was walking this path, but have no strength to go any farther; if you want, you must strengthen yourself and may God help you, for a great many ancestors took that burden upon themselves, traveled this road, but fell." Then he showed me through the window an abyss that was like the Black Sea, clothed in extraordinary darkness, and on the other side of the abyss, I saw a mountain that seemed to touch the clouds. And so I shouted, "Be that as it may, I will go with God's help!" And so I began to fly on a slant through the air into the abyss until I reached its very bottom, where, having touched the ground, I stopped. Walking in the dark, I came to the edge of the mountain. I realized that because of the steep smoothness of the mountain it would be very difficult to climb it. I would be forced to clamber up with my nails and use all my strength until I reached the top. As soon as I stopped there, a lovely fragrance surrounded me, and I saw many True Believers.[2] Seized by great joy, I did not yet want to climb to the very top of the mountain, saying to myself: "I will rest here

1. [I.e., Oriental.]
2. [I.e., Sabbatians.]

for a while." And sweat poured from my head like a river in flood because of the effort I had made in order to climb this mountain. [I said to myself:] "When I am well rested, then I will go up on the mountain toward all the good that is found there." And this is what I did: I let my feet hang down and sat with my body and hands on the mountain. Then I went up to the top of the mountain.

33. As I told you before, when I was taken to the rooms where all the kings and Patriarchs of Israel were, they told me: "Jacob, we have come so far, from here you must go on alone." "I am a *prostak*," I answered, "and have no wisdom; how will I go there?" "Don't worry about that," they answered, "it doesn't matter, for wisdom is hidden in the lowest of places." Nevertheless, I still held back. Suddenly the First [Sabbatai Tsevi], having put me on a table and having opened the window, showed me an abyss, saying: "Look at this impassable place. We cannot go there, but you, if you hadn't held back, would have had less difficulty in passing. Yet since you delay, you must suffer great sufferings." At that time I saw all the burdens that I would have to take upon myself. And so I was pushed into that abyss.

34. [...] What kind of an achievement would it be, if God lead the world with wise men and scholars? God wants to come forth in this world only with the meanest and the lowest, so that his power will be demonstrated. Just consider and look at me, there was no greater *prostak* than I, who was as if deprived of any sense; but wisdom, as I said, comes forth from nothing. When, at the age of eighteen, I was in Bucharest at the house of a certain lady, who was twenty-four years old, I had with me spools of gold and silver worth one hundred #.[3] I sold them to her for five hundred #. This greatly amazed me; yet not thinking much about it, I hid the money and went on my way, saying to myself: "If she gives [it to] me voluntarily, why shouldn't I take it?" The lady was very rich. She had about twelve hundred servants, all of them young people, especially chosen. Her husband was not present at that time and was away at his estates. She summoned me and asked me to sit near her. I did so and I saw that the servants started to slip out of the room one by one, till I was left alone with her. The servants closed the doors behind them, and the lady began to persuade me that I should spend the night with her, and demanded that I satisfy her desire. She offered me one thousand sacks of

3. [The symbol # can stand for any of several contemporary currencies appearing in the Frankist dicta.]

levs, saying that if I agreed to do that voluntarily and willingly, then I'd be given *in dublo*. "Look how many handsome and attractive slaves I have here, but I want only you, and I want you tonight. If in the future you have a desire for me, I will not deny you, but my need and desire must absolutely be quenched this night." I wanted to run away, but all the gates were locked. Then she said: "If you don't do it willingly, you will be forced to do it." Then I realized: if I break the window and jump out, I will make a lot of noise. I immediately gathered my valuables, asked her to keep them, and asked her permission to go out to the porch, to which she agreed and came out with me. That porch was very high above the ground, and the yard was full of sharpened poles; beyond the poles, the river flowed.

I tried to figure out how far I would have to jump to reach the water. Throwing off my shirt then, I jumped straight into the water, and swimming away, I went home. The following day I went to her and retrieved my valuables and my shirt. I did all this because I am a *prostak*. A long time afterward, I was told that she was a great astrologer and, having recognized me, desperately wanted to achieve union with me.

35. Once I was traveling with my business partner through some villages. He ran into peasants to whom he owed money, so they stopped us. I wanted to fight them, but they said: We have no issue with you; it is the other one who owes us nine hundred *levs*. My partner knew that I had six hundred *levs* with me. The peasants tied the debtor up, and he began to plead saying, "Jacob, for God's sake, give me four hundred *levs*; this will satisfy them and I will go free. As soon as I get home, I'll take my wife's corals, worth one hundred #, and I will give them to you." I agreed to this and gave him the money. When we got back home, I asked for the corals. My partner answered: "My wife is sleeping now; tomorrow morning I'll give them to you, and for the kindness you did me, I will also give you a cart with iron wheels, which is at my father's." In the morning, my partner fled with his wife and everything he had in the house. I went to his father with the note, which he had given to me to take the cart, but it wasn't given to me. His father told me that his son also owed him money and put the wagon in the yard surrounded by a high fence. At midnight I returned with two ladders. I tied them together and put them against the fence. I took the cart weighing one hundred *ok* on my back, carried it over the fence, and having descended the ladder with it, I carried it on my back for half a mile to Romani. The father ran after me, but everybody denied him the cart, saying that his son had done me greater injury by taking the four hundred *levs*. This was the second display of my simplicity.

36. Having come to the River Totroz, I found 150 wagons there, standing on the shore, afraid to go farther because of the high water. Without saying anything, I took my robe, put it and my sacks on my head, and in spite of the most terrible danger, I swam across the river with my horse. From the other shore, people shouted at me: "What are you doing?" "For God's sake, why are you taking such a risk?" Listening to no one, I swam across, and on the same day I traveled six miles to Romani. The people had to wait there for eleven days. When they reached Romani, they asked about me and were shocked to see me alive. And my simplicity caused this.

49. I was ordered to go to Poland, but I did not want to do it, saying: "How can I, such a *prostak*, go on this path. Here there are two scholars, Rabbi Issohar and Mardoch. Let them go." So I was told: "They won't listen to your advice here, you are chosen by God." When I remained unwilling, then they began to throw stones at me. "And since you are holding back," it was said, "you will have to go in poverty. If you delayed more, then you would be led in chains. You must do what is necessary. As for your heart, it is free and can do whatever you like." I was only shown the places and paths that I would have to tread, and all the obstacles that I would face. And I was told: "You are Jacob; fear nothing, do everything as far as your hand reaches."

57. In [1759] the Lord said in Iwanie, There was a man who had a pearl of inestimable value. It had not been pierced. He went with it from one great city to another searching for a master who could make a hole through it, promising to pay him lots of money for the work, if he undertook to do it without doing any damage to the pearl. None of the greatest masters wanted to undertake the job. Finally, he offered one thousand # for the work, but no one would dare do it. Not being able to do anything with his pearl, he went to an apprentice whose master had left his house, and without warning him of the danger of perforating a pearl, said: "Take this pearl and drill a hole through it for me; I will pay you well for it." The apprentice took the pearl and drilled a hole through it fearlessly. The man paid him well and, fully satisfied, went on his way. Thus it is here. Many wise men wanted to drill but could not, because they were afraid; but I was chosen, because I am a *prostak*, who with the help of my God, will drill through everything and will lead to everything.

103. As [you] see me before you as a *prostak*, you should have concluded from that that all laws and teachings will fall. If scholars were needed, then they would have sent you one who knows everything.

300. That same witty Jew, on seeing twelve pullets roasting on a spit at the home of another Jew, asked me: "Jacob, how do you want me to pay you to eat all these twelve pullets?" "Twelve *ok*," I answered. I sat down and ate all twelve of the pullets. Then the owner came with his wife, screaming: "What are you doing?!" But I pushed them all away, saying that I was hired to do so, because I was a *prostak* and did not understand their anger. I merely thought that I should do what I was hired to do. Having eaten, I went home for dinner. The Jew followed me and asked, "But Jacob, you just ate. Why are you going to eat dinner again?" I replied, "My first meal was for pay, and only now am I going to eat my own dinner."

515. I chose you and I wanted to lead you to a place that is not yet known to any man. Even though they would be displeased there, I would turn it into a joke. Only to shorten the road, I told about what I did to the king in Jassy. Several times I sent supplications through his ministers, but they did not reach him and my pleas were never shown to him. So I acted like a fool and, having caught him by the robe, I told him: "I made you a king over this land, and you pay no attention that justice be done; if it will continue to be so, you will no longer be king." The king and his ministers laughed at that. Then I gave him a supplication. Having read it, he rendered me justice. Therefore I was chosen, for I am a *prostak* and no other, learned, wise, and proud [person] could have performed such a trick.

579. In my youth, my member was so lively that when a man wanted to climb a tree I erected it for him, and he stood on it, and he climbed the tree. Also, in the coldest water it would still stand. And when I went among the maidens, I had to tie it up, because otherwise it would pierce through my trousers.

762. In my youth, I traveled to a village, where nobody had ever seen a Jew. I came to an inn where young boys and farmhands gathered. The girls were spinning there, and the boys were telling them stories to amuse them. When they saw me, one of them began to mock me and make fun of me in order to make me angry. He said: "Once the Jewish God and the Christian God went for a walk. The Christian God punched the Jewish God in the face, saying: 'Why do you wear on your head what I wear on my feet?'" I said to them: "I [will] also tell you a story.

Jacob Frank, The Words of the Lord | 155

Once St. Mahomet and St. Peter went for a walk. Mahomet said to Peter: 'I have a great lust to fuck you the Turkish way.' Peter didn't want to, but Mahomet was strong and tied him to a tree, and had his way. Peter screamed, for his butt hurt: 'I will accept you as a saint, but don't do that to me.'" Thereafter, the farmhand said: "You know what? We will make peace among us. We won't say anything about your God, and you won't say anything against our St. Peter."

1157. I was a *prostak* and didn't know anything but the verse: *Szama Isruel Adonai Elohaini, Adonai ehet.* Hear O Israel, our God, one God.[4] When I was fighting a powerful robber, I screamed out that verse. When I pronounced the word *ehet*, one, I cut off his head, so I said to myself that the *Echet* cut off his head.

Translated by Paweł Maciejko

4. [Shema Yisrael, Adonai Eloheinu, Adonai Ehad; Dt 6:4.]

28

Jacob Frank, Appendix to the Words of the Lord Spoken in Brünn

Source: Jakub Frank, *Życiorys i nauki Jakuba Franka, założyciela sekty Frankistów* [ca. 1772–1785], MS 2118, Biblioteka Publiczna im. H. Łopacińskiego, Lublin.

The Lord said on the twenty-third of October: "The whole world loathes Signor Santo [Berukhiah of Saloniki] for calling Sama[el] his brother. And just as you loathed him, you loathed that I called you my Brothers."

I am asking you: "Our fathers the Patriarchs did not have crowns on their heads, so from where did Esau get his crown? For it [is] written that those four hundred who went with him all had crowns on their heads, and all the more so he had a crown?" The Lord answered: "For as soon as he only put on those charming clothes, he went immediately and took them back to his land. Joseph, who was a king, came forth from Jacob." [...]

Why does the whole world pursue the Maiden? And the three persons who are one? This is the religion of Edom that believes in three that are one. Just so our Truebelievers believed in *Tlass Kiszre, ememchemnisse deienen chad*. Three knots of faith that are one.[1] Nobody knows who those three are who are joined in one. But I am telling you: it has been called out in Heaven: "Who would come into that world to lead it to eternal life?" King Solomon rose and said: "I will go and will bring eternal life into this world." But in the end he said, *Umarti ech keimo wehü rochoiko memeni.* "I understood that I was wise but it is far from me."[2] And he said these words: "Three are hidden from me and of four you do not know."[3] Why did he say that? You must know that there are three very powerful gods who lead the world. One is he who gives life to every man once he is born; that

---

1. [*Tlat kishrei [de-]mehimenuta de-inun had*, three knots (or bonds) are one, is the Sabbatian "credo," likely based on the "mystery of faith" that was revealed by God directly to Sabbatai Tsevi (see the introduction to part II, this volume). The expression is based on the Zohar (cf., for instance, Zohar III, 36a, 262b), but does not appear in it verbatim. The exact formulation quoted by Frank comes from Hayon, *Oz le-Elohim*, 87v: "Whoever does not believe in the three bonds of faith that are one has no share in Israel" (see part V, this volume).]

2. [*Amarti ehkhamah ve-hi rehokah mimeni*, Eccl 7:23.]

3. [Cf. Prv 30.18.]

one is very good because he grants life to all. The second is the one who gives riches. He doesn't give to everyone but only to those he chooses, to those he apportions affluence; and to that one to whom he doesn't want to give, that one must remain in poverty. The third is the Lord of Death, *Hamejłech hamuwes*.[4] That one is the most powerful of those three. When he pulls the soul from a man then he has no further need of riches and also loses life. Of the fourth you know nothing and that is the Good God himself. How could King Solomon go to the God of Life when he did not know where those three were? First he had to visit those three, and then he might have been able to come to the God of Life. And therefore, because he didn't know, he had to leave this world without achieving anything. And so he was not able to bring eternal life into this world. Accordingly, it was announced once more in Heaven: "Who is he who wants to go to this world and bring eternal life?" Jesus the Nazarene said: "I will go into this world and will bring eternal life into this world";[5] and he was at [the place of] those three, but he did not achieve anything. [. . .] Jesus was very learned. He saw that the Good God was not always at his side. He said in his heart: "Now [that] I have in me the power of the good God who gave it to me, I will go on my own." He then went to those three who lead the world. He began to heal the blind, resurrect the dead, and perform other miracles. But when those three who lead the world saw the power that Jesus possessed, the first one said to the second, *"Huwe, weneschakmu.*[6] Let us take counsel among ourselves. For that man came with such great power and wants to take from us all the governance of this world that we have in our hands." For those three leaders of the world know that there will come a messiah, and after inheriting their power, he will fulfill [the prophecy]: *Bile hamuwes leneicech* (Death will be swallowed up forever).[7] They are great sages. They took counsel among themselves. One said to the other: "The only way to the God of Life is through here. We shall do this: When he comes to us, then we will not permit him to go further." So they did. When Jesus came to the first, he sent him on to the second; he too sent him on, but when he came to the third, that one took him by the hand and asked him: "Where are you going?" Jesus answered him: "I will go to the fourth, who is the God of Gods." The God of Death told him: "There is no god higher than me, for I am the father of all the

4. [A pun on the Hebrew *melekh* (king) and *malakh* (as in *malakh hamavet*, the angel of death).]

5. [Mt 19:29, Jn 10:28.]

6. [*Havah nithakhmah*, Ex 1:10.]

7. [*Billa ha-mavet la-netsah*, Is 25:8.]

gods, and he showed him great fear in order to frighten him." Jesus realized that the Good God was not with him and was very frightened. Yet the God of Death had no power [to] take him. Thus he said to himself: "I will have to bribe him so he will stay with me." Then he said to Jesus: "Listen my son! Stay with me, and you will be seated to my right and you will be the Son of God and you will have the name of God over that world, just as it stands in the prayers: 'He sits to the right of God the All Powerful Father.'"[8] Jesus accepted that, for he was frightened because he went by himself and the Living God was not with him. So he said to the God of Death: "Let it be as you wish." After that the God of Death said to him: "Sign that for me." Then he signed his name in blood from his finger. Then the God of Death said: "Jesus, my son! You must sacrifice your flesh and blood for me!" Jesus responded: "How can I give my flesh to you when it was said about me that I will bring eternal life into this world?" The God of Death answered him: "It can't be that here, in this world, there will be eternal life." Jesus said to him: "But surely I had said that it is my teaching that I came to this world in order to bring eternal life here, into this world." So the God of Death told him: "Your teaching should be that there will be eternal life in another world, but not in this world." Therefore it stands in the daily prayer, "And after death, life eternal."[9]

So he went without the Living God and stayed with those three. He gave even more power to death over this world just like Moses himself. When the Jews are dying, then they call out in spite of dying, for they are frightened of God and don't know where they are going after death, whether to Hell or Paradise; therefore, they have no desire for death and die without desire. But the Christians die with joy, for they say that everyone will have his small share in heaven with Jesus the Son, who sits at the right of God. Therefore, Jesus went with nothing from this world and fell there. It was announced once more in Heaven: "Who is he who wants to go to this world and bring eternal life?" The Lord Sabbatai Tsevi responded: "I shall go." He also went; he raised up nothing and achieved nothing. Thereafter, I was sent that I might bring eternal life into this world. I was given power too, so that I might display the power that was given to me. [. . .] But I am a great *prostak* and will not go on my own, for Jesus was a very learned man and I am a great *prostak*; therefore, I will not go unless God himself leads me to the first step: from there I will go myself. For at first one needs to visit

8. [A paraphrase of the Apostles' Creed: "He is seated at the right hand of the Father."]
9. [The final words of the standard Polish version of the Apostles' Creed.]
10. [German: "without a murmur."]

those three who lead the world, and one needs to carry the burden of silence. *Es soll nich rauschen.*[10] For they are great sages and extremely intelligent, and they assume that the people come to them for that. Therefore, one must take power from them, from the hand with the power of the good God—*Wemen glüst sich ein so koich abzugeben*[11]—from the hand. For it was established that power has been given to them. Therefore, it is necessary to go to them in silence and not with a cry, *So thuen sie uns lechaches, Sie stossen sich; Drum will ech mech nit ruren ates boi dewurai,*[12] until the time comes for the letting out of my words. As *Gott wet mech unnehmen bey der hand und wet sagen: Jankiew geh trett auf der erste stabel, assoi eilech weiter mejacmi.*[13]

Adam, the first man, was not the first, for the world was created more than half a million years ago. And so why then was Adam called the first? For he was created from a man who came forth from a woman. Only for that [reason] was he called the first, for thanks to his creation there were people, men and women alike, who lived for eight or nine thousand years; and that first was the first who did not live the full ten thousand years, and therefore his years were decreased. It is for that reason that he was named, *Riszen* [*Rishon*], the first, but he was not *Udem Kadmon* [*Adam Kadmon*], the very first Adam.[14] The world *Teüwel* [*Tevel*] is not created by the Good God himself.[15] Similarly, Adam was not created by the Living God. For if Adam and the world had been created by the Living God, then the world would be stable forever and Adam would live eternally; since they were not created by the Good God, every man must die and the world cannot endure. The world and Adam are not created by the Living God; he must die and the world cannot endure, for it is created by a deputy. But my God is alive and is good and seeks to establish a stable world: *und die Menschen will Er derhalten auf der welt; dus will Gott allein.*[16]

Translated by Paweł Maciejko

11. [Yiddish: "How can one who gives up such power succeed?"]

12. [Yiddish: "So you do [this] to us just to make us angry, You escape; therefore, I will not budge until the time for my words arrives."]

13. [Yiddish: "Until God takes me by the hand and says: Jacob, go to the first rung, and then I will go further by myself."]

14. [Kabbalah distinguishes between "the first Adam (man)" (*Adam ha-Rishon*) and the "primordial Adam (man)" (*Adam Kadmon*).]

15. [In Sabbatian thought, the idea that the world was not created by the Good God originates in Cardozo; see part IV (this volume).]

16. [Yiddish: "And he wants to keep men alive in the world; that only God wants."]

29

Jacob Frank, The Red Letter

Source: Ben-Zion Wacholder, "Jacob Frank and the Frankists: Hebrew Zoharic Letters," *Hebrew Union College Annual* 53 (1982): 265–93.

ADDRESS

He who is the master of peace, may he give blessing and peace to you and to the entire House of Israel [who are] scattered in the lands of Hungary.

INTRODUCTION

Our beloved House of Israel! You should know that our holy lord, while still in the castle of Rome in Częstochowa, wrote a holy letter to the city of Brody, and these are his sacred words:

FRANK'S FIRST LETTER

Hear me ye stouthearted, you who are far from deliverance[1] and who are shrewd in their ways.[2] Who among you fears the Lord?[3] Who can hear the voice, the voice that comes from the wilderness of the nations? Woe unto you when the mighty lion awakens to remember the ram! It is written, For the Lord will not do anything unless He reveals His secret [to His prophets].[4] But if, indeed, you are the children of the Holy One Blessed be He, how is it that it has not been revealed to you what shall occur in the end of days, in these times? But surely the early predictions have already been fulfilled, and the new predictions[5] I foretell from beginning to end.[6] Therefore, let them be ready to weep and cry out concerning Kraków and its surroundings. Mourn, gird yourselves in sackcloth, cry

1. [Is 46:12.]
2. [Cf. Prv 2:15 (and Jb 5:13).]
3. [Is 50:10.]
4. [Am 3:7.]
5. [Is 42:9.]
6. [Is 45:10.]

out in the streets;[7] for a fire has gone forth from Heshbon,[8] [the number] of their sins, and it shall consume the city.[9] Who shall die by the sword, who by hunger, by plague or in captivity?[10] Their corpses shall lie like dung on the ground,[11] and dogs shall lick their blood.[12] Behold the storm of the Lord, His wrath has gone forth, a whirling tempest; it will fall upon the head of the wicked.[13] [For a fire is kindled by my anger] and it shall burn to the depths of Hell.[14] And it shall come to pass that the one who escapes the sword shall be caught in the trap.[15] Therefore, let them be ready to weep, to cry out for them. But let them be ready to cry out for your town and in your surroundings. A nation is about to rebel[16] [against] the nation of the sons of Edom with a battle cry as the king presses against the other king. Let them purify themselves and make themselves white[17] and condemn the guilty. But none of the wicked will understand, only those of real understanding will know[18] that anyone who has a spark of the seed of Abraham, Isaac, and Jacob must enter into the holy faith of Edom, and whoever will accept this creed with love will be saved from all of them [the persecutions] and will merit all of the consolations promised in Isaiah and in all the Prophets.

I would like to write at greater length, but a hint suffices for one of wisdom and understanding.[19] And I shall conclude with [the blessing of] life.

—*Jacob Joseph Frank*

INTRODUCTION TO FRANK'S SECOND LETTER

The preceding letter was written in 5527 [1766–67]. And in the year 5528 [1767–68], while he was still in Częstochowa, he wrote a second letter to all Jewry. And these are his holy words:

7. [Jer 4:8.]
8. [Nm 21:28.]
9. [Jer 4:8.]
10. [Cf. Unetaneh Tokef in the Rosh Hashanah liturgy.]
11. [Cf. Jer 16:4.]
12. [I Kgs 22:38.]
13. [Jer 23:19.]
14. [Dt 32:22.]
15. [Jer 24:18.]
16. [Cf. Targum Ps 55:7.]
17. [Dn 12:10.]
18. [Dn 12:10; cf. rabbinic commentaries referring to messianic computations.]
19. [Zohar I, 26b, 280b.]

A voice, a mighty voice was awakened from on high to the world below. Our eyes were opened when a ball[20] came down from on high to the many sides of the world. A mellifluous voice[21] came down from on high to the world below.

Awaken ye slumbering sleepers from the sleep that is in your nostrils, and you who do not know. They look but cannot see; their ears are closed; their hearts are heavy; they sleep and do not know the Torah that is standing in front of them, and do not pay attention, and do not know what they see; they look but cannot see.

The Torah has raised its voice, Look ye fools! Open your eyes and you shall know. There is no one who pays attention. Is there anyone to incline his ear? For how long will you be in the darkness of your willful evil? Seek to know, and light that is brilliant shall be revealed to you in time, etc.[22]

Surely you are wise and you know how to conduct a battle using a bow. When one pulls the bow lightly, it does not shoot far; when one pulls the bow with strength and lets them [the arrows] go, then the arrow shoots very far. Thus, know that at this time it moves slowly. You should know also that their time is beginning that you will forget your wives and your children on account of the evil decree, since it comes from the Lord Himself.

For all of the emperors and kings, even of the kingdom of Prussia, the dukes and the princes of all the world will hate you exceedingly. When they see a Jew they will direct their spittle at him; and pleasure will turn into a plague, and troubles will come, the likes of which have never been seen in the world.

You think that what I am writing you now resembles the first letter which has not been fulfilled so far. This is not the case. For what was said in the first letter was the awakener. And this epistle shall be your guide for what shall take place in the future in all of the countries, great and small: Poland, Lithuania and all of Russia, Hungary, Walachia, Moldavia, Tartary and the entire Ottoman Empire, France and all of Germany, Bohemia, Moravia, and the lands of Prussia, and in all places where Jews live. Woe, woe on this time! On account of what is intended against you, your wives and your children. Those who will be found in their houses will be slain in the houses and there will be no one to bury them

20. [Ball—planet, star, comet, etc.]
21. [Zohar I, 249a.]
22. [Zohar I, 161b.]

on account of the multitude of the corpses, and those in the fields will die in the fields and the dogs will devour them. I cannot write too much of what is about to happen to the world; a hint [suffices] for the wise. And if I were to write to you in detail, there would not be enough paper.

I am informing you that there shall be no order [literally, wheel] in the world until the Law of Moses is fulfilled, until they have entered the holy creed of Edom. As we find that Jacob had promised to Esau, Let my lord pass before his servant, and I will lead on slowly until I shall come to my lord in Seir.[23] And as it is written concerning Moses, And Moses dispatched messengers to Edom.[24] Anyone who is of the seed of Abraham, Isaac and Jacob must follow this holy creed of Edom. [The Lord comes from Sinai and shines forth to them from Seir] and he comes from his holy myriads.[25] Through his holiness there shall shine the primeval light; it shall come as a sign of the end of time. You shall make strife.

And it surely be clay, And as the toes of the feet were part of iron, and part of clay, so part of the kingdom shall be strong and part thereof broken.[26] And I say to you that the weak shall smite the strong.[27] Were they wise, they would understand this; they would perceive their end.[28] And he signed his holy name [Jacob Joseph Frank].

Translated by Ben-Zion Wacholder

23. [Gn 33:14.]
24. [Nm 20:14.]
25. [Dt 33:2.]
26. [Dn 2:42.]
27. [Cf. Joel 4:10.]
28. [Dt 32:29; cf. Targum Jonathan and Rashi.]

30

Eleazar Fleckeles, The Love of David

Source: Eleazar Fleckeles, *Ahavat David* (Prague, 1800), fols. 1v–6r.

Said the author: Lord, remember favorably my master, father, honorable teacher, may his name be a blessing and may he merit life in the world to come. I remember when I was a small boy, and riding on my father's shoulder; he instilled in my heart the love of the Torah and those who study it, and raised me on the confidence of delights,[1] and he separated me from those who wander [from the path of righteousness] and told me stories about the dog Sabbatai Tsevi, may his bones erode, who replaced the Lord and permitted the forbidden, he who believed in his words, God was not in any of his thoughts,[2] all of his actions were deceitful, he and his students were wicked, dogs, a pack of evil ones,[3] they say of his carcass that it is hidden and mysterious, and that his nakedness will swiftly be revealed and exhibited for all eyes, and they turn over the words of the living God and the Master of the Universe, they destroy the high and lofty walls and degrade the obligations of the fasts with their futilities and dreams.[4] And he brought me to the banquet room,[5] this Sinai and uprooter of mountains,[6] the pick of the officers[7] and the chief warrior,[8] our esteemed rabbi, who was great in Torah and importance, the light of the Diaspora, the genius among geniuses, the author of the responsa *Noda bi-Yehudah*, *Tsiyun le-Nefesh Hayah*, may he rest in Eden,[9] he too told me many tales of those who detest justice,[10] from the evil sect of Sabbatai Tsevi, whose injury is grievous, for generations and in their own times. And when I took the seat of judgment in the holy community of Goitein [Kojetín] in Moravia, there too trustworthy men spoke ill of them to me,

1. [After Prv 8:30.]
2. [Ps 10:4.]
3. [Ps 22:17.]
4. [Ecc 5:6.]
5. [Sng 2:4.]
6. [BT Berachot 64a and elsewhere.]
7. [Ex 15:4.]
8. [1 Chr 11:10.]
9. [Rabbi Yehezkel Landau, the chief rabbi of Prague between 1755 and 1793.]
10. [Mi 3:9.]

all of their paths are bad and bitter, they mislead people with their lies and their recklessness, and even more than them, my sons, beware[11] of bad mischance, this crazy sect, which is an affliction of leprosy, their belief is in a worm,[12] Jacob the smooth-armed,[13] his roots are in Amalek,[14] his heart has departed from our Father in heaven, he has supplanted them twice, in both worlds, they will be uncovered and unraveled, they will plunge down to the depths, their souls will disgorge their misery,[15] for their intentional and unintentional sins, for in the arrogance of the wicked one, he who is ruthless, the poison of vipers,[16] who mocks all those who remain loyal, they all walk in blindness, the Jews, the Christians, and the Egyptians,[17] and all of the people of the lands were struck with blinding light,[18] and he invented a new religion, in order to extract the glimmers of holiness, and they expound on the subject of forbidden relations in the presence of three,[19] they are sorcerers and they cause man and woman to be adulterous; what is more, a stake is standing[20] that was prepared for hanging, all are bound to appear,[21] there they question and inquire of the dead[22] in the depths of the underworld, and similar unfamiliar abominations, they go daily in the place where the dead are buried, so that they will reveal secrets to them, as the birds of prey came down upon the carcasses,[23] that is the predatory bird, and deposited venom—the augury in Jacob[24] is their messiah, may their spirits expire. And their deeds were undertaken in darkness for several years, and in most cases they inherited utter delusions from their fathers[25] and walked in their footsteps, and chose their ways and their fetishes,[26] and they did not incite and seduce others,

11. [After Eccl 12:12.]

12. [From Lam 4:5, with a meaning different from the verse.]

13. [Gn 27:11.]

14. [Jgs 5:14.]

15. [Ps 107:26.]

16. [Dt 22:23.]

17. [I.e., He was a heretic against Jewish, Christian, and Muslim beliefs—an allusion to Frank's repeated conversions.]

18. [Gn 19:11.]

19. [BT Hagigah 11b.]

20. [Est 7:9.]

21. [Mishnah Hagigah 1:1.]

22. [Dt 18:11.]

23. [Gn 15:11.]

24. [Nm 23:23.]

25. [From Jer 16:19.]

26. [Possibly an allusion to Amon, as found in 2 Kgs 21:21.]

in their abominations and detestations, and only a small number were captured in their traps,[27] but these two years they have been plotting craftily against the people of God,[28] and building traps and fetters[29] in which to entrap upright and blameless people, to hew out broken cisterns for them,[30] and they sent out foreign and rebellious missives to all the towns, full of nonsense and ignorance, and they are a proverb and a byword,[31] [in] every city and in every province,[32] [they are] poor and empty of all understanding and wisdom and have invented a religion and a faith, and everyone who hears and sees and can read the matters written in these missives will laugh[33] and ridicule immeasurably,[34] until his voice will be heard in the distances, and will say the eye sees and the ear hears,[35] because their soul is stuck in madness and blindness[36] and insanity; they chirp and moan[37] in a stammering jargon and in a garbled tongue,[38] their faces were covered with chickweed,[39] utter futility,[40] it is all garbled, their language is not Hebrew and not Aramaic, not Spanish and not French, not Ashkenaz and Riphath, not from the descendants of Japheth,[41] that they sound in their throats,[42] like one of their multitudes, in fake and crazy words, like the speech of one of the cooks or bakers, and I saw an example of the openings of the letter and it bears witness for the whole, that the mind is wild, and the truth is lacking, without wisdom and knowledge—their skin has erupted in malignant leprosy, in unintelligible speech and a difficult foreign language,[43] that is: "know, that when our impure

27. [Lam 4:20.]
28. [Ps 83:4.]
29. [Eccl 7:26.]
30. [Jer 2:13.]
31. [Dt 28:37.]
32. [In the language of Esther, see for example Est 9:28.]
33. [After Gn 21:6, where Sarah says that everyone will laugh or ridicule her for her pregnancy with Isaac, whose name is the basis for the play on words here.]
34. [Is 5:14.]
35. [Prv 20:12.]
36. [Dt 28:28.]
37. [Is 8:19.]
38. [After Is 28:11.]
39. [Prv 24:31.]
40. [Ecclesiastes 1:2.]
41. [Gn 10:2.]
42. [Ps 115:7.]
43. [After Ez 3:5.]

lord sat in Tara Rome, in Częstochowa he wrote,"[44] young men laughed at them, [saying] that they were not proficient in the language of the Hebrews (and meant to say: know that when our impure lord was sitting at the gates of Rome),[45] and all those possessed of knowledge would respond and say that they are crazy people, bitten by a rabid dog and walking in darkness regarding a simple Aggadah, that which our rabbis of blessed memory said (in Tractate *Sanhedrin* 97a of the Babylonian Talmud) that the messiah sits at the gates of Rome, anyone who has but half a brain understands that it is merely a proverb and an epigram, from the words of the sages and their riddles, and thus too interpreted Rashi and the Marsha in these words: in his place, not literally at the gate of Rome, but rather in the Garden of Eden, at the southern entrance, and these matters are very deep, and you should seek them out there. And now see this great madness: they gave their corpse the name of a messiah, he who is anointed in filth, and they call Częstochowa the big city of Rome, woe to him who has no courtyard,[46] for he is descending into the netherworld, into hell beneath, and he made a gate for his courtyard,[47] and thus too the other words of the missive, [which cause] panic and frustration, threatening and frightening, [saying] that all of the Jews should be ready, they will come, rams of Bashan and he-goats,[48] streaked, speckled, and mottled,[49] in the way of the foolish who frighten children, [saying that] you will meet wildcats and hyenas[50] and sons of Ethiopia,[51] black people, whose skin glows like an oven,[52] and they spread nets in which goat-demons will dance, each one holding two sticks, and other similar mad things and folly [. . .].

But despite all this, this threat has the tiniest amount [in common] with he who is like an ass, who has no heart at all to understand, who will be misled by the dung, and the Name of God might, God forbid, be desecrated, [therefore] myself and my fellow distinguished rabbis (and we took sweet counsel with the leaders of our city, the exalted students of Torah, may God save and preserve

---

44. [See chap. 29, "The Red Letter" of Frank (this volume).]

45. [Tar'a in Aramaic means "the gate of," but the missive phrased this incorrectly, such that it sounded like Tar'a was the name of a place.]

46. [BT Shabbat 31b.]

47. [Ibid.]

48. [Dt 32:14.]

49. [Gn 31:10.]

50. [After Is 34:14.]

51. [Am 9:7.]

52. [Lam 5:10.]

them) and we stood in the breach, so that the vermin which swarm upon the earth should not spawn [more vermin],[53] and we preached in assemblies that all of their deeds are madness and folly, their traditions? stupidity and foolishness, and we made known their disgrace, that they are confused and corrupt in all their doings, and they pursue delusions with all their belongings, and there is falsehood in their right hands, they will pine away for their sins,[54] and the wicked will be no more,[55] and they are hypocritical snakes, bad and crazy, depraved children, brood of evildoers,[56] and I, praise God, gave three explicitly zealous sermons, for it is not a time for silence,[57] woe unto the evildoers, who are inclined after the carcass of an impure bird, and a winged swarming thing that walks[58] in four worlds, and his thoughts are impure and full of materialistic matters, full of idols and pictures that are their folly [...].

And I know that when they went crazy regarding this year, using despicable hints of secrets, there will yet come eras and times when they will say the years have arrived, and they will bring signs and erect signs from the secrets of wise and knowledgeable men,[59] as they did for the year 1740, they will find a clue in the Zohar [...] and turn the hearts of the multitudes and tempt [them] with their mouths and their slippery tongues, after receipts of delusion and deception,[60] from three instigating inciters, Sabbatai, Berukhiah, and Jacob, the last of the odious messiah, three who are lopped and flawed, who vaunt their idols[61] and walk after the Baalim, and worship the household idols and the fetishes; therefore, I wrote the aforementioned sermons for a decree and a memory, in the assembled congregation of Jeshurun, so that it will be known until a future generation,[62] and they will not be able to dissuade you with deceitful clues,[63] even though they are rhymed, in the words of the prophets and the seers, and don't believe he who says, "I have the secret, I have the secret, and I am the sage of the secrets" [...].

53. [After Gn 7:21.]
54. [Lv 26:39.]
55. [Ps 104:35.]
56. [Is 1:4.]
57. [After Eccl 3:7.]
58. [Lv 11:21.]
59. [A reference to the High Holy Day prayer service.]
60. [Lam 2:14.]
61. [Ps 97:7.]
62. [After Ps 98:6.]
63. [After Ex 5:9.]

And since these fools bring proof texts from the Zohar and calculate the end of these horrors[64] in acronyms and numerical values [of words], I too will bring evidence from the Zohar, that they are mistaken and cause others to mistake and are crazy in all of these calculations and imaginations and visions and imagined dreams. [...]

And I called this little composition by this name "the Love of David" [...] since it is for the love of David, the messiah of God, in order to uproot and weed out the thorns from the vineyard of the Lord of Hosts, who distances the end of these horrors, in other words, the believers in Sabbatai Tsevi, may his spirit be frustrated, and all of his wicked students who act in his name, who pluck salt-wort and wormwood,[65] who have flung abuse at your anointed[66] and breached breach after breach,[67] and purified the vermin and cheapened every nation and language in the country and world. [...]

According to the voice of the tumult of the city,[68] scoundrels exist, who are few and not counted and not a part of the community, who have banded together and made a connection and an association in order to involve themselves in delusions and deceptions[69] received from Sabbatai [Tsevi], an ousted gazelle and a broken one,[70] and the band of his believers,[71] who are evil and sinful before God, Beru-khiah from Saloniki who was blessed,[72] because he blessed God and would say his Name, in names and combinations and curses and abuse, and Jacob Minai,[73] he is Jacob Achnai,[74] who circled his words like a snake surrounding the Rock of the Worlds. And although all [the names] of these sinful people are not known, I said but today I will reveal two handbreadths, the disgrace of the evil faith, from three shepherds of the evil spirit, and I will publish their infamy in public, regarding them and their students who will all inherit hell, may God remember

64. [According to Dn 12:6.]

65. [Jb 30:4.]

66. [Ps 89:52.]

67. [Jb 16:14.]

68. [Jb 39:7.]

69. [Lam 2:14.]

70. [A play on words based on Sabbatai Tsevi's last name, which means "gazelle" in Hebrew.]

71. [Based on Gn 26:26.]

72. [This is a play on words based on Berukhiah's name, which means "one who blessed God," here used as an antiphrase for cursing.]

73. [I.e., the "min"—heretic.]

74. [I.e., "the snake."]

the sins of their fathers in addition to their own, and may Satan stand on their right,[75] may sinners disappear from the earth and the wicked be no more[76] [. . .].

These wicked people, who say to the "dry"[77] wood "you are my father,"[78] they appear as righteous ones, people of deeds and people of [good] characteristics and merits, the meek of the earth, well-cared-for cattle,[79] they bent their shoulders to the burden[80] of the yoke of God's word and they have no anger or pride, no jealousy and no lust, they do not search for honor or chase after fame, whose mouths are full of the fear of God, all day [they speak] rebukes that discipline,[81] [in order to] guide people and lead them to waters in places of repose,[82] to take off garments soiled[83] in bad attributes from them and to dress them in sacral vestments, the beautiful attributes, from the secrets of the wise and sagacious,[84] to hear their disgrace but refrain from responding, and similar fine garments[85] that clothe a man in honor and splendor, which bring him to the end goal of happiness, until he abides in the protection of Shaddai,[86] and all of their dealings are in haggadic matters, which appeal to the hearts of people who live in the deepest darkness,[87] on whom no glimmer of the Gemara and *poskim* touches [. . .];[88] and they deceived them with their speech, lied to them with their words[89] of idol worship, [they are] within reach of all who desire them,[90] to hold the corpses of their abominations,[91] [. . .] and all of their words are [spoken] in patience and in joy, without anger and wrath, so that the people will hear

75. [After Zec 3:1.]

76. [Ps 104:35.]

77. [In Hebrew this word serves as an acronym for Jacob (Frank), Berukhiah, and Sabbatai (Tsevi).]

78. [Jer 2:27.]

79. [Ps 144:14.]

80. [After Gn 49:15.]

81. [Prv 6:23.]

82. [Ps 23:2.]

83. [Zec 3:4.]

84. [A reference to the High Holy Day service.]

85. [After Gn 26:15.]

86. [Ps 91:1.]

87. [Ps 107:10.]

88. [After Am 5:20.]

89. [Ps 78:36.]

90. [Ps 111:2.]

91. [Jer 16:18.]

and their hearts will be drawn, and after they, with their slippery tongues, have surrounded the man with a net on all four sides, and he is caught in their web, then they tell him my secret, the fraudulent writings, the letters of mischief and evil,[92] from the three idolatrous shepherds, who vaunt their idols,[93] in household idols and fetishes, and permit forbidden sexual partners and every abhorrent act that the Lord detests,[94] and they are thistles and thorns[95] to all the nations, take note[96] of the last one of them, he is "Akov Yaacov,"[97] who plotted to make all of the nations of the world a disgrace, and of all of the kingdoms an ignominy, he wrapped himself in the wrappings of the Ishmaelites and girded himself with a belt around his waist and a flowing turban on his head,[98] and in his hand a cross like a Christian, and on his head phylacteries like a Jewish man; he is nothing but a clown and a scoundrel, who laughs at all the religions of the nations and the languages of the world, and he wanted to invent a new religion, and when matters became known, his works of mockery,[99] to the Christian priests, and they investigated and inquired, they put him in custody and jailed him in the Częstochowa fortress, to be held there forever, for all the days of his life, [but] because the Russian soldiers captured it, that fortress, and proclaimed release to the captives, liberation to the imprisoned,[100] and he also was released with them, he returned to his evil ways and became a skillful hunter with his mouth,[101] to destroy his fellow man, and he captured many souls, senseless people,[102] with clues and with futile and false dreams, [so] that he was held in the prison for seven years, seven months, seven days, seven hours, seven minutes, for seven abominations are in his mind,[103] and in seven he will fall and not get up;[104] and

92. [Ps 10:7.]
93. [Ps 97:7.]
94. [Dt 12:31.]
95. [Ez 2:6.]
96. [Ps 48:14.]
97. [A reference to Jacob Frank, containing an allusion to Jer 9:3, where the phrase translated to "takes advantage."]
98. [Ez 23:15.]
99. [After Jer 10:15; 51:18.]
100. [Is 61:1.]
101. [After Gn 25:27–28.]
102. [Ps 95:10.]
103. [Prv 26:25.]
104. [As opposed to the righteous man, who will fall down seven times and get up— Prv 24:16.]

riffraff and scoundrels gathered around him,[105] and they followed him, corrupted and perverted [themselves] in the ways of the abominations, blessed is God who killed him, for this rabid dog died like a defeated corpse, but afterward it became known by the scientists that he who has been bitten by a rabid dog will himself bite, and this bad dog bit many dogs, and furthermore, the dogs lapped up his blood,[106] and they seize the dog by its ears,[107] which in this world has stronger venom than the venom of a viper, a seraph, and a scorpion.

Translated by Sara Tova Brody

105. [After 2 Chr 13:7.]
106. [After 1 Kgs 22:38.]
107. [Prv 26:17.]

VIII | Literary Accounts of Sabbatianism

Sabbatianism inspired numerous works of fiction. One of the earliest literary treatments of Sabbatai Tsevi was composed by Leopold von Sacher-Masoch (1836–1906), mainly known for his erotic fiction that gave source to the term "masochism." Masoch's father was a police commissioner in Austrian Galicia and was directly involved in the feuds between the Hasidim and the Maskilim (representatives of the Jewish enlightenment). His son had an intimate knowledge of Hasidism and had visited the court of the tsaddik of Sadigura (he provided in an article one of the earliest and most accurate descriptions of a Hasidic court ever penned by a non-Jewish observer). Von Sacher-Masoch's fascination with the world of Judaism expressed itself in a series of stories and reportage based on both direct contact with Jews and wide reading in several languages. Many of these feature strong and independent Jewish women whose actions determine the course of history at its critical junctures. Sacher-Masoch's women are always on the forefront of social change and, as such, are invariably linked with motifs of crossing boundaries through religious conversion, intermarriage, or erotic involvements transcending the limits of class, faith, and nationality. Masoch's novella *Sabbathai Zewy* (1874) is arguably the first attempt to romanticize the messiah, an approach that would have been unthinkable to Jewish authors of the same period. The plot revolves around Sabbatai's relationship with his third wife, Sarah (in Masoch's story renamed "Miriam"). In the work, Tsevi is a saintly figure who, in attempting to prove himself, chose as his first two wives beautiful women whom he did not touch. His third marriage to Sarah/Miriam is supposed to provide final proof that he is able to withstand temptation, thus confirming his messianic mandate. Driven by his messianic delusions, Sabbatai prepares to face martyrdom. In trying to save her husband, Sarah/Miriam endeavors to "transform him into a man" by forcing him to sin. The encounter with powerful female eroticism puts an end to Sabbatai's messianic delusions and paves the way for his conversion.

The erotic element of Sabbatianism also stands at the center of the interest in the movement of the great Yiddish writer and Nobel Prize winner Isaac Bashevis Singer. Singer's first novel, *The Satan in Goray*, describes the religious and sexual fervor that overwhelms a small Jewish settlement in the wake of their receiving the news of Sabbatai Tsevi. Less known than *Satan in Goray* are Singer's two novels drawing upon the exploits of Jacob Frank and his followers, *Der zindiker moshiekh* (*The Sinning Messiah*) and *Der man fun khaloymes* (*The Man of Dreams*). While the former is merely a not-very-successful fabularization of historical scholarship, the latter is an ingenious take on the Frankist milieu of nineteenth-century Warsaw. The novel takes the form of a memoir (the narrator claims to have written it in Polish, which would make Singer's novel a Yiddish translation) of one Tuvia Yerachmel Alter Ben-Zion Cohen. Born into a strictly observant Jewish family, Tuvia first becomes a Maskil, and then a convert to Protestantism named Peter Morrison. Having met the leader of the Roman Catholic Frankists in Warsaw, Mieczysław Majewski, Tuvia converts to Catholicism, adopts the name Adam Stanisław Kordecki, and joins a group of Frankist remnants. Kordecki does not hail from the families of Jews who converted to Christianity in the 1750s; almost a century later, he elects to become a Frankist. In Singer's novel, Frankism is the ideology of choice for a person who permanently shifts his identity and lives a life of sexual promiscuity involved simultaneously with several women.

In "Knots upon Knots," written by another Nobel Prize winner, Shmuel Yosef Agnon, the figures of the two protagonists of one of the great Sabbatian controversies, Jonathan Eibeschütz and Jacob Emden, are brought together. The narrator of the story, in many ways Agnon's alter ego, attends a "craftmen's convention," where he meets two persons bearing the names of Emden and Eibeschütz, who in the story are also given Agnon's first names (Samuel Emden and Joseph Eibeschütz). The narrator is acquainted with both of these characters, yet he fails to talk to them. Agnon's Emden and Eibeschütz emblematize the impossibility of human communication. The dreamlike setting of the story presents the world tangled beyond comprehension, full of undecipherable connections between words, things, and persons. While the story contains not a single overt reference to Sabbatianism, the feud between these two rabbinic giants seems to drive the vision of the world the story portrays.

31

Leopold von Sacher-Masoch, Sabbatai Tsevi

Source: Leopold von Sacher-Masoch, *Sabbathai Zewy: Die Judith von Bialopol*
(Berlin: R. Jacobsthal, 1886), 26–38.

On the twentieth day of the month of Tevet of the year 1666, Sabbatai Tsevi
festively entered Constantinople. The Jews there greeted him with fanatic cheer-
ing. He sat in an open gold-plated sedan chair and was carried by his followers,
followed by the Queen of Israel, Miriam,[1] richly dressed and also in a sedan chair.
The people prostrated themselves in front of him so that those who carried him
had to walk over the bodies of the enthusiasts.

Sultan Mehmed VI was at that time in Adrianople. The grand vizier swiftly
reported to him that Sabbatai Tsevi, whose name had already reached the Great
Lord's ears, had arrived in Constantinople and had requested an audience with
him. Mehmed ordered the grand vizier to immediately take the pretended messiah into custody. The grand vizier sent off an aga with fifty janissaries to arrest
Sabbatai. However, Sabbatai's appearance so completely disarmed the aga that
the latter explained to the grand vizier that he was unable to offend Sabbatai:
Sabbatai resembled an angel and was certainly sent by God. A second aga with
two hundred janissaries also returned without having achieved his purpose.

Subsequently, Sabbatai himself went to the grand vizier to be imprisoned.
Also, the first dignitary of the Turkish Empire became entirely enchanted by
him. Although the vizier, following the sultan's order, sent Sabbatai to one of
the castles on the Dardanelles, the Cesto Castle, Sabbatai was kept and there
served as a king while his followers were allowed to visit him. From his prison
he released the following writing: "My brethren and my people! My loyal fellow
religionists! I order you to celebrate a great festival of joy on the next ninth of
the month Av. For this day is the birthday of Sabbatai Tsevi, your King, the most
exalted king of all kings on earth. I make an eternal covenant with you, with the
loyal grace I promised David. So says the man who is highly elevated over all
fame and praise, he, the anointed of the God of Israel. Sabbatai Tsevi."

1. [Sacher-Masoch changed the name of Sabbatai Tsevi's wife, Sarah, to Miriam to con-
form to the prophecy of Nathan of Gaza that the messiah would marry a woman named
Miriam.]

A famous Polish rabbi, Nehemiah, came to Sabbatai at the Cesto Castle and tried to prove to him that the portents the Talmud specified for the arrival of the messiah were not met yet. Sabbatai tried to convince him in vain. The Polish rabbi called him an impostor, and when Sabbatai threatened him with death he fled, pursued by Sabbatai's followers. In the moment when he was overtaken and saw himself lost, he threw his Polish hat on the ground, tore the turban from the nearest Turk's head, put it on his own, and shouted that he was becoming a Muslim. Thus he saved his life. Sent to the sultan in Adrianople by the grand vizier, he once again declared Sabbatai an impostor.

Consequently, Mehmed ordered that Sabbatai be brought to Adrianople. On the sixteenth day of the month of Elul, he and his wife Miriam were escorted there and imprisoned in a house that was tightly secured and surrounded by janissaries. On the next day Sabbatai was led before the mufti, who received him in a friendly manner, told him to seat himself, and asked him a number of questions. This happened only as a pretense. In that same hour Sabbatai's wife Miriam was led in front of the consort of the sultan, who received her, seated on silken cushions, in a green velvet kaftan trimmed with ermine fur. The consort observed Miriam attentively, and the eyes of the Jewess were equally attentive resting on her. Both women were beautiful, smart, and experienced. For a long time the conversation therefore concerned only trivial matters. Eventually, however, the sultana lost her patience.

"You call yourself the Queen of Israel," she said. "Is your husband truly the messiah?"

"He says so," responded the smart Jewess, "and Nathan of Gaza says so, and a hundred prophets and prophetesses."

"They are all wrong," spoke the sultana, "but even when true no one could save him from the wrath of the Great Lord, save by God alone performing a miracle."

"That miracle He will do."

"I tell you, your husband Sabbatai Tsevi will die tomorrow."

Both women were silent for a long time.

"However," the sultana said after a while, "Sabbatai Tsevi can save his life when he accepts our faith."

"He would never do that," spoke Miriam. "If he is not the messiah, then he still is a saint."

"Who tells you that?"

"I am his third wife, Lady, and he had never known a woman."

"Do you love him?"

"I love him."

"Then, Jewess, turn your saint into a man before tomorrow and you can save him, otherwise you cannot. Use all your guile and the force of your beauty and say no word to him that it was me who advised you to do so." A careless hand gesture of the sultana sent off Miriam, who kneeled down for her with arms crossed on her breast and on one knee, and then quickly left the seraglio.

[...]

Miriam was the perfect woman to transform Sabbatai from a saint into a man. Her real story was that she had been stolen from her parents during a Russian attack in Poland, baptized, and raised in a monastery. Her further history was nonetheless neither as supernatural nor as saintly as the followers of Sabbatai had embellished it. Miriam had escaped from the monastery straight into a house of ill repute. As priestess of the goddess of love, she had roamed all over Poland, Germany, Italy, and Holland. In Amsterdam she found her brother, with whom she sailed to the Levant to try her luck there. Against her plan to become a pasha's favorite, her fate decided that she become the wife of Sabbatai Tsevi and make out of a wanton girl the Queen of Israel. Familiar with all the enticing tricks of woman and with all secrets of love, she could easily suit herself to Sabbatai's holy madness and feign a cold, haughty demeanor, which in truth was far from her feelings for her angelically beautiful husband.

This treatment tortured her pious, fanatical husband far more than Sarah's passion and Hanna's tears[2] had been able to achieve. Miriam's cold awoke the love in his heart and brought all his senses to turmoil. More than once she had brought him to despair, more than once had the saintly man, whose feet the people kissed, been close to flinging himself facedown on the ground in front of the erstwhile maiden to beg her for pity. But she had thus far believed in his divine mission and had also been steadfast toward the one begging for love, from the fear of committing a mortal sin and making him forfeit Jehovah's forgiveness.

Now, however, she began to doubt. She repeated to herself the words of the beautiful sultana and the proof of the wise Rabbi Nehemiah from Poland, and finally told herself: Sabbatai is not the messiah. What therefore remained was to save the man she loved; he could, however, only be saved when he sinned, when he fell. Therefore, he had to fall. She wrote to the sultana, who promised her in everything her help. That same night Miriam set to work.

2. [The names Sacher-Masoch gives to Sabbatai's first and second wives. Their true names are lost to historical record.]

An hour before midnight she woke Sabbatai and shouted: "The Spirit has come over me, I have seen the Lord of the World, surrounded by the ten Sephirot as by ten radiant arches, come, Sabbatai, follow me and do as I tell you."

Sabbatai dressed himself and followed her. When he, however, saw that she was dressed in her most expensive clothes, he said: "For which purpose have you adorned yourself so?"

"The Lord has ordered me so!"

It was strange to see how the janissaries guarding the house withdrew in front of Miriam as before a heavenly appearance, and let her and her husband freely go.

"You are working miracles, woman!" exclaimed Sabbatai Tsevi, astonished.

"The Spirit of the Lord, who is in me, is doing them," Miriam said with calm grandeur, "and you will see more miracles by the power that God has given me."

And it was a rare sight to see how the beautiful majestic woman strode on as a queen in the trailing velvet garment, her proud and delicious limbs nestled in her dark fur, her flaming red hair braided with pearls and with shining gems, her face shrouded in a white veil through which burned the dark, burning eyes, and the angelically beautiful holy man following, having no will of his own, like a child, like a lamb.

There, at the confluence of the three rivers Arda, Tundscha and Marizza, she halted and spoke: "Here is the place."

Sabbatai looked at her and groaned—he was suffering unspeakable torments.

"Will you obey me?" She began.

"I will obey you."

"In everything?"

"In everything."

"So do as the Lord orders through my mouth: you will stand tomorrow in front of the sultan, Sabbatai Tsevi, therefore it is my will that you sanctify yourself for the exalted work. You will do horrendous penance, but then you will also be rewarded, Sabbatai Tsevi."

"I will do as you order me."

"You will bathe here, Sabbatai," Miriam continued, "here, where the three rivers meet, now, at midnight."

In silence Sabbatai did as he was told and descended into the waves. It was on the night following the twenty-third day of the month of Elul, September 10. The air was cold and the water icy, but Sabbatai did not shudder and obeyed. Suddenly he saw that Miriam had also thrown off all her clothes and had dived into the river.

"What are you doing?" he asked trembling, for at once the water seemed to flow around her.

"Do not ask, Sabbatai. I only obey the Spirit in me."

She remained for a while in the water and then exclaimed: "Now the hour has arrived, go to the shore, man, and dress yourself."

When Sabbatai was dressed, she came out of the water herself, beautiful like Aphrodite born of the foam, and he threw himself down in front of her.

"What are you doing?" she asked.

"I worship God in his works."

"This the Spirit has spoken to you, because such is the will of the Lord," she responded. "Come, help me dress." At her gesture Sabbatai handed her the precious fur and put the gold-stitched slippers on her. "Follow me," she ordered him and walked toward the Great Lord's garden, whose gilded iron gate glimmered through the trees. The gate opened when her hand touched it, and when they arrived at a pavilion illuminated by a standing lantern, its door jumped open and they stepped inside.

"You work miracles, woman," said Sabbatai in astonishment.

"The spirit of the Lord that is in me is working them," Miriam responded, "and you will see even greater wonders from the power that God has given me." She reclined on the cushions at the wall, and Sabbatai stood in front of her, shaking in unspeakable torment.

"Woman!" he shouted suddenly. "You are a murderous scourge to me!"

"Thus wants the Lord," she said, "bare your back, man, and kneel down, for it is His will that you kneel before me."

Sabbatai bared his back and lowered himself in front of her on both knees.

"You have to confess your sins and do penance, the Lord orders through my mouth," she shouted. "Pray the Wido³ confession."

Sabbatai began to pray the Wido. Miriam, however, grabbed the twigs covered with sharp thorns that were lying prepared on the cushions and braided from them a crown and a whip. She pressed the crown of thorns on Sabbatai's head so that red blood flowed down his forehead and began with the whip of thorns to savagely beat him so that red blood streamed down his back. But Sabbatai felt no pain. He only saw the woman standing in front of him, like the one born of the foam, whose body shone from the dark fur like a light from heaven, and whose loosened red hair lit her up like divine flames.

3. [Hebrew: *vidui*, confession.]

"You are the woman whom *bat kol* has destined for me," he shouted as in rapture.

"You have spoken rightly," answered Miriam, "because it is thus, and thus the Lord desires, and this, Sabbatai Tsevi, must be your reward." She tossed the whip away, tore the crown of thorns from his head, and with wild tenderness threw her white arms around him."

"My God! My God!" stammered Sabbatai Tsevi.

—He was suddenly overcome—

When he came to his senses, the hot tears streamed from his cheeks. "Woman, what have you made me into?" he groaned, down at her feet, and hid his face.

"A man, you saint," she responded with proud laughter, "and this is the greatest miracle that I have wrought. For, Sabbatai Tsevi," she continued, "you are not the redeemer of Israel, you are not the messiah."

Sabbatai did not answer; he remained lying at her feet, mute and without moving.

Translated by Alexander van der Haven

Source: I. B. Singer, "Der man fun haloymes," published in installments in *Forverts* (November and December 1970).

On the way back to the hotel I reconsidered my situation. First, it became clear to me that the revulsion I felt toward Ewa didn't mean that I had become a *baal-tshuve*, [a penitent] but rather resulted from the heights she'd climbed and the low rung I was stuck on. A woman desires a man who stands higher than her. But when a man is forced to look up to a woman, it impedes his love.

The whole time that Yente was Yente, Reb Yisroel's daughter, or even old Dzialski's wife, I felt powerful with her. But now that she had become a countess —a lady of a manor with servants and horses—I began to feel inferior. I silently protested against her. She had sought greatness for herself and married me off to an ugly woman nearly devoid of means.

The Frankist ecstatic enthusiasm disappeared with Dzialski.

But would I be able to return to Judaism? I didn't believe in either Jewish or Christian dogma. Besides that, the law forbade a convert to Christianity from returning to Judaism. And, well, what would I do if I went back to being a Jew? Go begging door-to-door?

I crept along the dark alleys of Lublin, and though I wore a fur coat and felt boots, the cold tore at me. I peered into a bar. Men sat in the dark light of an oil lamp and forgot their gloom with schnapps, but alcohol was never my passion.

It then became clear to me that I would not find a community in Poland. Born Christians held converts at arm's length, especially ones who, like me, still speak Polish with a Yiddish accent. And even if I found some down-and-out nobles, what would I talk to them about? They were interested only in politics, affairs of state, cards, horse races, hunting—but none of these things were of interest to me. Rich converts shied away from people like me. They wanted to ingratiate themselves to the Gentiles.

I was not a Christian and not a Jew, but a Frankist, and the fall of the sect was my downfall. Majewski, one could say, was the last of the Frankists. But I had tied myself to a woman who had no understanding of these matters.

All my woes befell me at once. I had a young daughter in England, but I didn't know where. My brother Shimele died. My sister Khame was struggling, and

I didn't know how to help her; I hadn't brought much extra money with me, only what I needed for expenses. My mother had died, unquestionably from the shame that I had caused her. Perhaps, if my brother Shimele were still alive, my mother would not have left this world. I betrayed my people, murdered my family, and what did I get in return? The right to live like a parasite off an ugly goy?

That night I did not eat dinner. I was a mourner, in truth I had just started mourning: I needed to sit shivah, tear my clothes. On cue, Antoni had already become acquainted with a fresh *shiksa*, and the look he gave me was wonder: how had I been beaten so low, and why wasn't I eating supper. Hunger had long kept me from falling asleep. Bedbugs bit me—despite the fact that I was staying in a hotel intended for nobles. It was also cold in my room.

"Perhaps I should put an end to all this?"—the idea came to me. But how?

In the morning I ordered Antoni to ready the sleigh for the return to Warsaw.

It happened by chance—or perhaps it was an act of Providence—that Antoni stopped in a shtetl named Marków. A part of the sleigh had broken. One of the horses also needed to be outfitted with a horseshoe. Dusk fell, a cold wind blew, and it began to storm. We made it to a tavern at the edge of the shtetl. I took a room and ordered a meal.

Dark fell after the meal, and I went out into the streets and asked someone where one could find a rabbi. The man answered me that there were two rabbis in Marków: one that serves the city and a second, a holy man, a miracle worker (a master of wonders), and I told him that I would go to the miracle worker. I could have saved myself the trouble of asking. I saw a group of Hasidim on their way to a building not far from the market. That was where, it appeared, the rabbi lived.

I entered a courtyard. There was a study house, another house, and a building that was, apparently, the ritual bath. Smoke rose up from the chimney. I entered the study house: walls covered with soot, shelves with torn books. Young men sat at long tables: young men with beards and long, curled sidelocks, dressed in tatters. Some of them swayed to and fro, made wild gestures, sung the texts they studied to a melody, a *nign*. Others stared at the pages in silence.

I had reasoned that it would be well after the afternoon prayers. But a prayer leader took his place at the lectern and quickly started to recite the Ashrei. Everyone else murmured and buzzed like bees. People washed their hands in a dismal barrel and dried them with their sleeves or with a handkerchief as dirty as a sack. Only a few lights shined in the whole room. The students illuminated the holy books with tallow candles.

I stood by the door not knowing what to do with myself. An old Jew approached me and asked:

"Do you want to say Kaddish?"

He apparently took me for a Jew—one of those Gentiled ones who enter holy places only once a year, on the anniversary of a loved one's death, or when they have to recite Kaddish.

I answered, "Yes, Kaddish."

He found me a prayer book and leafed to the Kaddish. I said Kaddish together with the other mourners. I snuck a crumb of Jewishness into the middle of my Christianity. Soon we were done with the afternoon prayers.

A door opened and the rabbi appeared. He was short, meager; a grey beard completely covered his cheeks. He had thick grey eyebrows, grey sidelocks. He wore a wide-brimmed hat far too big for his head and a coat that came down past his ankles. The rabbi, it seemed, had prayed in a small house next to the study hall. He took short steps. He was immediately surrounded by a group of Hasidim to greet him. I, too, approached him and extended my hand. The rabbi took my hand in his and held it for a while.

"Where does a Jew such as yourself come from?" He asked with a weak voice, barely audible. And those words strangely moved me.

"From Warsaw."

"And what does a Jew such as yourself do?" the Rabbi asked. "A merchant?"

"Yes, a merchant."

"Where is your beard?" The call came at me from one of the Hasidim. He was thickset with rosy cheeks and with a round beard as black as pitch. His appearance exuded power.

The rabbi defended me. "According to the law, one is permitted to cut."

"He is freshly shaven," the black Hasid said.

"We do not know that, we do not know," the rabbi mumbled. After a while he said, "What are you doing here?"

"I was traveling through, and I came here to say Kaddish."

"As long as a Jew wants to say Kaddish, he has faith," the rabbi said to the black Hasid, to me, and to himself.

After a while, other Hasidim pushed their way toward the rabbi.

I stood in the half-dark study house and looked every which way. The young men at the tables had gone back to studying. One of them twirled a sidelock. Another seized his partner by the lapels. A third shook his head side to side and grimaced. I overheard one of them explain to another a difficult commentary by the Maharsha.

I told myself not to be impressed by anything taking place. People were studying sacred books that were almost two thousand years old. The students were almost all dressed in rags. They made wild gestures. Most of them had squealing and grating voices. The Polish writers who claimed that the Jews in Poland—and especially the Hasidim—were a wild tribe, no better than the Hottentots or the Zulus in Africa, were not without justification.

But an otherworldly warmth gleamed from under the disheveled exterior, a silent love, a feeling of comfort, indescribable with words. Here a people sentenced to decline almost two thousand years ago continued to reckon its accounts with God and with the world. Here the law was not something to break with lawyerly manipulations, but was holy, a part of the soul.

A passion seized me—the desire to grab a book and peer into it, even to sit down and study in singsong. I blindly pulled out a tractate of the Talmud. It was *Masekhet Beitsa*, the laws pertaining to holidays. I sat down at the table.

The sight of a "German," fresh-shaven, dressed like a noble, studying Talmud, roused the interest of the crowd.

I heard one of them say to another, "He looks clueless, like a rooster staring at the Jews about to swing 'em over their heads."

"I'm nothing like an ignorant rooster," I said. "Listen—I know this whole portion by heart."

He motioned as if drawing back. He said, "I also know it by heart. Close the book and say the words."

I closed the Talmud and began to recite, first the Mishnah, the law, and thereafter the Gemara, the interpretation. A circle of students and men formed. I glanced and saw the rabbi standing near me. I recited the entire column and started to recite the next one. I heard the rabbi's voice.

"There is no estimating a Jewish soul!"

And the Hasid with the black beard answered, "The teaching is not the essence, rather the deed."

"So, it seems you know a page or two of Talmud," the rabbi said to me. "In that case, let's start over. How do you do!"

He took my hand and a warmth flowed into me from his small, thin hand—not the warmth that comes from health, wine, whiskey, but rather the kind given off by someone in fever. He lifted his thick eyebrows, and I saw a pair of almondlike eyes, half-mournful, half-joyful with a paternal softness. The look in his eyes was almost indescribable: the sorrows of a man of flesh and blood who had taken upon himself the heaviest of all burdens: the burden of the kingdom of heaven.

The rabbi said, "The Torah purifies. As it is written in the Torah, 'You have forsaken me and have not kept my laws.' The Gemara responds to this verse . . ."

"'*If only* you had forsaken me and kept my laws.'"

"*Gevalt!* He is a learned man," the rabbi said in a whispery voice that nonetheless contained within it a scream. He continued, "Where, young man, did you study? In a yeshivah?"

"With my father."

"Where did he live?"

I did not want to say Lublin, so I called out the name of a random town in Poland.

The Hasid with the black beard asked, "Seeing as you studied Torah, how did you become a 'German'?"

"My business demanded it," I answered, astonished at how quickly I found an answer. I knew well that Jews consider "business" the best possible answer. That is something that a Jew understands.

The Hasid with the black beard asked, "What is your business?"

I answered, "I travel around and sell goods in Russia."

"How are the Jews of Russia?" the rabbi asked.

"Jews are Jews."

"Of course that is so!" the rabbi said. "The God of Israel will not fail."

Everyone was silent for a time. Thereafter the rabbi asked, "Do you have many children?"

And I answered, "No, I am a bachelor."

"Is that so? A Jew must have a family," the rabbi said. "The Gemara calls it 'With bread in his pocket.' When one has bread in his basket, one does not lust after another person's bread. Without a match, a man is only one-half of a body."

I was at once encircled by love — not a conditional love that lasts for a minute and which is in essence hatred (the hatred of those who want to take more and more and give less and less) — but the love of brotherhood.

The rabbi said, "Perhaps you can stay here for a while?"

And I answered, "Yes."

The rabbi asked me my name, and I told him that it was Baruch Levi. The lies came to me without effort. I had the feeling that my tongue was capable of inventing lies on its own.

The rabbi said to me, "Visit me after the evening prayers. I want to chat with you."

What could the rabbi want to talk to me about? I asked myself. I recited the evening prayers with the Jews. I said the opening words, *ve-hu rachum yihaper avon ve-lo yashhit* [And He the Merciful forgives sins and He does not destroy], and I was amazed at how familiar they sounded to me, but also, at the same time, how strange. I had never once thought about them. And I especially ignored the last words: *ve-lo yair kol hamato* [He will not awaken all of his wrath]. That is to say, that Jews expect *a portion* of God's wrath. But why should God be grieved about them? Do they not suffer enough already? The Christians request only mercy in their prayers, forgiveness. They may commit the most heinous murders; you can be a murderer, a rapist, a thief, a criminal—so long as you believe in Jesus. He absolves you of all sins. But the Jewish God, it seems, is in truth angry when one does wrong . . .

I stood for the Amidah, looked at the others deep in prayer, and grew amazed. How had this people withstood persecutions, libel, all manners of expulsions and edicts for close to two thousand years? Where did they gather their powerful faith in a God who is always silent and who always punishes? They mesmerized themselves. (I am nowhere near certain that I thought all of these things in the moment. It is possible that these are my thoughts now.) The Bible, the Talmud, their holy books have the rare power to convince all who immerse themselves in them. Even the New Testament was written by Jews, even the Qur'an—I read somewhere—is said to have been written by a Jew. Even Jewish atheists have more strength of conviction than Gentile atheists . . .

After the evening prayers, I went out and met the rabbi. In addition to the prayer house adjacent to the study house, the rabbi had a house. The rabbi was a widower. He had four daughters, but three of them lived in other cities. The rabbi had no sons. Downstairs the rabbi had a library, a parlor in which to receive his Hasidim, and a kind of private room, or room of solitude, where the rabbi could seal himself off. The rabbi's servants and a few residents stayed on the other side of the corridor.

How strange it was that the rabbi dined with me. I was given a ladle to draw water to wash my hands. I was given bread, buckwheat with milk, and a tray with fruit. The rabbi had not eaten meat in a week. As soon as we sat down, the rabbi asked me about my mother and father, grandmother and grandfather, where I lived in Warsaw, and did I regularly go to shul? I answered that I prayed in the Reform shul only on Rosh Hashanah and Yom Kippur.

The rabbi said, "That may suffice for an ignoramus, but not for a scholar."

"Rabbi, my faith has been wounded," I answered him.

"What do you mean, 'wounded'?" the rabbi asked back. "The world didn't create itself."

"If there is a God," I said, "there isn't a single person who knows what He wants."

"The Torah."

"There isn't a person who was there when God gave the Torah," I said, knowing that I was hurting a holy man. "We have our Torah, the Christians have their Torah. Scientists have discovered that the earth is millions of years old. We've found skeletons of animals who lived tens of thousands of years ago . . ."

I worried that the rabbi would scream: "Sinner—Get out of my home! Impure!" But he looked at me with his mild eyes and there at his mouth, in the thick of his beard, something like a smile appeared.

The rabbi said, "That isn't news. There have long been those who maintained that Moses was—God forbid—a liar. So, let's say for a moment that that is, God forbid, the case. Can we derive from it that there is no Creator?"

"No, Rabbi, it cannot be derived from that that there is no God. I myself believe in God. But as we do not know what God wants, we must listen to our own minds, to our own bodies, our own passions. When one is hungry, one has to eat; when one is thirsty, one has to drink. And when one wants a woman, one must have a woman—"

I myself was astounded that I said such things to the rabbi. Where could it all lead? He won't turn me into a saint, and I won't turn him into a heathen. But just once in my life I had to express all of my doubts, and all of my pain.

The rabbi asked, "And what is a person to do if he wants to murder? Does he also have to obey that?"

"One is punished for killing," I said.

"Not always. Suppose a strong man was to go into the forest, and there he saw a noblewoman dressed in gold and laden with jewels. He could be filled with the desire to rape her, steal her jewels, and then kill her, throw her into the water somewhere or bury her in the ground. No one would probably ever find out who did it. Would you, God forbid, do such a thing?"

"No, Rabbi."

"Why not? If we listen to the body, and the body wants it—why not act on such a desire?"

"My body does not want such things."

"Another body *does* want them," said the rabbi.

I remembered something I read in Hobbes, in Rousseau, in Spinoza, and said: "If human society is to exist, the urges to kill and to rob must be fenced off. Today I want to rob someone, tomorrow he will rob me."

"Not necessarily. In this world, not all criminals are punished."

I knew that the rabbi had posed a difficult question, a question which no secular philosopher or ethicist has been able to fully answer. I said, "Some people have the attribute of mercy, others do not."

"How could you, according to what you've just said, object to a cruel person? You listen to what your body desires, and he listens to what his body desires."

The rabbi continued. "One person is by nature cruel. Another is by nature a sexual deviant. The third person is a thief by nature, or a swindler. Insofar as the Torah is, God forbid, not from the heavens, whence can it be derived that your nature is superior to his? Look, Chmelnitsky, may his name be blotted out, was driven by nature to drill his Cossacks, to order them to flay people, to burn people alive, to subject them to all kinds of torture. As long as he ignored them, the great nobles rejoiced, got drunk, and feigned ignorance. When it reached *them*, they set out against him and went to war. Meanwhile whole towns of Jews —and also many Gentiles—were murdered. The Cossacks and the nobles all listened to their bodies, their passions . . ."

"Joshua the son of Nun and King David did just the same—in the name of God."

The rabbi furrowed his brow. "The Seven Nations were immersed in all the abominations that exist in this world. They sacrificed their own children to Moloch. But let's accept, for a moment, that Joshua and King David were, God forbid, sinful. How can you be the judge if, as you say, man must accord to his own body? Where is the line?"

"There is no line," I said.

"If so, then the world is anarchy."

"Yes, Rabbi, the world is anarchy."

"Even heretics have their own customs. *Were it not for the fear of* [government], *one person would eat the other alive.*"

That night we talked at length. Before I said good-bye to him, the rabbi said something to me that I will never forget: "If—God forbid—the voice of God were to pronounce that the murderers were in the right and that Moses was— God forbid—a liar, I would still shout that it was heavenly by Rabbi Reb Bunem in Pshiskhe and it was hell among the well-to-do young people in Germany."

I wanted to leave the rabbi a gift, but he refused to take my donation. Quickly he said, "Young man, I pity you."

"What should I do, Rabbi?"

"Come to me for the holiday. There, where Jews gather, is the true world."

I had already started to rise to leave when the door suddenly opened and a woman entered whom, even now, I still consider the most beautiful woman I have ever seen. How can I describe her? She wore a hat and a dress that reached to the ground—just like my mother, may she rest in peace. But she looked no older than seventeen. Her face was bright, but she had two black eyes, deep as night. They smiled with goodness and the kind of modesty that only the tradition of dedication to Torah and self-sacrifice could have produced, an age-old tradition now miraculously rejuvenated in this otherworldly female form. She carried a glass of tea and a bottle of medicine. I heard her say, "Father, take your prescription."

And her voice comforted me. There was a gentleness reposed inside it, a tenderness, a musicality that I never knew existed until that moment. Her features were classical, without even the mildest flaw: her nose, her forehead, her chin, her throat. She wore her loose, old-fashioned clothing so well, I could tell that her figure was as perfect as her face. She had no hair. Jewish women shaved their heads after they were married, but her brows testified to the kind of hair she could have if she let it grow. She left me flustered.

I forgot to mention her hands. Her sleeves extended to her knuckles, but she couldn't hide her fingers, which expressed the essence of femininity, the secret of coupling, godly grace. I embarrass myself with these embellishments, but there is no other way for me to express the emotions that she evoked in me that night.

The rabbi said, "Devorale, not now."

"Father, it's already been four hours. The doctor said, every four hours."

And the way those simple words resounded in my ears, it was as if the Matriarch Rachel had risen from the dead, stepped out of her grave and let her voice be heard—(*a voice is heard in Ramah, Rachel weeping for her children, she cannot be comforted*).

The rabbi looked at me with a sort of embarrassment. "My daughter wants to make me healthy. Oh well . . ."

He extended his hand to me, and Devorale glanced at me, half-amazed, half-bemused. The rabbi said to her: "He's a modern man, but with a Jewish soul."

I left punch-drunk. Not a single lantern blazed outside. A few stars shimmered between the clouds. I shook as I walked. I reached a well and stopped to drink in the darkness. The water reflected a tear in the clouds and a shred of purified heaven. I stood there intoxicated. I breathed in the cold and clean air. My own behavior baffled me. Why would a convert to Christianity step into a study house, recite the Kaddish, and in addition, play tricks on a holy Jew? Did I become a penitent? And, well, what was the sense behind my present drunkenness? She is a forthright daughter of Israel. Women like her throw themselves into the fire to avoid breaking a rule from the Shulhan Arukh.

I lay down to sleep in my hotel, but the grey daylight hours had started to appear by the time I drifted off to sleep. I dreamed that I wandered along narrow alleys with blind, brick buildings. The pathway was sloped. I reached a stone wall, which reached up high, without windows, without a doorway. I stretched out my arms and touched the stones and asked, "Where does one go now?"

Antoni was bent over my bed. He announced that it was the time I requested he wake me.

When I arrived home in Warsaw the next day, I had the dark feeling that this was not my home and that I didn't belong there. The servant told me that the lady of the house was suffering from migraines. She slept and made me promise not to wake her. Helena was away at a dance lesson. Several new paintings hung in my chambers. Teresa had also changed the carpeting. Someone knocked on the door. A servant brought a letter from Mr. Mieczysław Majewski. He invited me to come meet him at Lurs's. He hoped, of course, that I had brought Ewa with me. I sent word that I would come.

Translated by Eitan Kensky

Shmuel Yosef Agnon, Knots upon Knots

Source: Shmuel Yosef Agnon, "Kisherei Kesharim," in *Kol sipurav shel Shai Agnon*, vol. 6 (Jerusalem: Schocken, 1964), 186–89.

Even I was invited to the craftsmen's convention. Since they had invited me I said, I'll go. I gathered my overnight things and wrapped them in paper and took along several copies of my new book, for several of those who had requested copies of my book were sure to be at the convention and by giving it to them I would not have to bother with the mails. It would have been good had I put my belongings in a satchel, except that a satchel is useful only as long as it carries your belongings. Once empty it is simply a load to be carried.

I came to the city and left my things at the bookbinder's place as I always do when I come to town, and then I set out for the convention building.

The hall was filled to overflowing. With difficulty I found myself a cramped spot among the many visitors, some invited and some uninvited. When my eyes had become clear of the stuffiness in the air I saw Joseph Eibeschütz standing before me. And since he is smaller than I in height, it seemed to me that I was sheltering him. His ears were red out of the strain of his effort to listen closely. But don't be surprised, for at that moment the elder of the craftsmen was lecturing about all that had been introduced in his generation, and here Eibeschütz wanted to grasp the essence of the era's innovations.

I greeted him with a nod, but did not ask him, Surely you wanted to visit me, so why didn't you come? Nor did he apologize that he had not come. Others came and pushed their way between us and I was pushed from my spot. And as long as I had been pushed, I left.

Since I had come for the sake of the convention but had not found myself anything to do, it appeared to me as if I had been blessed with a day that was entirely my own. I said to myself, As long as that's so, I'll take a little walk.

I took myself towards the Gates of Mercy and went down into the valley behind the houses and from there I went up the hill that overlooks the valley.

The month of Heshvan was already over. Bands of clouds lay beneath the heavens and hung over the low trees on the hill. Their branches lowered themselves to the earth to form a kind of booth. And within that booth sat a group of men, among them Samuel Emden, who was striking out at adherents of the known craft. It was easy to understand his coming to the craftsmen's convention but difficult to understand why he was here and not there. Since I knew him I went up to him.

At that moment he was sitting and discussing a matter which as yet had no interpreters, although a few people had begun to be aware of it. As soon as he saw me he greeted me and made room for me at his side. And he went on speaking, setting forth hidden matters as if they were explicit. When he paused I said to him, That was a nice letter you wrote me, perhaps I was supposed to have answered it? This question was hardly necessary, for there had been nothing in the letter that required an answer. But when I asked him his face whitened like that of one who has been insulted. And I knew that I had not done well to leave his letter unanswered.

After a short while he and all the members of the group stood up and went on their way.

I too stood up and went on my way.

It would have been good had I returned home, but the day was drawing to a close and my house is far from the city and the coaches to my neighborhood had already stopped running. There was nothing for me to do but to look around for an inn to find myself a place for the night. I went to the bookbinder's to get my overnight things before he locked up the workroom.

Upon entering the bookbinder's place I found several members of Emden's group. From their manner it was apparent that they too had deposited their things there. And they whose feet were lighter than my thoughts had gotten there before me.

The old bookbinder stood in the entrance, twisting his sash on his loins in the manner of one who prepares himself for prayer. Afterwards he took a bunch of keys and handed them over to him to whom he gave them and went on his way. When the one had gone, the other got up and gave each and every one his belongings. Finally, with his keys in his hand, he showed me a many-chambered chest that held the articles I had brought today as well as those I had left there days and weeks and months before. Not only many articles, but numerous books that the binder had bound for me were piled in several places. I had no need of them at that moment, nor did I have a satchel or suitcase at hand to hold them. Consequently I kept my hands off them and took my overnight things.

Meanwhile the members of the group had gathered their things and were taking out their wallets to pay a storage fee. I was amazed that they were paying a storage fee, for the binder had never asked a fee of me for anything I had left with him. Since I saw that all were paying I rummaged in my pocket and asked, And how much must I pay? And I thought, without a doubt this fellow is going to ask a fee for each and every package. I became enraged that for the sake of one piece of rope with which I had not tied all the packages into one, I was to be charged who knows how much. He shook his head at me by way of saying no and did not request a fee. But he urged me to clear out my things, for the painter was to come the next day to paint the workroom and he could not guarantee that my things would not be lost, and even if they were not lost they were sure to be messed up.

I looked at the members of the group to see if they might leave with me. They left without me. And even the holder of the keys went out. Maybe he left to accompany them or maybe he went out for his own purposes. One who is not burdened with things is free to do whatever his heart desires.

I stood among my things and thought to myself, When did I ever have need of you and when will I ever need you. And there they lay, casting a shadow upon themselves, a thick and thickening shadow. And if there is no substance in a shadow, substance there is in those who cast shadows.

The holder of the keys returned to rap with the keys whose sound became increasingly angry. But don't be surprised, for tomorrow's a hard day, the day they're painting the workroom and he wants to rest and renew his strength and at the last minute he's held up by me. My hands weakened and my fingers became intertwined as if they had been tied with ropes.

I stretched out my hands to stir them from their sluggishness and took package after package and tied them one to another, because packages have a way of being easier to carry when they are tied together which is not so when they are separate. When I noticed that fellow's eyes as he waited impatiently, my fingers lost all their strength and the packages fell from my hands. And even the books that were wrapped and tied ripped out of their cords, the paper that covered them tore and they fell.

I went over to the biggest of the packages and took the rope that was on it in order to tie one package to another. The rope was old and knotted in knots upon knots, and on every knot that I unraveled I bruised my hands and tore my fingernails. And when I had finally unraveled all the knots, the rope fell apart. Its mate that I untied from a different package was no better. I unraveled it and it weakened, I knotted it and it disintegrated.

I took the pieces that had separated themselves and joined one to another to make one long rope out of them. And once I had a long rope in my hands, I used it to tie one package to another, all together, until they formed one package. The man locked the workroom after me and went his way, talking to himself and saying, I hope it doesn't rain tomorrow.

It would have been good had I found myself an automobile to take me to an inn, but it was time for the evening session and all the visitors who had come to the convention had grabbed all the vehicles in the city to get to the convention building. I bent my back to the package that weighed me down more and more. And as it was with the package, so it was with its shadow. I am not saying that the shadow weighed me down, but it is terrifying when it is thick and lacks a head. And don't be surprised, for the load reared itself up above the head of the one who carried it so that his head entered into his burden.

In the meantime I heard a dull noise and saw that my things were falling. The rope I had worked so hard to assemble had been weak from the start and when I began to move, the package on my shoulders shook, the rope tore and the articles scattered.

I bent down to the ground and began to collect my things. I would lift one thing and its mate would fall from my shoulders. I would lift it and it would fall again. I had nothing left but the rope with which I had tied my package. To add to this drops of rain began to fall. The rains that had hidden by day in the clouds emerged from their hiding places. And there was no automobile around to take me to the hotel nor was there anyone to help me. And don't be surprised, for the craftsmen's convention was a large convention and all who were able went to the convention and whoever didn't go to the convention hid at home from the rain.

The rains that had pattered softly at first began to descend heavily. And in the midst of the rain, as in a vision, two men ran in great haste. I am not saying that they were Joseph Eibeschütz and Samuel Emden. But if I were to say that one of them was one or the other, it would not be far from the truth.

Translated by Anne Golomb Hoffman

Suggestions for Further Reading

Baer, Marc David. *The Dönme: Jewish Converts, Muslim Revolutionaries, and Secular Turks.* Stanford, CA: Stanford University Press, 2010. A monograph of the Dönmeh focusing on their role in the modernization of the Turkish state.

Cardoso, Abraham Miguel. *Selected Writings.* Translated by David J. Halperin. Classics of Western Spirituality. New York: Paulist Press, 2001. Translation of several of the most important Cardoso tracts.

Carlebach, Elisheva. *The Pursuit of Heresy: Rabbi Moses Hagiz and the Sabbatian Controversies.* New York: Columbia University Press, 1990. The best available account of anti-Sabbatian polemics.

Duker, Abraham G. "Polish Frankism's Duration: From Cabbalistic Judaism to Roman Catholicism and from Jewishness to Polishness: A Preliminary Investigation." *Jewish Social Studies* 25, no. 4 (1963): 287–333. A fundamental account of the survival of Frankism in the nineteenth century.

Goldish, Matt. *The Sabbatean Prophets.* Cambridge, MA: Harvard University Press, 2004. Survey of the Sabbatian interpretation of biblical prophecy and the renewal of prophecy during the height of the Sabbatian movement.

Halperin, David J., trans. and ed. *Sabbatai Zevi: Testimonies to a Fallen Messiah.* Oxford: Littman Library of Jewish Civilization, 2007. An anthology of English translations of several primary documents from the early phase of Sabbatianism.

Idel, Moshe. "Saturn and Sabbatai Tsevi: A New Approach to Sabbateanism." In *Toward the Millennium: Messianic Expectations from the Bible to Waco.* Edited by Peter Schäfer and Mark Cohen, 173–202. Studies in the History of Religions. Leiden, The Netherlands: Brill, 1998. A fascinating analysis of the astrological backdrop of Sabbatianism.

Lenowitz, Harris, ed. and trans. *The Collection of the Words of the Lord [Jacob Frank].* 2004. A translation of all dicta of Jacob Frank; not free of some mistranslations of the idiomatic text.

Maciejko, Paweł. "The Jews' Entry into the Public Sphere: The Emden-Eibeschütz Controversy Reconsidered." In *Special Issue: Early Modern Culture and Haskalah.* Edited by Dan Diner. *Simon Dubnow Institute Yearbook* 6 (2007): 135–54. A discussion of the newspaper coverage of the Emden-Eibeschütz controversy.

Maciejko, Paweł. *The Mixed Multitude: Jacob Frank and the Frankist Movement, 1755–1816.* Jewish Culture and Contexts. Philadelphia: University of Pennsylvania Press, 2011. The only monograph of Frankism in English.

Rapoport-Albert, Ada. *Women and the Messianic Heresy of Sabbatai Zevi: 1666–1816.* Translated by Deborah Greniman. Littman Library of Jewish Civilization. Oxford: Littman, 2011. A systematic discussion of the role of female personalities and the gender theology of Sabbatianism.

Scholem, Gershom. "Redemption through Sin." Translated by Hillel Halkin. In Gershom Scholem, *The Messianic Idea in Judaism and Other Essays on Jewish Spirituality*, 78–141. New York: Schocken, 1995. An English translation of the essay that launched modern research on Sabbatianism.

Scholem, Gershom. *Sabbatai Tsevi: The Mystical Messiah, 1626–1676*. Rev. ed. Translated by R. J. Zwi Werblowsky. Littman Library of Jewish Civilization. London: Routledge and Kegan Paul, 1973. The English edition of Scholem's monograph on Sabbatai Tsevi. The most fundamental work on the subject.

Wolfson, Elliot R. "The Engenderment of Messianic Politics: Symbolic Significance of Sabbatai Tsevi's Coronation." In *Toward the Millennium: Messianic Expectations from the Bible to Waco*. Edited by Peter Schäfer and Mark Cohen, 203–58. Leiden, The Netherlands: Brill, 1998. A discussion of the gender aspect of Sabbatian Kabbalah and the concept of the androgyny of the messiah.

Index

similarities to Sabbatianism as issue, 88. *See also* transreligious (syncretic) facet of Sabbatianism

Christians, nonconfessional, Sabbatians and, xxx–xxxi

Coenen, Thomas, 2, 8–11

commandments, Dönmeh's rejection of, 48

Cordovero, Moses, 82

creation: Eibeschütz on, 117; of humankind, Frank on, 160

Destruction of the Wrongdoers, The (Hagiz), 88, 104–9

Divrei Nehemiah (Hayon), 87

Dönmeh of Salonika: beliefs of, 48–49; conversion to Islam, xvii, 47–48; leaders of, 48; songs and poems of, 53–58; splintering of sects in, 48; as still-existing sect, 49

Dubnow, Simon, xvi

Eibeschütz, Jonathan: and amulet controversy, 116, 117–18, 124–27, 133–35, 136–37; *And I Came This Day unto the Fountain*, 115, 117, 119–22; as atheist, 118; on creation, 117; as crypto-Christian, 118, 133–35, 137–38; Emden's attacks on, 116, 117–18, 123–28, 136–39; eminence as scholar, as shield against condemnation, 115, 116–17, 123–24; on God, nature of, 119–22, 119n1; idiosyncratic worldview of, 117–18, 119–22; letter to Jacob Falk, 129–32; literary works about, 176, 193–96; ongoing debate about, 115; public condemnation of Sabbatians, 115–16, 117; response to Emden's attacks, 129–32; rumors of misconduct haunting, 115; on Sabbatai Tsevi, 122, 122n17; on salvation, 117; on Shekhinah (female aspect of God), 117, 119–22, 119n1; as suspected Sabbatian, 115–16, 117–18; and tension between personal relationship with God and established religious doctrine, xxviii;

and transreligious facet of Sabbatianism, xxiv; and Tsevi's mythological messianism, xxvii

Emden, Jacob: attacks on Eibeschütz, 116, 117–18, 123–28, 136–39; *The Bridle for the Deceiver*, 145–50; on Christianity, authority of Torah moral laws for, 147–49; on Christianity, prohibitions beyond Torah in, 146; criticisms of Sabbatians, xxviii–xxix, 2; Eibeschütz's response to attacks from, 129–32; fictional works about, 193–96; on Frankists, 145–50; on Jews, authority of Torah moral laws for, 149–50; *Purim's Letter*, 123–28; *A Whip on the Fool's Back*, 136–39

Emden-Eibeschütz controversy, 116, 117–18, 123–28, 136–39; literary works about, 176, 193–96

Enriques, Baruch, Cardozo letter to, 76–80

Escapa, Joseph, xii

Esther, Cardozo on, 74

exile, Jewish experience of: Cardozo on, 68–69; Eibeschütz on, 119–20; Nathan of Gaza on, 43; transreligious facet of Sabbatianism and, xxix–xxx

Fading Flower of Tsevi, The (Sasportas), 3

Falk, Jacob Yehoshuah, Eibeschütz letter to, 129–32

fiction. *See* literary (fictional) accounts

Fleckeles, Eleazar, 165–73

Frank, Jacob, 141–43; background of, 141; conversion to Christianity, 141; deliberate violation of religious and moral norms by, 141, 142, 146, 172; Emden's criticisms on, 145–50; Fleckeles's criticisms of, 166–73; on four gods, 157–60; on God's messengers as lowest of humankind, 152; on his sexual potency, 155; on humankind, creation of, 160; idiosyncratic doctrine of, 142–43; imprisonment as heretic, 141, 172; literary works on Frank and

Frankism, 176, 183–92; prophesies of God's wrath, 161–64; *The Red Letter*, 161–64; as self-declared messiah, 159–60; self-presentation as simpleton (*prostak*), 142, 152–56, 159–60; on three knots of faith, 157; and transreligious facet of Sabbatianism, xxiv; and Tsevi's mythological messianism, xxvii; vision of Sabbatai Tsevi, 151–52; wholesale rejection of religion by, 142–43; *The Words of the Lord Spoken in Brünn*, 141, 142, 151–56; *The Words of the Lord Spoken in Brünn*, appendix to, 157–60

Frankists: communities, 141; literary works on, 176, 183–92

Galante, Moses, 32
"Gazel" (Tovah), 57–58
"Gazel on Love" (Tovah), 56–57
"Gazel Tovah" (Tovah), 55–56
God: Eibeschütz on nature of, 119–22, 119n1; Hayon on nature of, xxviii, 69, 111–12; Hayon on origin of, 112–13; in Sabbatian theology, as God of living experience, xxix; Tsevi's claims to be, xiv, 32, 33. *See also* Holy Ancient One; Sabbatian theology

Gods, four, Frank on, 157–60
Graetz, Heinrich, xvi

Hagiz, Moses: concerns with Sabbatianism apostasy, xxviii–xxix; *The Destruction of the Wrongdoers* (Hagiz), 88, 104–9; Hayon and, 87–88

Halevi, Joseph: letter to Nantawa, 27–30; on Tsevi's conversion, 23

Hasidism, influence of Sabbatianism on debate on, xii, xix

Haskalah, influence of Sabbatianism on debate on, xii, xix

Hayon, Nehemiah Hiyya ben Moses: Ashkenazi-Sephardic tensions and, 88, 111; *Bet Kodesh ha-Kodashim*, 110; and

Christian overtones of Sabbatianism, xxiii–xxiv; conflict with rabbinical authorities, 87–89, 102–9, 111; *Divrei Nehemiah*, 87; Eibeschütz and, 117; life of, 87; on nature of God, xxviii, 69, 111–12; on origin of God, 112–13; *Raza di-Yihudah*, 87; rejection of Kabbalah secrecy, xxviii, 88–89, 91–101; Sabbatian works by, 87–89, 91–101. *See also Oz le-Elohim* (Hayon)

Hazzan, Israel, 51–52
Hidden Testimonies for the Truth of the Christian Religion Deduced from Twenty-Four New and Rare Jewish Amulets (Megerlin), 133–35
Hiyya, Maimon, 16
Holy Ancient One: Eibeschütz on, 119, 119n1, 120, 120n6, 122; Nathan of Gaza on, 5, 5n1

In the Sight of All the House of Israel (Hakham Tsevi), 87–88, 102–3
Isaac de Alba, xii
Islam, Sabbatians' conversion to: debate on necessity of, xvii, 47; Tsevi's call on followers to convert, xiv–xv; Tsevi's inconsistent views on, 47
Islam, Tsevi's conversion to, xiv; call on followers to convert, xiv–xv; Cardozo on, xxvi, 67, 69, 72–74, 79–80, 84; and condemnation as false messiah, xv, xvi; debate on followers' need to emulate, xvii; Eibeschütz on, 122n17; fiction account of, 175; Nathan of Gaza on, xi, xxvi, 24–25, 39–46; ongoing practice of Jewish rituals following, xiv; range of interpretations of, xvii, 23, 27–30, 47; Sabbatian theology on necessity of, xvi, xvii; Tsevi's account of, xxvi, 23–24, 25, 34–35; unknown details of, 23
Islam: Nathan of Gaza on, 25; Sabbatians' engagement with Christianity and, xxiii, xxv; Tsevi on God's conversion to, 24; Tsevi's views on, xxvi

syncretism of Sabbatianism. *See* transreligious (syncretic) facet of Sabbatianism